## Springer Series in Synergetics

Editor: Hermann Haken

Synergetics, an interdisciplinary field of research, is concerned with the cooperation of individual parts of a system that produces macroscopic spatial, temporal or functional structures. It deals with deterministic as well as stochastic processes.

Volume 40 **Information and Self-Organization**
A Macroscopic Approach to Complex Systems By H. Haken

Volume 41 **Propagation in Systems Far from Equilibrium**
Editors: J.E. Wesfreid, H.R. Brand, P. Manneville, G. Albinet, N. Boccara

Volume 42 **Neural and Synergetic Computers** Editor: H. Haken

Volume 43 **Cooperative Dynamics in Complex Physical Systems**
Editor: H. Takayama

Volume 44 **Optimal Structures in Heterogeneous Reaction Systems**
Editor: P.J. Plath

Volume 45 **Synergetics of Cognition** Editors: H. Haken, M. Stadler

Volume 46 **Theories of Immune Networks** Editors: H. Atlan, I.R. Cohen

Volume 47 **Relative Information** Theories and Applications
By G. Jumarie

Volume 48 **Dissipative Structures in Transport Processes and Combustion**
Editor: D. Meinköhn

Volume 49 **Neuronal Cooperativity** Editor: J. Krüger

Volume 50 **Synergetic Computers and Cognition**
A Top-Down Approach to Neural Nets By H. Haken

Volume 51 **Foundations of Synergetics I** Distributed Active Systems
By A.S. Mikhailov

Volume 52 **Foundations of Synergetics II** Complex Patterns
By A. Yu. Loskutov, A.S. Mikhailov

Volume 53 **Synergetic Economics** By W.-B. Zhang

Volume 54 **Quantum Signatures of Chaos** By F. Haake

Volumes 1–39 are listed on the back inside cover

Hermann Haken

# Synergetic Computers and Cognition

## A Top-Down Approach to Neural Nets

With 163 Figures

Springer-Verlag

Berlin Heidelberg New York London
Paris Tokyo Hong Kong Barcelona

Professor Dr. Dr. h.c. Hermann Haken
Institut für Theoretische Physik und Synergetik der Universität Stuttgart,
Pfaffenwaldring 57/IV, D-7000 Stuttgart 80, Fed. Rep. of Germany and
Center for Complex Systems, Florida Atlantic University,
Boca Raton, FL 33431, USA

ISBN 3-540-53030-4 Springer-Verlag Berlin Heidelberg New York
ISBN 0-387-53030-4 Springer-Verlag New York Berlin Heidelberg

Library of Congress Cataloging-in-Publication Data. Haken, H. Synergetic computers and cognition : a top-down approach to neural nets / Hermann Haken. p. cm.–(Springer series in synergetics ; v. 50) Includes bibliographical references (p. ) and index. ISBN 0-387-53030-4 (U.S.) 1. Neural networks (Computer science) I. Title. II. Series. QA76.87.H35 1991 006.3–dc20 90-10387



54/3140-543210 – Printed on acid-free paper

# Preface

This book will be of interest to graduate students, researchers and teachers in the computer sciences, in the cognitive sciences and in physics. It provides the reader with a novel approach to the design and study of neural nets. The applicability of this approach is shown explicitly by means of realistic examples. In addition, detailed models of the cognitive abilities of humans are included and compared with the performance of the synergetic computer presented in this book.

The work presented here would not have been possible without the important help of my coworkers. Dr. Arne Wunderlin has helped me in many respects over many years and has made essential contributions, in particular to the slaving principle of synergetics. Drs. Michael Bestehorn, Rudolf Friedrich and Wolfgang Weimer have applied the methods of synergetics to spontaneous pattern formation in fluids and have further developed these methods. Armin Fuchs has not only implemented my algorithm on a VAX computer, but has also made his own important contributions, in particular to pattern recognition that is invariant with respect to translation, rotation, and scaling. Thomas Ditzinger, Richard Haas, and Robert Hönlinger have contributed within the work on their diploma theses to the application of our approach to a number of problems that are shared by humans and computers in the field of pattern recognition. I wish to thank all of them. Chapter 14 is the result of a most fruitful cooperation with my colleague and friend Scott Kelso to whom I am most grateful, also for highly stimulating discussions on a variety of problems in sensory-motor control, and for his constant encouragement. I extend my thanks to Ms. Irmgard Möller, who has not only prepared various versions of the manuscript with great diligence, but also helped very efficiently in a variety of ways to bring the manuscript into its final form. I am indebted to Karin Hahn and Maria Haken-Krell who assisted me in many respects. Last but not least I owe thanks to the staff of Springer-Verlag for their excellent cooperation, in particular to Dr. Angela Lahee, who made numerous highly valuable suggestions for the improvement of my manuscript.

Stuttgart and Boca Raton, FL
November 1990

*H. Haken*

# Contents

# 1. Goal

The purpose of this book is at least three-fold.

1) It presents a new computer concept with explicit examples of its applications.
2) It shows how synergetics leads us to the idea that pattern recognition and, more generally, cognitive processes can be conceived as spontaneous pattern formation.
3) It provides the reader with new models of cognitive processes.

In this way the book will offer new insights into the principles used by nature in the inanimate and animate world, and it may help us to construct novel technical devices. Let us discuss these goals in somewhat more detail.

## 1.1 Why a New Computer Concept?

Up to now, the field of computers has been dominated by serial computers based on the concept of the universal Turing machine and on the von Neumann architecture. Serial computers may process numbers as well as symbols and they are thought to be universally applicable, at least in principle. In practice, however, there are some limitations, which become evident when certain specific tasks are to be fulfilled by computers. For instance, in vision an enormous number of bits must be processed and, if real time processing is required, even our fastest computers are far too slow. Quite evidently biology has mastered this problem. In spite of the fact that neurones are slow, having processing times of the order of milliseconds, we can recognize patterns within a fraction of a second. Thus the brain works by means of a different principle, which can only be parallel processing. So the question arises of how to find the basic ideas for the construction of parallel computers. A possible answer is provided by the Hillis machine (or the hypercube) but this has the drawback that it requires heavy programming. As nature teaches us, there must be realizations in which learning, or in other words self-programming, takes place rather easily. This has led scientists to devise neural computers constructed in a manner analogous to the nets of neurones of human or animal brains.

Present day concepts rely heavily on the model of McCulloch and Pitts (1943) who represented neurones as two-state elements which receive inputs and have outputs. A neurone is activated only if the sum of the input signals exceeds a specific threshold. Early attempts to realize these basic ideas, in particular by Rosenblatt, who constructed the perceptron, were not followed up for a while because Minsky had shown that the perceptron cannot learn certain logical tasks such as the "exclusive or". Over the last decade, however, there has been an enormous revival of this field initiated by several groups of researchers. Their concepts are still based on the fundamental idea of McCulloch and Pitts but with some slight modifications; in particular, with respect to the shape of the threshold curve. At present, no unique opinion exists among the experts as to how far this approach may go. On the one hand, there are some beautiful results, for instance, those of Sejnowski, who trained a neural net to learn spoken language so that the net could perform like children in the first one or two years of school. On the other hand, there is no general theory of what a network can really do, or of how it can be trained in a reliable and fast manner. In fact, learning is still a major problem and, at present, predictions for the future of these devices are difficult to make. Thus the novel concept of a synergetic computer must be viewed against this background.

The concept of the synergetic computer stems from the interdisciplinary field of synergetics which we shall discuss below. The synergetic computer utilizes far-reaching analogies between spontaneous pattern formation and pattern recognition. In this book we shall become acquainted with the basic equations of the synergetic computer. These equations may be solved on a serial computer, but they also provide us with the construction principle of a new type of parallel network, in which the individual nodes or neurones have quite different properties to those of the previous neural computers in the sense of McCulloch and Pitts. The most prominent feature of our approach will be the following: We can treat the behavior of our network rigorously in the mathematical sense so that we know precisely what its performance will be. In particular, there are no so-called spurious states which are unwanted and in which the system can become trapped. This difficulty, which occurs in both pattern recognition and learning, and which has been a major problem in traditional neural computers, does not appear in the synergetic computer. In contrast to the bottom-up approach of neural computers, where one starts with the properties of the individual neurones, and then tries to fix the links between them in such a way that the network performs specific tasks, the approach to the construction of a synergetic computer is top-down. One first identifies the desired properties and then an algorithm is established which eventually leads to a technical realization.

We shall provide the reader with a number of explicit examples of the performance of our synergetic computer. We use the example of associative memory and pattern recognition and present results on the recognition of faces and city maps. We will show how recognition can be made invariant with respect to position, orientation, and the size of the objects to be recognized. Scenes composed of several faces can also be recognized. A number of further applications which relate to psycho-physical experiments or to the performance of logical operations will be pesented in Parts II and III of this book.

## 1.2 What is Synergetics About? Pattern Recognition as Pattern Formation

Because the synergetic computer relies heavily on basic concepts and methods of synergetics and utilizes the analogy between pattern recognition and pattern formation, a few words about synergetics may be in order. (More details will be given in Chap. 4.) The word synergetics is taken from Greek and means cooperation. Thus synergetics is an interdisciplinary field of research which deals with the cooperation of the individual parts of a system. This cooperation may lead to the formation of spatial, temporal, or functional structures.

**Fig. 1.1.** Top view of a liquid in a circular vessel. When the liquid is heated from below and the temperature gradient exceeds a critical value, hexagonal cells are formed. In the middle of each cell the liquid rises, sinking back down at the edges of the hexagon. From Koschmieder (1977)

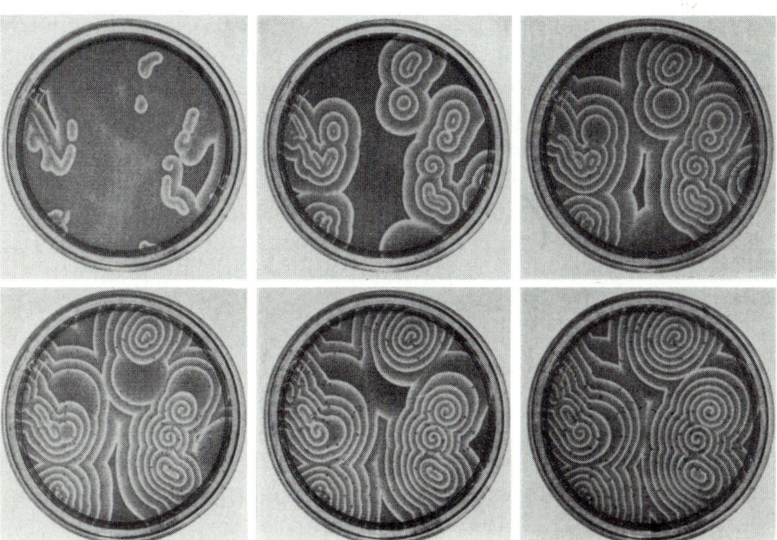

**Fig. 1.2.** Formation of spirals in a chemical reaction. (Winfree, private communication)

A simple example is the case of a fluid heated from below which may spontaneously form patterns in the form of hexagons or rolls based on an upwelling of the fluid (Fig. 1.1). Further examples are provided in physics by the production of the coherent light of lasers, in chemistry by the macroscopic rings or spirals formed in chemical reactions (Fig. 1.2), and in biology by morphogenesis during the growth of plants and animals. Another example is in behavioral patterns which may range from the gaits of horses to specific movements of human beings. In all these cases the systems acquire their structures as a result of rather *unspecific* changes of their environment, for instance when the fluid is heated more strongly or when the concentration of a chemical is changed, etc. In other words, the structures evolving in the system are not prescribed in a specific manner from the outside. More precisely, the system forms its new structure by *self-organization.* In a more abstract sense, the formation of a structure can be interpreted as the emergence of new properties of a system. As was shown in synergetics, there are a great variety of phenomena in physics, chemistry, and biology where the spontaneous formation of patterns or the emergence of new properties by means of self-organization is governed by the *same basic principles.* In Chap. 5 we shall show how these principles may be used to formulate our approach to a synergetic computer.

## 1.3 Cognitive Processes and Synergetic Computers

The simulation or, still better, the understanding of human behavior by means of machines has a long tradition. Just think of clockwork dolls built to mimic human motions such as dancing, etc. We live in an age in which the simulation and understanding of human activities, especially of cognitive processes, is undergoing a revolution that began with the advent of the electronic computer. Because it was soon recognized that computers cannot only process numbers but also symbols, simulations of the tasks performed by humans, for instance playing chess, or the solution of the tower of Hanoi problem were tackled by means of electronic computers. Cognitive processes were modelled by strings of symbols which were processed consecutively. Among the early pioneers, Herbert Simon and Allen Newell as well as Marvin Minsky may be mentioned. After an initial period of great enthusiasm we are presently witnessing a rather critical debate about the success of their concept of Artificial Intelligence. I am sure that a similar debate will occur about connection machines, i.e. "neurocomputers", (and synergetic computers) in the future, especially if we are making far fetched claims about their role in *fully* understanding or simulating human intelligence. It was at the time AI was defined that connection machines, in particular the perceptron, came into existence, were then abandoned, and are presently experiencing an enormous revival. We shall not discuss this exciting development here (but see references cited in Sect. 1.1).

One might reasonably ask whether connection machines, or in other words neural computers, can, in a single step, conceptually bridge the enormous gap between microscopic events taking place in the real neurones of the brain and the macroscopic phenomena of cognition, or whether intermediate steps are required. The latter point of view has been clearly expressed by Smolensky. I am also inclined to support this latter view. It is here that the synergetic computer comes in. Being based on a top-down approach we study macroscopic events and try to simulate them by a network which in turn may combine the functions of subunits composed of a greater or lesser number of neurones. Nevertheless, we wish to demonstrate that our approach allows us to make quite specific predictions that can be compared with psychological findings. We shall show how our computer can recognize patterns, and how the process is made invariant with respect to displacements, rotations, and scaling. It will turn out that these invariance properties can be devised in different manners.

A comparison with experimental psychological data will tell us that one of these approaches can be followed up as a model of cognitive processes whereas the other is certainly less applicable (Sect. 12.2). We shall also see how a parameter, which may be directly related to psychological attention, is responsible for the recognition of scenes by a computer. This may shed new light on the way humans perceive complex scenes. The same attention parameters will turn out to be responsible for oscillations that occur in human perception of ambiguous figures such as Fig. 2.5. The application of the synergetic computer to the recognition of movement patterns, for instance the distinction between the different gaits of horses, leads us to ask whether or not humans perceive these patterns in a similar manner.

We have chosen vision as an example of cognitive processes for several reasons. First of all pattern recognition can be easily performed by our computer and the results can be readily compared with those of psycho-physical experiments, even in a quantitative manner. At the same time we believe that vision is a useful paradigm for higher mental processes, such as reasoning, problem solving, etc. Interestingly, this is also mirrored in language by the existence of expressions such as "to gain insight" and "to develop a picture of a situation", etc.

Our approach "sheds new light" on the question of mental maps or mental representations. Surprisingly, the approach allows two interpretations:

1) By a completely parallel network in which mental maps or representations must be stored in the connections or "synapses" between different "neurones".

2) An alternative interpretation in terms of the "grandmother cells" which have occasionally been postulated in brain theories. But most probably our grandmother cells are different from neurones and represent whole assemblies of neurones. We shall also show how we can model assimilation and adaptation and how these two concepts are related to one another. I do not believe that our approach, or any other contemporary approach, will be the ultimate step towards a full understanding of brain functions. On the other hand, I am convinced that it is an important step possessing much future potential.

In many, if not all cases, I believe that the processes of cognition may be thought of as pattern formation by self-organization. This must occur at the abstract level as far as concepts are concerned, and at the material level in cognitive processes related, for example, to firing patterns in neural nets. As the reader will see, a number of our results can be tested experimentally so that a sound basis for future work is established. Our results can also be related to Gestalt-theory. Indeed, more recently psychologists such as Stadler and Kruse have underlined pronounced analogies between the behavior of the systems dealt with in synergetics and phenomena found in perception. As we shall see, a key to cast the concept of "Gestalt" into a rigorous form is provided by the order parameter concept of synergetics.

# Part I

# Synergetic Computers

# 2. What are Patterns?

> One of the most interesting aspects of the world is that it can be considered to be made up of patterns. A pattern is essentially an arrangement. It is characterized by the order of the elements of which it is made rather than by the intrinsic nature of these elements.
>
> *Norbert Wiener*

These sentences by the famous mathematician Norbert Wiener may serve us as a first guideline in defining a pattern. The idea that the nature of the elements is irrelevant for a pattern raises an important issue; namely, a pattern is defined on a specific length scale, on which the nature of the elements is irrelevant. Clearly we may focus our attention on the structure of these elements, but then the elements become the pattern and in turn are composed of still smaller elements. Rather than attempting a final definition of a pattern, let us consider instead a series of examples.

The animate world provides us with a huge variety of different patterns which on occasion may be quite bizarre as is demonstrated by Fig. 2.1. This figure shows the spherical eye of a tropical fly and exhibits the fine hexagonal structure of the facets. Figure 2.2 shows a number of butterflies and moths with their beautifully patterned wings. We recognize these animals in spite of their rather different shapes and their different markings. Apropos shape and coloring: quite often shape and coloring of animals and plants serve special purposes, e.g., to attract a sexual partner or to hide from an enemy by an adequate camouflage or mimicry. Figure 2.3 shows a variety of dogs. We recognize them all as dogs although they may be of different ages, may belong to different breeds, are photographed in different locations, and are in different states of movement or rest. Thus our recognition evidently has a very pronounced capability of categorizing.

Human beings have a highly developed ability to recognize faces, and there is even a specialized center in our brain to do so. Figure 2.4 shows a scene that can be easily decomposed by our brains such that the individual faces can be recognized. There are also patterns that cannot be interpreted in a unique fashion. An example is shown in Fig. 2.5, a drawing by the famous artist Escher. When we consider the white dots as foreground, we recognize angels; when we consider the black dots as foreground, we recognize devils. As we are told by psychologists, and as our own experience teaches us, our perception of these patterns oscillates, i.e. we first recognize the devils for a while, then they are replaced by angels, then the devils will reappear, etc. Patterns need not be static, they may also be dynamic, e.g., when we watch the gaits of horses or dancing people, their movements follow specific patterns. Therefore, one may speak of behav-

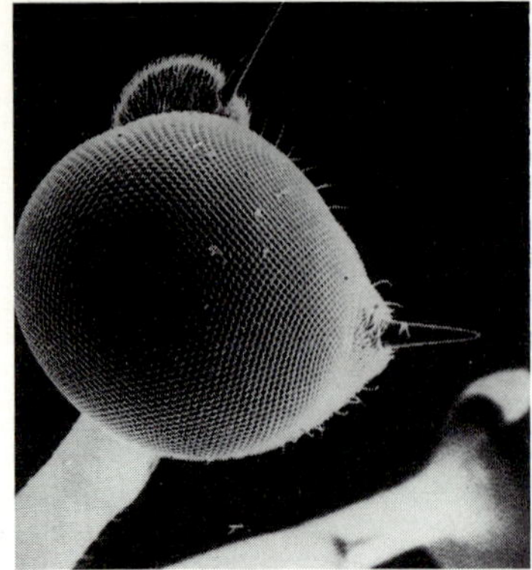

**Fig. 2.1.** Spherical eye of a tropical fly. From Scheibelreiter (1979)

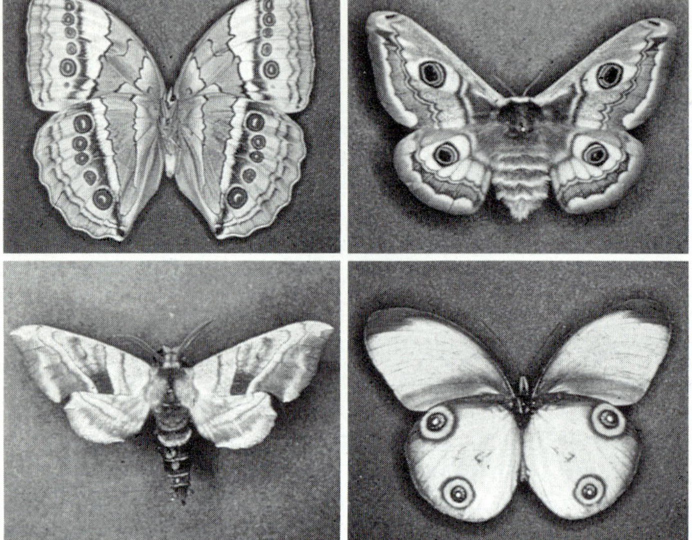

**Fig. 2.2.** Biologists believe that the eye-like patterns on the wings of these butterflies and moths serve to deter predatory birds from attack

ioral patterns. We can often identify people by the way they walk and sometimes even by the sound of their footsteps. At a still higher level we find behavioral patterns in gestures, in facial expressions, and in the kind of speech (for instance pronunciation). Cases of mental illness show characteristic types of behavior, and may also be associated with sudden switching from one type to another.

Science and technology confront us with a great variety of patterns. Such patterns may be the blue-prints for houses, for tools, or for devices (Figs. 2.6, 7). To use these blue-prints a variety of recognition processes must occur, e.g. the blue-print of a house determines what parts must be ordered – steps of staircases, windows, etc. – and where they are to be located. In the case of a circuit

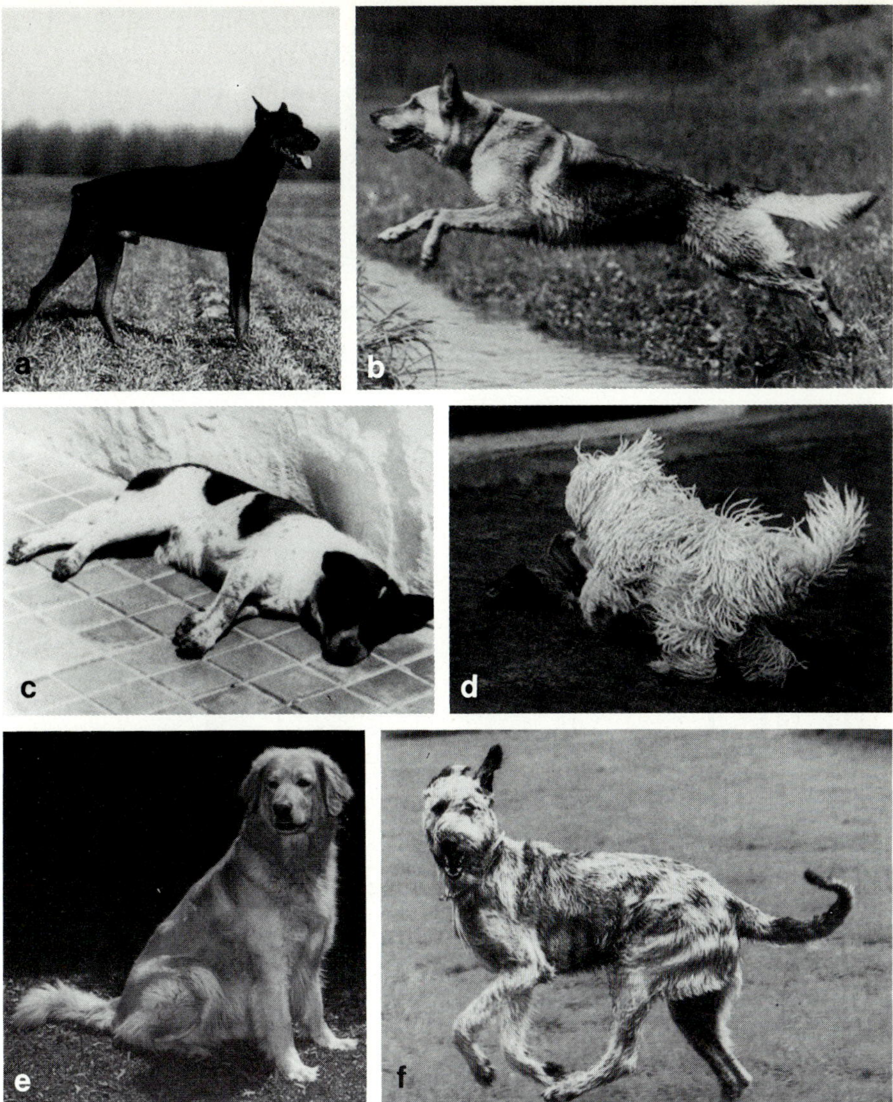


**Fig. 2.3 a – f.** Some examples of the category "dog"

board we must recognize which parts have to be used and where they have to be implemented. Other kinds of patterns are represented by maps, e.g. city-maps, and one wishes to use these maps as guides when walking or driving a car. Meteorology provides us with a great variety of cloud patterns which must be interpreted and analysed for weather-forecasting.

Let us consider some further examples of the patterns produced in science and technology. Figure 2.8 shows an infrared spectrogram of isobutyraldehyde,

Fig. 2.4

Fig. 2.5

**Fig. 2.4.** Scene composed of two faces. From Fuchs and Haken (1988a)

**Fig. 2.5.** A drawing by M.C. Escher: angels or devils. From Escher (1975)

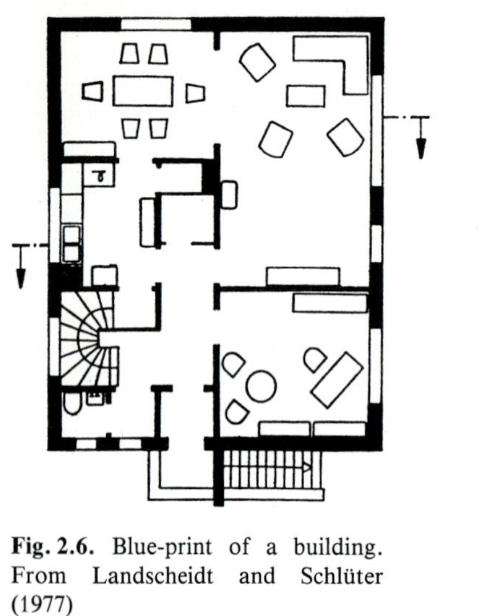

**Fig. 2.6.** Blue-print of a building. From Landscheidt and Schlüter (1977)

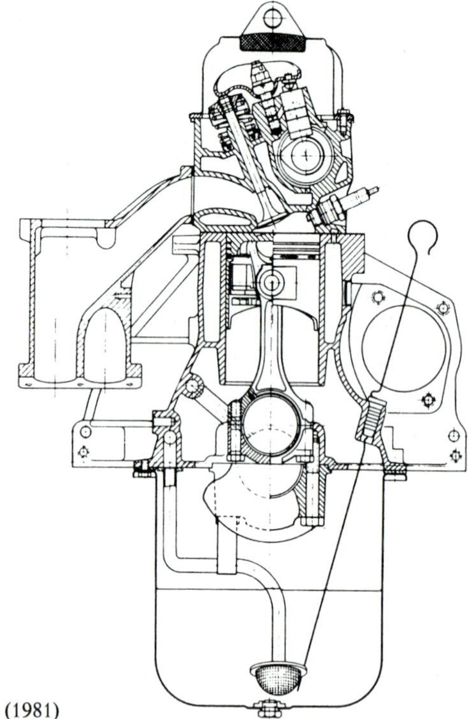

**Fig. 2.7.** Blue-print of an engine. From Grohe (1981)

whereas Fig. 2.9 shows the nuclear magnetic resonance spectrum of the same molecules. Clearly the task will be to devise machines that recognize these patterns and identify the corresponding molecules.

In medicine a number of methods exist for producing pictures or, in other words, patterns. Figure 2.10 shows the electroencephalogram (EEG) of a healthy

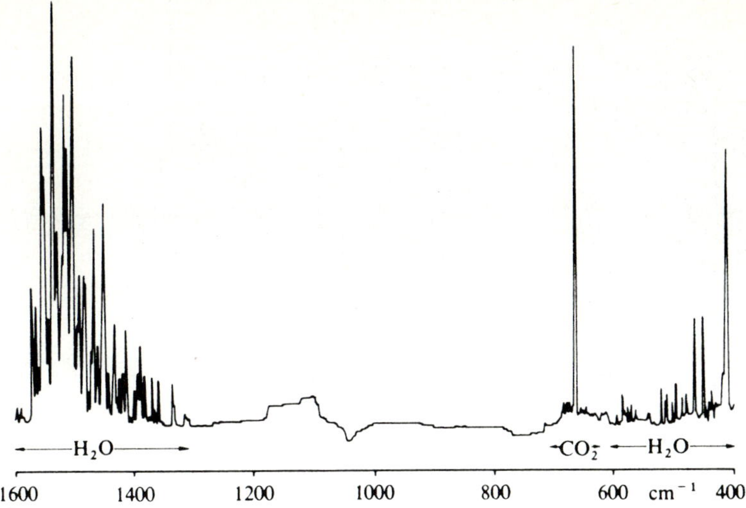


**Fig. 2.8.** Example of an infrared spectrogram. From Banwell (1983)

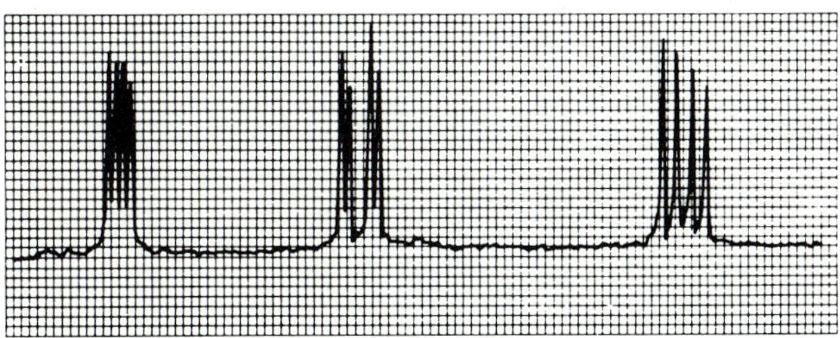

**Fig. 2.9.** Example of a nuclear magnetic resonance spectrum. From Banwell (1983)

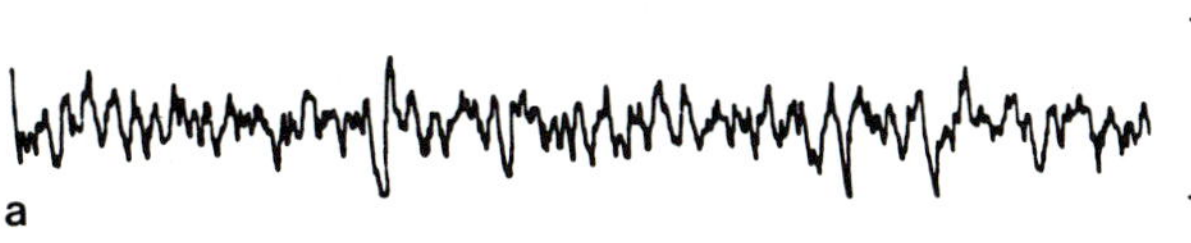


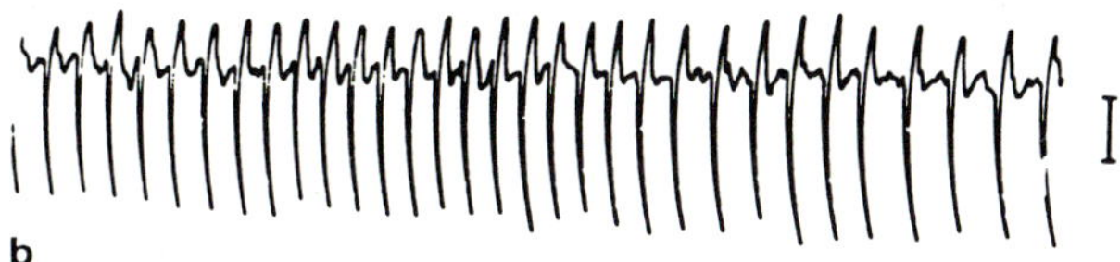


**Fig. 2.10 a, b.** Human electroencephalograms. (**a**) A healthy person thinking. (**b**) A sick person experiencing an epileptic seizure. From Babloyantz (1980)

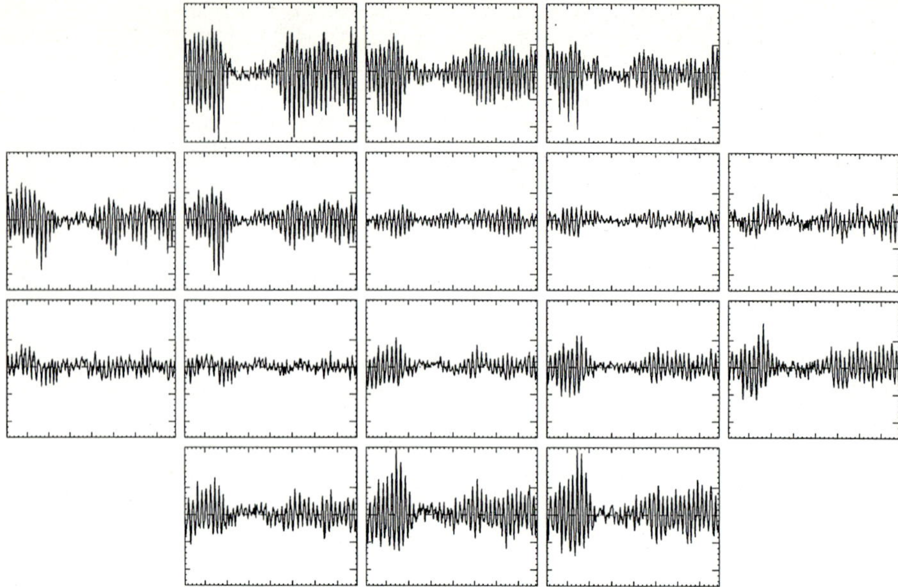

**Fig. 2.11.** Series of EEG recordings taken at 16 different locations on the scalp. (Lehmann, private communication)

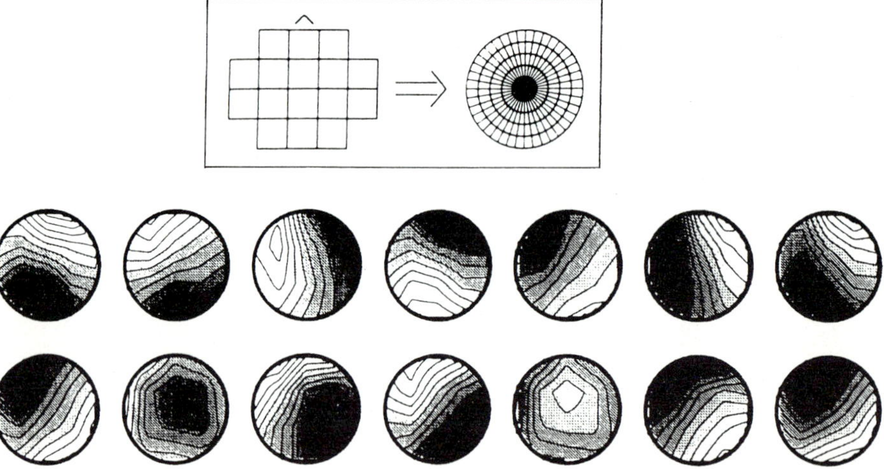

**Fig. 2.12.** *Upper part*: The recordings shown in Fig. 2.11 are mapped from the arrangement shown on the left to a circular arrangement in order to find smooth variations. *Lower part*: Time sequence of EEG activity as a function of space mapped according to the upper part of this figure. Light regions code for high intensity, dark regions for low intensity. The rotation of a wave can clearly be seen. From Friedrich et al. (1987)

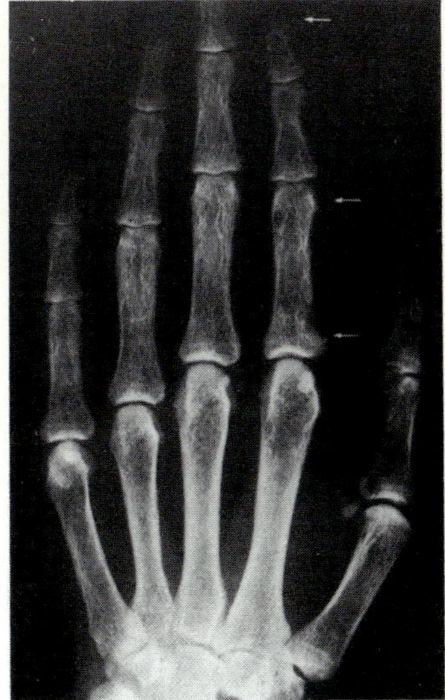

**Fig. 2.13.** X-ray photograph of a hand. From Thurn and Bücheler (1982)

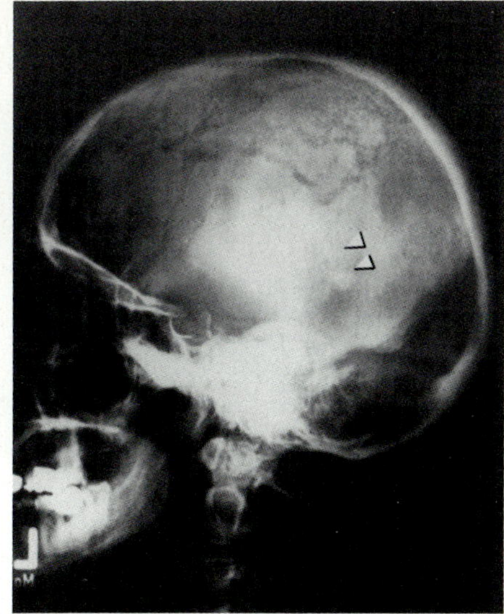

**Fig. 2.14.** X-ray tomograph image of a skull. From Thurn and Bücheler (1982)

person (upper part) and of a person during an epileptic seizure. In medicine attempts are made to analyse these EEG data to draw conclusions about mental illnesses, about the existence of tumors, etc. Multi-electrode electroencephalograms may also be made. Figure 2.11 shows a series of such measurements from sixteen different positions on the scalp. Taking the position and the time-dependence together, spatio-temporal patterns of electrical brain activity can be reconstructed as shown in Fig. 2.12. Experiments by Lehmann in Zürich show that adequate EEG measurements can be correlated to the object of the person's thought. For example, one can establish whether the person is thinking about abstract or concrete events. Another class of patterns important in medicine are X-ray images and images produced by X-ray tomography. Some examples are shown in Figs. 2.13 and 2.14. Again one wishes to discover tumors, tuberculosis, or bone fractures, etc. Finally, a more recent development in medical imaging is the study of various parts of a body by nuclear magnetic resonance or nuclear spin tomography. Here the protons of the hydrogen atoms resonate with electromagnetic waves and produce specific patterns indicating the density of hydrogen in the body (Fig. 2.15). This method can be used for diagnosis, for instance of the existence of tumors.

Of the many experiments in physics which produce an enormous number of data, we mention only high energy physics. Here the paths of the individual elementary particles produced in high energy collisions can be made visible in bubble chambers and with other kinds of detectors (Fig. 2.16). The numerous photographs then have to be studied in the search for new particles, which manifest themselves by specific kinds of traces. It would be desirable, of course,

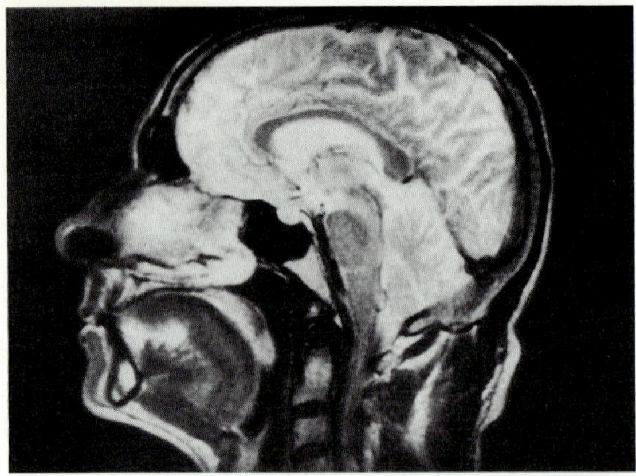

**Fig. 2.15.** A nuclear spin tomograph of a healthy person. From K. Hauser, private communication

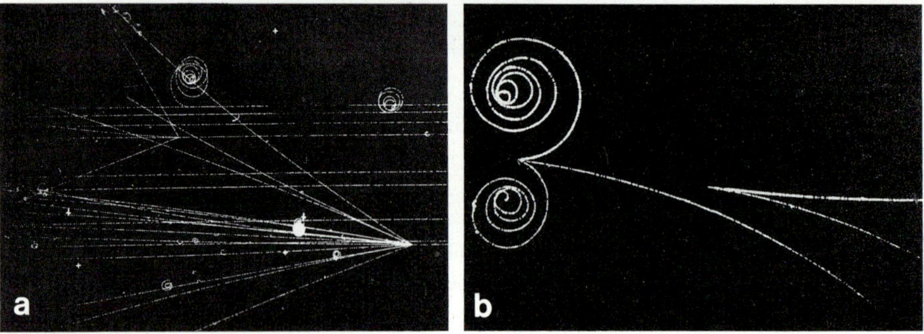


**Fig. 2.16.** (**a**) and (**b**) Typical photographs of traces of particles in bubble chambers. From Close et al. (1989)

if this very labor-intensive job of highly trained humans could be done by computers.

The above examples obviously represent only a very small selection of the patterns we are confronted with in our daily life and in science. Quite clearly patterns have specific meanings for man, animals and even plants. If we think of the position of the sun as a specific pattern, it is clear that a plant has to recognize where the sunshine comes from so that it can adjust its leaves correspondingly. Patterns cause reactions which may be immediate or may be delayed; in either case the result may be stored in a memory. There may be also cases in which a pattern does not cause any reaction. This may be due to a lack of the corresponding senses or to the absence of attention. As we shall see later, attention plays a decisive role in the learning of patterns as well as in their recognition.

Occasionally in this book it will be useful to have a look at biology. Pattern recognition has been essential for survival from the very beginning of the existence of life. All living things rely on pattern recognition in their search for food or prey, to recognize enemies, to search for their sexual partners, etc. Pattern recognition exists at the lowest levels of life; there are bacteria which react to optical signals, although their kind of pattern recognition is obviously quite different from that of, say, an animal. But here again we must be aware of the fact that different creatures recognize and interpret patterns in different ways. A frog, for example, reacts to small and quickly moving objects as being prey, to large objects, however, as being an enemy. Thus, quite generally, according to the pattern and the observer, different behavior may result, such as attack, flight, etc.

We have already alluded to the highly developed ability of humans to categorize, e.g. to recognize a dog irrespective of its bread, age, etc. It is often believed that in this recognition process an enormous number of details are analysed. On the other hand, the evolutionary process suggests the opposite. A light-sensitive bacterium, for instance, reacts to the incoming light in a rather global fashion. Even a frog reacts to objects in a rather global fashion and classifies them on the basis of certain global features. One might thus suppose that human beings, too, classify according to rather global features, and do not rely on a detailed analysis of specific properties. This concept, in fact, comes close to that of Gestalt-theory.

# 3. Associative Memory

A simple example of an associative memory is a telephone dictionary. When we look up a name, we can read off the telephone number belonging to that person. When we use the telephone dictionary, we do this in sequential order. We first look for the first letter of the family name, then for the second letter, etc., and finally we must also, in general, look for the first name. Another example is provided by the identification of a smell, e.g. the smell belonging to a rose. In such a case, on perceiving the smell we immediately associate it with a picture of a rose. A further example might be the face of a person known to us. In such a case we associate a name with this face. In a more formal manner, we may characterize the property of an associative memory as follows: Let a set of data, which we symbolize by $x$ and $y$, be given. We then wish to find a rule or a procedure by which the set of data is complemented:

$$(x, y, \bullet) \Rightarrow (x, y, z) \ . \tag{3.1}$$

An associative memory needs not be unique. For instance we may have two different kinds of substitutions for the empty place on the left-hand side of

$$(a, b, \bullet) \begin{array}{l} \nearrow \ (a, b, c) \\ \searrow \ (a, b, d) \end{array} \tag{3.2}$$

by data $c$ *or* $d$. Such ambiguities occur for instance in language where e.g. the word 'plane' may mean flat or may denote an aeroplane. Ambiguities are also well-known in visual perception as exemplified by Escher's picture of devils or angels (Fig. 2.5). Nature has provided us with different means of resolving such ambiguities. In language it is done by the context, or, in other words, by a hierarchization (letters → words → sentences). In optical perception, on the other hand, oscillations will often occur such that we observe first angels, then devils, then angels again. We shall come back to this latter case in Chap. 13. The addition or multiplication of small numbers can also be considered as an application of associative memory. According to the idea of (3.1), the addition

$$3 + 5 = 8 \tag{3.3}$$

can be expressed in the form

$$(3, +, 5, \bullet) \Rightarrow (3, +, 5, 8) \ . \tag{3.4}$$

To store such rules for arbitrary numbers by an associative memory would evidently require an infinitely large storage. This may be a reason why humans have invented rules for multiplication, addition, etc., where symbols replace numbers. But we may nonetheless interpret such rules as being stored by an associative memory which manipulates symbols. In the context of the development of neural computers, the concept of associative memory is used to train computers to recognize general laws, such as symmetries in figures, topological properties such as interior vs exterior, relations between positions, concepts such as continuous or discontinuous, etc. This raises the question of how far the concept of associative memory can be stretched.

Let us consider the example of a mathematical proof. Clearly at each step certain mathematical rules are used, but the skill of the good mathematician consists in knowing which rule to use when. In general, there are always a number of different possibilities. A simple example is given by convergence criteria for series. One may argue that in such cases some kind of associative memory is again at work but at a higher level. In this author's opinion, the exact relationship between intelligence and the use of associative memory is not entirely clear. At any rate it may be stated that the concept of associative memory is more general than the simple provision of computational rules.

# 4. Synergetics – An Outline

## 4.1 Some Typical Examples

Synergetics is an interdisciplinary field of research concerned with the spontaneous formation of spatial, temporal or functional structures by self-organization. Synergetics focusses its attention on situations where the macroscopic properties of a complex system change qualitatively. Instead of trying to confront the reader with still more definitions, let us rather consider some typical examples. We shall start with physics.

When a liquid in a vessel is heated from below, the heat is transported by heat conduction on a microscopic level and no macroscopic motion can be seen initially. When the temperature difference between the lower and upper surfaces of the liquid exceeds a critical value, suddenly a macroscopic motion can be observed, e.g. in the form of rolls as shown in Fig. 4.1. The fluid rises at specific positions, cools down at the upper surface, and then sinks down at different positions. Perhaps surprisingly, a well-ordered pattern emerges. Such rolls may also develop in a circular vessel. Figure 4.2 shows a computer simulation based on methods of synergetics which will be outlined below. For the time being, it is sufficient to observe the following: When an initially random pattern is given, the fluid organizes itself after a while into a specific roll pattern with a special orientation of the rolls. When a different random initial pattern is given, the rolls will develop again but now with a different orientation.

The system thus shows *multistability*. What causes the different orientations of the rolls can be made clear by the following computer calculation. We set the temperature difference somewhat beyond the critical temperature difference and superimpose an upwelling fluid motion along a line on an otherwise random velocity field as is shown in Fig. 4.3 upper left. The time evolution of the motion in the fluid is shown in the left column from top to bottom. In the next run, a new initial state is prescribed with a different orientation of the line along which upwelling occurs (Fig. 4.3 middle column, upper part). The time evolution is shown in that column. A final state is reached with a roll system which points along the initially prescribed preferred direction. Finally, an initial state was prepared in which two "lines" of upwelling fluid were superimposed on the random velocity field, one "line" being 10% stronger then the other (right column, upper part). Interestingly, the fluid does not make any compromise but develops into a roll system which corresponds to the stronger of the original lines.

We may interpret these findings as follows: The initial state may be considered (or even mathematically represented) as a superposition of all possible final roll systems and of further configurations of the fluid. In this superposi-

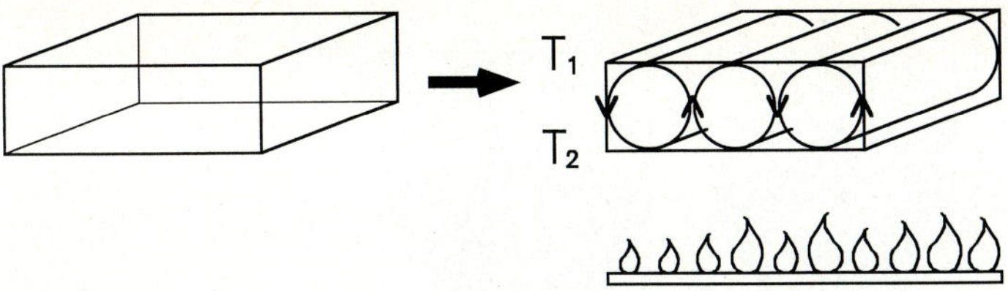


**Fig. 4.1.** Left: When a fluid is heated from below such that there is only a small temperature difference between the lower and upper surface, heat is transported by conduction and no macroscopic motion becomes visible. Right: When the temperature difference $T_2 - T_1$ exceeds a critical value, a macroscopic motion may set in in the form of rolls

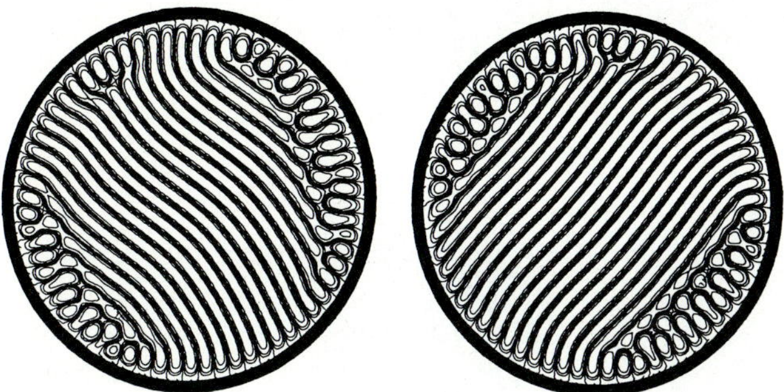

**Fig. 4.2.** Top view of a circular vessel containing a fluid which is heated from below. Depending on initial conditions, the roll system may adopt various orientations

tion, one state, i.e. a roll system in a specific direction, prevails to some extent. This is the one which then gets amplified, while all other configurations are suppressed, so that, eventually, all the parts of the system are pulled into this specific ordered state. As the reader may notice here, this behavior is reminiscent of that of associative memory. Once a set of data is given, the set will be complemented in a specific fashion. As we shall see later, this idea will play a fundamental role in the formulation of a synergetic computer.

Let us consider, as a second example, chemical reactions. When chemicals are poured together, the usual result is a homogeneous end product. There are, however, some specific chemical reactions which can produce rotating spirals, or concentric rings moving outwards, or immobile stripe patterns. Examples are presented in Fig. 4.4. To analyse how these patterns are produced we decompose the whole volume into small volume elements (Fig. 4.5). In each of these elements chemical reactions are happening in which the concentrations of the individual chemicals are changing. The temporal rate of change of their concentrations can be described by addition or multiplication of concentrations. In other words, specific 'computations' are going on in each volume element. Furthermore, the individual volume elements are coupled to one another by the diffusion of chemicals. In this way, information is transferred from one cell to the next. Thus the processes we are considering here provide us with a nice example of a parallel computer. In each of the volume elements computations are going on in parallel

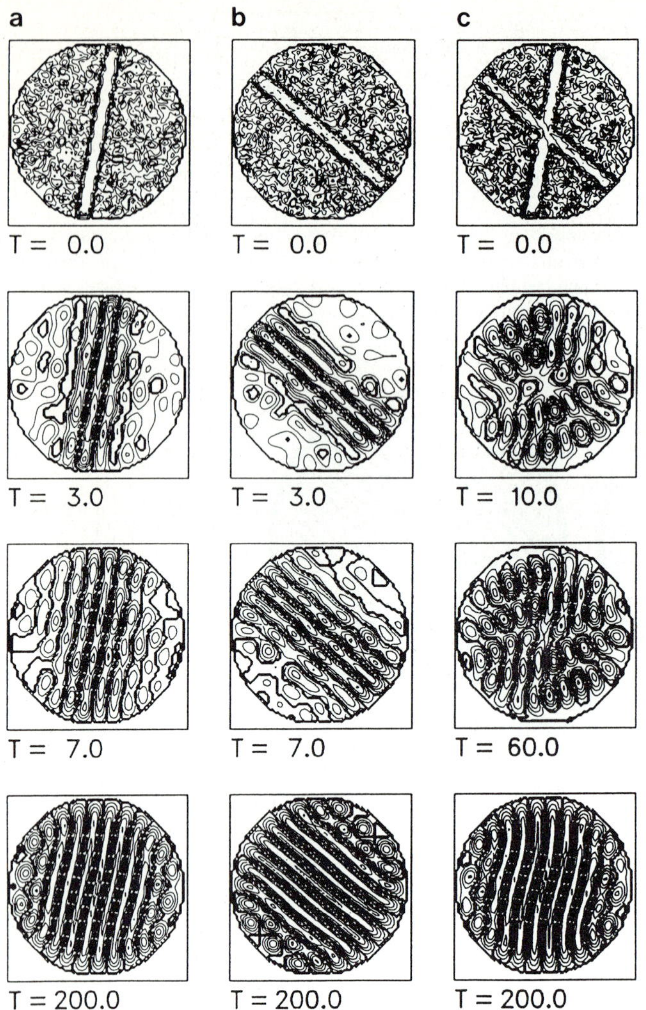


**Fig. 4.3 a – c.** Computer simulation of the development of rolls in a liquid heated from below (top view of the vessel). (**a**) The first frame ($t = 0$) shows the initial orientation of the upwelling, which develops in the course of time into a specific final roll state. (**b**) Same as (a) but which a different orientation of the initially prescribed upwelling of the fluid. (**c**) The initial state consists of a superposition of two lines of upwelling fluid with different strengths. Eventually only one pattern survives to win the competition. (Bestehorn and Haken, unpublished)

and information is exchanged at the same time. The outcome of these processes is then the macroscopic pattern we may observe.

To give the reader a feeling of the breadth of the field of synergetics, we mention a few further examples. In biology we have to deal with morphogenesis at various levels of an organism. Simple examples are the formation of a zebra's stripes and the ring patterns on the wings of butterflies (Fig. 2.2). Other questions concern the growth of neural nets under the impact of incoming signals.

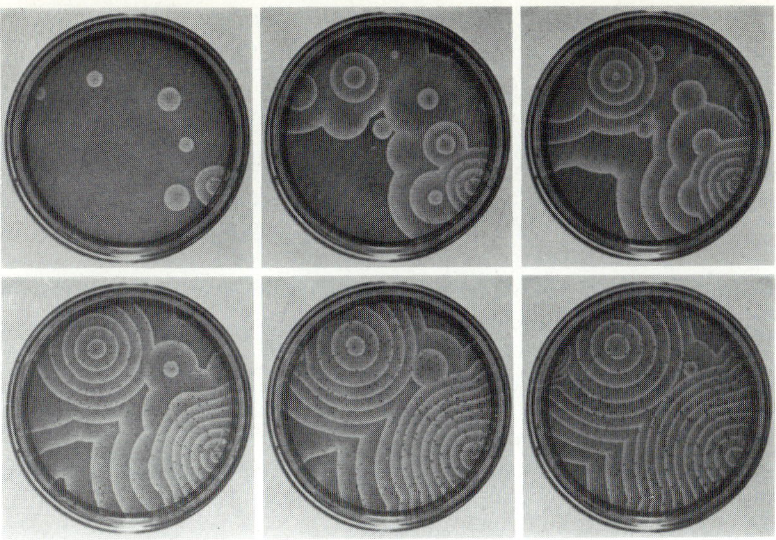

**Fig. 4.4.** Chemical ring patterns formed in the Belousov Zhabotinski reaction

**Fig. 4.5.** Visualization of the chemical reactions in a vessel by dividing the whole volume into individual volume elements. The lines between the elements indicate the path of diffusion of chemicals

Synergetics provides us with models of EEG-patterns, of changes in hand movements, and of changes in the gaits of quadrupeds, just to mention a few typical examples. Synergetics has also found applications in other fields such as economy and sociology, but we shall not dwell here on these aspects. Instead we wish now to deal with its basic concepts and its general mathematical method.

## 4.2 Reminder of the Basic Concepts and Mathematical Tools of Synergetics

Let us now deal with the mathematical formulation. We describe a system by a state vector having components

$$q = (q_1, q_2, \ldots, q_M) \ . \tag{4.1}$$

When we treat pattern formation in continuous media, the individual components $q_j$ are not only dependent on time, $t$, but also on space

$$q_j = q_j(\boldsymbol{x}, t) \tag{4.2}$$

where $\boldsymbol{x} = (x, y, z)$.

Examples for the possible meanings of the components are provided by the case of fluids, where the individual components $q_j$ may mean density $\varrho(\boldsymbol{x}, t)$, velocity field $\boldsymbol{v}(\boldsymbol{x}, t)$, and temperature field $T(\boldsymbol{x}, t)$.

In chemistry the symbols may represent the concentrations, $n$, of different kinds of chemicals labeled by indices $j = 1, \ldots, M$,

$$\boldsymbol{q} = (n_1, n_2, \ldots, n_j, \ldots, n_M) \tag{4.3}$$

which again depend on space and time.

In biology the components could be the density of specific cells, the firing rates of neurones, etc. In the following we shall use an abbreviation for the time derivative of $\boldsymbol{q}$, namely

$$\frac{d\boldsymbol{q}}{dt} = \dot{\boldsymbol{q}} \ . \tag{4.4}$$

In all cases considered by the mathematical theory of synergetics, the state vector (4.1) undergoes a time evolution according to equations of the form

$$\dot{\boldsymbol{q}}(\boldsymbol{x}, t) = \boldsymbol{N}[\boldsymbol{q}(\boldsymbol{x}, t), \nabla, \alpha, \boldsymbol{x}] + \boldsymbol{F}(t) \ . \tag{4.5}$$

Here $\boldsymbol{N}$ is a vector which depends on the state variable $\boldsymbol{q}$ at the same or at different space points as those occurring on the left-hand side of (4.5). In continuously extended media diffusion or wave propagation will take place so that the nabla operator $\nabla = (\partial/\partial x, \partial/\partial y, \partial/\partial z)$ appears. The system is subject to external controls, e.g. to the temperature difference in the Bénard instability, to the rate at which chemicals are poured into the system undergoing chemical reactions, etc. The control parameters are denoted by $\alpha$. In general, $\boldsymbol{N}$ may also depend on spatial inhomogeneities as indicated by $\boldsymbol{x}$. The function $\boldsymbol{F}(t)$ represents fluctuating forces which stem from internal or external fluctuations. Their properties will be specified later. In a number of cases the fluctuations may be neglected, in others they play a decisive role. We shall indicate below what happens in each case.

Let us consider some explicit examples of equations of the type (4.5). In chemistry as well as in biological population dynamics we deal with numbers or concentrations of molecules (individuals of a species). A typical equation for the rate of change of the concentration $n_j$ is given by the form

$$\dot{n}_j = \alpha n_j - k n_j + k' n_l n_m \ . \tag{4.6}$$

The first term on the right-hand side corresponds to a so-called autocatalytic multiplication, because the growth rate of $n_j$ is proportional to its own concentration $n_j$. The next term stems from a spontaneous decay of this type of molecule (or the death of individuals of a species). The last term describes the production of a molecule of type $j$ by the interaction of molecules of type $l$ and $m$. Equation (4.6) may be written in short in the form

$$\dot{n}_j = R_j(\boldsymbol{n}) \tag{4.7}$$

where the vector $\boldsymbol{n}$ is given by

$$\boldsymbol{n} = (n_1, n_2, \ldots, n_M) \ . \tag{4.8}$$

In general, not only reactions but also diffusion processes take place. In such a case $n_j$ becomes a function of space and time

$$n_j = n_j(\boldsymbol{x}, t) \ . \tag{4.9}$$

The temporal change of the concentration $n_j$ is then determined by

$$\dot{n}_j = R_j(\boldsymbol{n}) + D_j \nabla^2 n_j \tag{4.10}$$

in which $D_j$ is the diffusion constant and $\nabla^2$ the Laplace operator. Equations of the type (4.10) are called reaction-diffusion equations. They express in mathematical form what we have discussed in Sect. 4.1.

Quite naturally, it is not possible to solve the Eq. (4.5) for the general case. However, the basic idea of synergetics is as follows: When a system is driven only weakly by external controls, there will be a time-independent state $\boldsymbol{q}_0$ which, in the case of a homogeneous system, is even space-independent

$$\alpha_0 \Rightarrow \boldsymbol{q}_0 \ . \tag{4.11}$$

From many experiments we know that the state (4.11) can change qualitatively when the control parameter is changed from $\alpha_0$ to $\alpha$. In order to check the stability of the solution (4.11), we make the hypothesis

$$\alpha \Rightarrow \boldsymbol{q}(\boldsymbol{x}, t) = \boldsymbol{q}_0 + \boldsymbol{w}(\boldsymbol{x}, t) \ . \tag{4.12}$$

Inserting (4.12) on the right-hand side of (4.5), where we neglect the fluctuating forces for the time being, and expanding the nonlinear function $\boldsymbol{N}$ as a power series in $\boldsymbol{w}$, we obtain

$$\boldsymbol{N}(\boldsymbol{q}_0 + \boldsymbol{w}) = \boldsymbol{N}(\boldsymbol{q}_0) + L\boldsymbol{w} + \hat{\boldsymbol{N}}(\boldsymbol{w}) \ . \tag{4.13}$$

$L$ on the right-hand side of (4.13) is a matrix

$$L = (L_{ij}) \tag{4.14}$$

which may contain spatial derivatives. The matrix elements are defined by

$$L_{ij} = \frac{\partial N_i}{\partial q_j} \quad \text{at} \quad \boldsymbol{q} = \boldsymbol{q}_0 \ . \tag{4.15}$$

$\hat{N}(\boldsymbol{w})$ is a nonlinear function containing the second and/or higher powers of $\boldsymbol{w}$. Since we are, at least for the moment, interested only in the onset of instability, we may assume that $\boldsymbol{w}$ is small so that we can neglect the nonlinear term in (4.13). Because $\boldsymbol{q}_0$ was assumed to be a stationary solution, which changes uniquely with the control parameter $\alpha$, we have

$$\dot{\boldsymbol{q}}_0 = \boldsymbol{N}(\boldsymbol{q}_0) = 0 \ . \tag{4.16}$$

Consequently, in the linear stability analysis we are left with

$$\dot{\boldsymbol{w}} = L\boldsymbol{w} \ . \tag{4.17}$$

The solutions of (4.17) can be written in the general form

$$\boldsymbol{w} = \mathrm{e}^{\lambda t}\boldsymbol{v}(\boldsymbol{x}) \tag{4.18}$$

provided the eigenvalues $\lambda$ of $L$ are nondegenerate. Otherwise $\boldsymbol{v}$ may contain powers of $t$. For sake of simplicity we shall focus our attention on the non-degenerate case. We shall distinguish the eigenvalues and eigenvectors by the index $j$

$$\lambda_j, \boldsymbol{v}_j(\boldsymbol{x}) \ . \tag{4.19}$$

We now wish to solve the fully nonlinear equations (4.5) taking care also of the fluctuating forces. To this end we make the hypothesis

$$\boldsymbol{q} = \boldsymbol{q}_0 + \sum_j \xi_j(t)\boldsymbol{v}_j(\boldsymbol{x}) \ . \tag{4.20}$$

Inserting it into (4.5), where we use the decomposition (4.13), we obtain

$$\sum_j \dot{\xi}_j(t)\boldsymbol{v}_j(\boldsymbol{x}) = \sum_j \xi_j(t)L\boldsymbol{v}_j(\boldsymbol{x}) + \hat{N}\Big[\sum_j \xi_j(t)\boldsymbol{v}_j(\boldsymbol{x})\Big] + \boldsymbol{F}(t) \ . \tag{4.21}$$

As one may show, it is always possible to construct a set of adjoint functions $\boldsymbol{v}_k^+(\boldsymbol{x})$ with the property

$$\langle \boldsymbol{v}_k^+ \boldsymbol{v}_j \rangle \equiv \int \boldsymbol{v}_k^+(\boldsymbol{x})\boldsymbol{v}_j(\boldsymbol{x})dV = \delta_{kj} \ . \tag{4.22}$$

where $\delta_{kj}$ is the Kronecker symbol, $\delta_{kj} = 1$ for $k = j$ and 0 otherwise. We multiply (4.21) by $\boldsymbol{v}_k^+(\boldsymbol{x})$ and integrate over the space. Using the property

$$L\boldsymbol{v}_j(\boldsymbol{x}) = \lambda_j\boldsymbol{v}_j(\boldsymbol{x}) \tag{4.23}$$

and the definitions

$$\int \boldsymbol{v}_k^+(\boldsymbol{x})\boldsymbol{F}(t,\boldsymbol{x})dV = F_k(t) \tag{4.24}$$

and

$$\int \boldsymbol{v}_k^+(\boldsymbol{x})\hat{N}\Big[\sum_j \xi_j(t)\boldsymbol{v}_j(\boldsymbol{x})\Big]dV = \tilde{N}_k[\xi_j(t)] \ , \tag{4.25}$$

we may cast the equations (4.21) into the form

$$\dot{\xi}_k = \lambda_k \xi_k + \tilde{N}_k(\xi_j) + F_k(t) \ . \tag{4.26}$$

We now distinguish between two cases depending on the sign of the real part of the eigenvalues $\lambda_j$. If the real part is non-negative, we shall call the corresponding configurations $\boldsymbol{v}(\boldsymbol{x})$ *unstable modes*, and in the opposite case we shall call them *stable modes*; we distinguish them by introducing the abbreviations u (unstable) and s (stable). According to this discrimination we may split the equations (4.26) into two sets, namely

$$\dot{\xi}_{\mathrm{u}} = \lambda_{\mathrm{u}} \xi_{\mathrm{u}} + \tilde{N}_{\mathrm{u}}(\xi_{\mathrm{u}'}, \xi_{\mathrm{s}'}) + F_{\mathrm{u}} \tag{4.27}$$

and

$$\dot{\xi}_{\mathrm{s}} = \lambda_{\mathrm{s}} \xi_{\mathrm{s}} + \tilde{N}_{\mathrm{s}}(\xi_{\mathrm{u}'}, \xi_{\mathrm{s}'}) + F_{\mathrm{s}} \ . \tag{4.28}$$

Note that the indices u and s serve a double purpose: the u and s of $\xi_{\mathrm{u}}$ and $\xi_{\mathrm{s}}$, respectively, label the variables where $\mathrm{u} = 1, \dots, n$, and $\mathrm{s} = n+1, \dots, K$, (where $K$ is the number of modes), whereas in $\xi_{\mathrm{u}}$ and $\xi_{\mathrm{s}}$ the index distinguishes between the set of unstable and stable modes, respectively. Because we are operating the system in a situation where the real part of $\lambda_{\mathrm{u}}$ is still small, we may apply the *slaving principle* of synergetics. We shall not derive it here because of its very lengthy proof, but rather we wish to give the reader a feeling how it works. For simplicity, let us consider the case where $\lambda_{\mathrm{u}}$ is real. Let us treat a special case of (4.28), namely

$$\dot{\xi}_{\mathrm{s}} = \lambda_{\mathrm{s}} \xi_{\mathrm{s}} + \xi_{\mathrm{u}}^2 + \dots \ . \tag{4.29}$$

Because $\lambda_{\mathrm{u}}$ is small (and $\xi_{\mathrm{u}}$ is assumed to be small also), we conclude from (4.27) that $\xi_{\mathrm{u}}$ changes only very slowly in time. According to equation (4.29), $\xi_{\mathrm{u}}$ drives $\xi_{\mathrm{s}}$, and thus we find that $\dot{\xi}_{\mathrm{s}}$ is of the order of

$$\dot{\xi}_{\mathrm{s}} \approx \lambda_{\mathrm{u}} \xi_{\mathrm{s}} \ . \tag{4.30}$$

But because $\lambda_{\mathrm{u}}$ is much smaller that $\lambda_{\mathrm{s}}$, we may neglect $\dot{\xi}_{\mathrm{s}}$ on the left-hand side of (4.29) entirely:

$$\dot{\xi}_{\mathrm{s}} = 0 \ . \tag{4.31}$$

This allows us to replace the differential equation (4.29) by a normal algebraic equation which can be solved immediately

$$\xi_{\mathrm{s}} = -\frac{\xi_{\mathrm{u}}^2}{\lambda_{\mathrm{s}}} - \frac{F_{\mathrm{s}}}{\lambda_{\mathrm{s}}} \ . \tag{4.32}$$

Actually, a detailed discussion shows that this approximation is even permissible for the fluctuating force $F_{\mathrm{s}}$ since it is taken care of in (4.32). Our example shows us that $\xi_{\mathrm{s}}$ can be expressed by $\xi_{\mathrm{u}}$ explicitly, and with the same time argument as

$\xi_u$. In other words, $\xi_s$ follows $\xi_u$ instantaneously. Under the assumption that the real parts of $\lambda_u$ are small, one may show quite generally that $\xi_s$ can be expressed explicitly by $\xi_u$ and with the same time argument:

$$\xi_s(t) = f_s[\xi_u(t); t] \ . \tag{4.33}$$

The additional explicit time-dependence appearing in (4.33) stems from the fluctuating forces; if they are absent, this time-dependence vanishes. By means of (4.33) we may eliminate $\xi_s$ in (4.27) which leaves us with an equation of the form

$$\dot{\xi}_u = \lambda_u \xi_u + \bar{N}_u(\xi_{u'}) + F_{u,\text{tot}} \ . \tag{4.34}$$

The general case, in which $\boldsymbol{q}_0$ may be periodic or quasiperiodic in time, and where the $\lambda$'s are complex is treated in the literature (see references). For our present purpose, a consideration of (4.34) will be sufficient. Because of (4.20) and (4.33), the evolving structure or, in other words, the ordering of the system is determined by $\xi_u$, and thus these variables are called *order parameters*. Equation (4.33) is known as the *slaving principle*.

In order to derive a typical explicit form of (4.34), let us consider a simple case in which $\xi_u$ obeys the equation

$$\dot{\xi}_u = \lambda_u \xi_u - \xi_s \xi_u \ . \tag{4.35}$$

Using (4.32), we find

$$\dot{\xi}_u = \lambda_u \xi_u - \beta \xi_u^3 + F \tag{4.36}$$

where $F$ is a fluctuating force.

In order to grasp the meaning of (4.36), we write it in the form

$$\dot{\xi}_u = -\frac{\partial V}{\partial \xi_u} + F \ , \tag{4.37}$$

i.e. we introduce a potential function $V$. By adding an acceleration term $m\ddot{\xi}_u$, where $m$ has the meaning of a mass of a particle, to the left-hand side of (4.37), we may interpret the latter as the equation of the overdamped motion of a particle in a potential $V$ subject to a fluctuating force $F$. For the case of a single order parameter $\xi_k$ the potential is plotted in Fig. 4.6 for positive and negative values of $\lambda_u$. Quite evidently, the potential changes qualitatively. We immediately see that for $\lambda_u < 0$ the particle remains close to the minimum and is only displaced slightly by the fluctuating forces $F$. For the case $\xi_u > 0$, two minima occur, i.e. $\xi_u$ adopts non-vanishing stable displacements which are subject to small fluctuations. The behavior of the variable $\xi_u$ exhibits features which are well-known from systems in thermal equilibrium when they undergo *phase transitions*, e.g. when a magnet goes from its unmagnetized state into a magnetized state or a superconductor from its normal state into the superconducting state. Here one expects the following phenomena: The formerly stable position $\xi_u = 0$ becomes

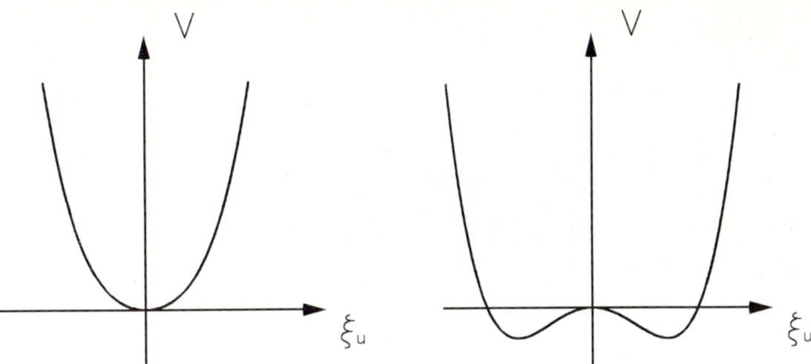


**Fig. 4.6.** The potential $V$ as function of the order parameter $\xi_k$ for a negative control parameter (*left*) and for a positive control parameter (*right*)

unstable and is replaced by two new stable positions according to Fig. 4.6. The two states are totally equivalent, or, in other words, symmetric with respect to one another. Nonetheless, the system has to decide between these two states and can adopt only one state. Therefore it has to break the symmetry. Such a transition is thus called a *symmetry breaking instability.* Furthermore, when we let $\lambda_u$ grow starting from negative values, the potential curve of Fig. 4.6 (left) becomes flatter and flatter. Thus the particle, which is kicked away from the equilibrium point by the fluctuating force, relaxes back more and more slowly. This, too, is well-known from equilibrium phase transitions as *critical slowing down.* Furthermore, because the restoring force is becoming weaker and weaker, the fluctuations of the "particle", i.e. of $\xi_u$, become more and more pronounced. Thus *critical fluctuations* occur. Since these phenomena, which are all typical for the conventional phase transitions of systems in thermal equilibrium, now also occur in systems far from equilibrium as treated by synergetics, we shall call the change in the behavior of $\xi_u$ a *nonequilibrium phase transition.*

As we were able to show by the explicit treatment of numerous examples, the number of order parameters is generally much smaller than the number of mode amplitudes $\xi_s$ which are also called the *enslaved modes.* In a number of cases the right-hand side of (4.34) can be written as a derivative of a potential function $V$, even if several order parameters are present [cf. (4.37)], where $V = V(\xi_u)$. The potential can be visualized as a landscape having hills and valleys (Fig. 4.7). The bottom of each valley represents a *stable fixed point*, the top of each mountain an *unstable fixed point.* Because the stable fixed points seem to attract the "particle", they are also called *attractors.* (Note, however, that a fixed point is a special case of an attractor.) All points in the landscape from which the particle can roll down into the same attractor form the *basin of attraction.* Points of minimal height on ridges may be described as *saddle points.* When we plot the trajectories of $\xi_u$ in two dimensions, we obtain pictures such as those in Fig. 4.8. Equations of the type (4.37) will turn out to play a decisive role in our approach to pattern recognition.

Once we have solved (4.34) or (4.37) and calculated $\xi_s$ according to (4.33), we may construct the desired solution $\boldsymbol{q}(\boldsymbol{x}, t)$ by means of (4.20), where we now

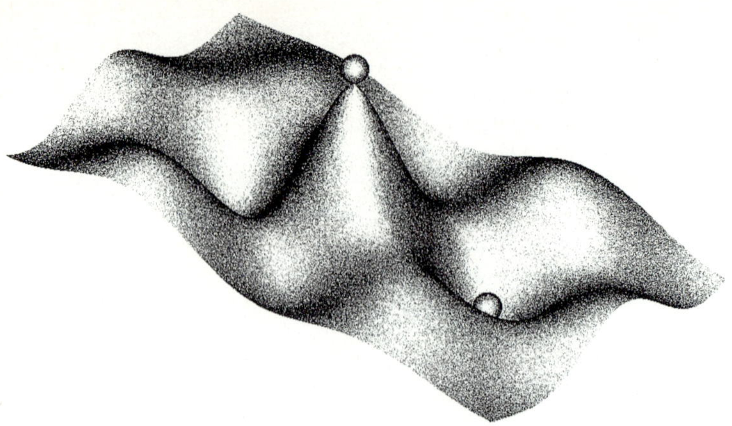

**Fig. 4.7.** Example of potential landscape in a space of two order parameters

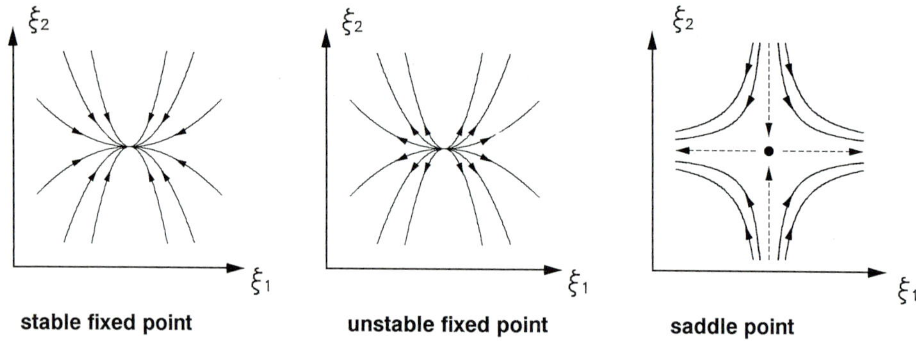


**Fig. 4.8.** Fixed points in two dimensions: A stable node (*left*), an unstable node (*middle*), and a saddle point (*right*). The lines with arrows are the trajectories followed by the system

distinguish between the order parameters $\xi_u$ and the amplitudes $\xi_s$ of the enslaved modes. We obtain

$$q = q_0 + \underbrace{\sum_u \xi_u(t) v_u(x)}_{\text{mode-skeleton}} + \sum_s \xi_s(t) v_s(x) \ . \tag{4.38}$$

Close to the transition point the order parameters $\xi_u$ are much bigger than the amplitudes $\xi_s$, and thus the pattern is described by the first sum in (4.38); this sum will therefore be called "the mode-skeleton".

In order to prepare for our section on pattern recognition, we consider (4.38) more closely. For sake of convenience we put

$$q_0 = 0 \ . \tag{4.39}$$

When we multiply (4.38) by $v_j^+$ and use the identity (4.22), we readily find

$$\xi_j = \langle \boldsymbol{v}_j^+ \boldsymbol{q} \rangle \ . \tag{4.40}$$

Since in the following we shall only be interested in the behavior of the mode-skeleton, we shall change our original equations so that the last sum in (4.38) tends to 0 for $t \to \infty$

$$\sum_s \xi_s(t) \boldsymbol{v}_s(\boldsymbol{x}) \to 0 \ . \tag{4.41}$$

For $\xi_u$ we shall adopt the Eqs. (4.34), i.e.,

$$\dot{\xi}_u = \lambda_u \xi_u + \hat{N}_u(\xi_{u'}) + F_{u,tot} \ , \tag{4.42}$$

whereas we replace the equations for $\xi_s$ by

$$\dot{\xi}_s = -g_s(\xi_{u'}, \xi_s) \tag{4.43}$$

where $g_s$ is a function with the property

$$\xi_s \to 0 \quad \text{for} \quad t \to \infty \ . \tag{4.44}$$

We now multiply (4.42) and (4.43) by $\boldsymbol{v}_j(\boldsymbol{x})$ and sum up over $j$. We readily obtain

$$\begin{aligned} \dot{\boldsymbol{q}} = & \sum_u \lambda_u \langle \boldsymbol{v}_u^+ \boldsymbol{q} \rangle \boldsymbol{v}_u + \sum_u \boldsymbol{v}_u \hat{N}_u(\langle \boldsymbol{v}_u^+, \boldsymbol{q} \rangle) \\ & + \sum_s \boldsymbol{v}_s g_s(\langle \boldsymbol{v}_j^+ \boldsymbol{q} \rangle) + \hat{\boldsymbol{F}}(t) \ . \end{aligned} \tag{4.45}$$

We shall utilize (4.45) as the starting point for our formalism on pattern recognition. Before doing so, however, we will illustrate the meaning of the order parameter equations (4.37) by means of an explicit example taken from fluid dynamics. We imagine a fluid heated from below and consider the situation in which the temperature of the fluid is somewhat above the threshold temperature for the onset of macroscopic motion. As one may show, a linear stability analysis of the Navier-Stokes equations leads to a velocity field described by

$$\boldsymbol{v}(x,y,z) = \exp\left[\mathrm{i}(k_x x + \mathrm{i} k_y y)\right] \boldsymbol{g}(z) \tag{4.46}$$

when we utilize a complex representation. The function $\boldsymbol{g}(z)$ which we shall not specify here, describes the change of the velocity in the (vertical) $z$-direction, whereas the exponential function describes a wave propagating in the (horizontal) $x-y$ plane.

In the following we shall use the notation

$$\boldsymbol{k} \cdot \boldsymbol{x} = k_x x + k_y y \ . \tag{4.47}$$

We focus our attention on a horizontal plane, i.e., a constant value of $z$, and we identify the vertical velocity $v_z$ with a component of $\boldsymbol{q}$ in Eq. (4.38). This leads to the hypothesis

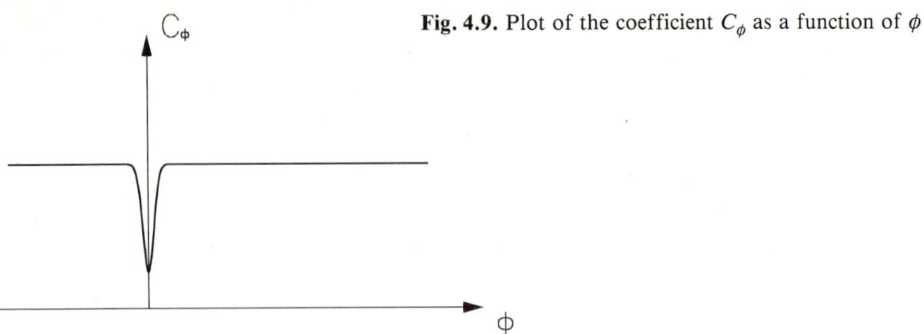


**Fig. 4.9.** Plot of the coefficient $C_\phi$ as a function of $\phi$

$$v_z = \sum_k \xi_k(t) e^{i k \cdot x} , \tag{4.48}$$

where the $\xi_k$ play the role of order parameters. As a detailed calculation in fluid dynamics, which we shall not repeat here, shows, these order parameters obey the following set of equations

$$\dot{\xi}_k = \lambda(k)\xi_k - \xi_k \sum_{k'} C_{k,k'} |\xi_{k'}|^2 \tag{4.49}$$

where

$$|\boldsymbol{k}| = k_0 . \tag{4.50}$$

These calculations show further that $C_{k,k'}$ depends only on the angle $\phi$ between the wave vectors $\boldsymbol{k}$ and $\boldsymbol{k}'$ in a way shown in Fig. 4.9. But this dependence has a very important consequence, namely that the only stable solutions of (4.49) are those in which only one $\xi_k$ does not vanish; all other $\xi_k$ must be zero in a stationary state. In other words, (4.49) provides the "mode" selection, i.e., the selection of a specific roll system (cf. Fig. 4.2). At the same time it describes multistability because any direction $\boldsymbol{k}$ of the roll pattern can be realized. The time evolution of the roll patterns according to (4.49) was represented in Fig. 4.3 for various stochastic initial conditions of the velocity field $\boldsymbol{v}$. As we shall show in Chap. 5, this property of specific mode selection remains valid if $C_{k,k'}$ is replaced by

$$C_{k,k'} = \begin{array}{ll} A & \text{for} \quad \boldsymbol{k} = \boldsymbol{k}' \\ B > A & \text{for} \quad \boldsymbol{k} \neq \boldsymbol{k}' . \end{array} \tag{4.51}$$

This means that the functional dependence on $\boldsymbol{k}, \boldsymbol{k}'$ is now given by Fig. 4.10.

Let us summarize the results of this chapter. When a system is controlled from the outside by means of a control parameter, it may be driven into an unstable state. In this state a number of modes tend to grow, whereas all others remain damped. The amplitudes of the growing modes are called the order parameters, since they determine the dynamics of the whole system and the mode-skeleton. Whereas below the instability point there exists only one stable state, beyond it several states become accessible but only one of them can be selected

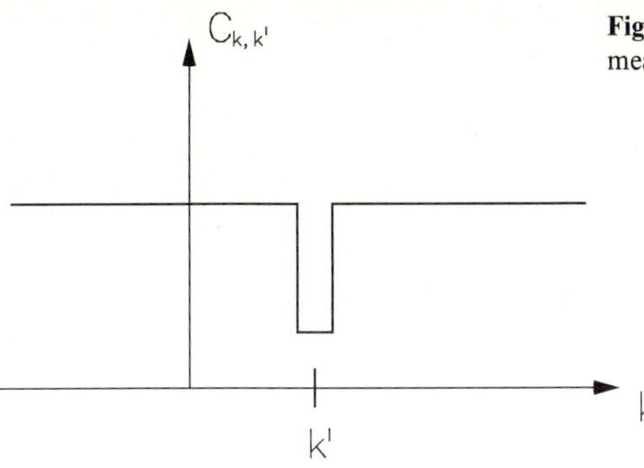


**Fig. 4.10.** Idealization of the curve of Fig. 4.9 by means of the coefficient $C_{kk'}$, as a function of $k$

(symmetry breaking). The actual choice depends on the state produced initially, e.g. by fluctuations. Once the order parameters are determined, the patterns defined by (4.38) are fixed. When an order parameter or a set of order parameters grow, the corresponding patterns (4.38) also grow in the course of time. Examples are shown in Fig. 4.3.

The rest of this chapter is devoted to the Fokker-Planck equation, which will play an important role when we study the learning mechanisms of synergetic computers. In what follows, it will not be important whether we deal with the original vector $\boldsymbol{q}$ or with the order parameters $\xi$. Therefore, we shall again denote our variables by $\boldsymbol{q}$. In the case of a single variable, the equation for $q$ acquires the form

$$\dot{q} = K(q) + F(t) \quad , \tag{4.52}$$

where $K$ is a deterministic force, whereas $F$ represents a fluctuating force. We shall assume here that $F(t)$ obeys the relations

$$\langle F(t) \rangle = 0 \quad , \quad \langle F(t) F(t') \rangle = Q\delta(t-t') \tag{4.53}$$

where the angle brackets mean the statistical average over the stochastic process which produces the fluctuating force $F$. Its strength is given by $Q$, while the Dirac $\delta$-function expresses its short memory.

Readers who are not familiar with fluctuating forces can safely read this chapter by ignoring their occurrence totally; their significance will merely be alluded to occasionally.

Instead of tracing the different paths described by $q(t)$ and followed by the particle under the influence of the random forces $F$ (Fig. 4.11), we may look for an ensemble of such paths, and ask for the probability of finding the particle at a time $t$ in the interval $q \to q + dq$. The corresponding probability function will be denoted by $f(q,t)dq$ (Fig. 4.12). As is well known in physics and mathematics, this probability function $f$, which belongs to (4.52), obeys the Fokker-Planck equation

$$\dot{f}(q,t) = -\frac{\partial}{\partial q}(Kf) + \frac{1}{2} Q \frac{\partial^2 f}{\partial q^2} \quad . \tag{4.54}$$

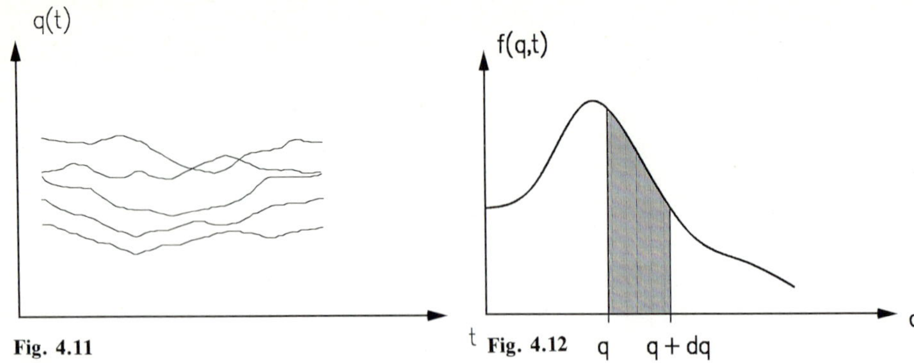


**Fig. 4.11.** Different realizations of the time evolution of the variable $q(t)$

**Fig. 4.12.** The probability distribution function $f(q,t)$ versus $q$ for a fixed time. The shaded area is the probability of finding the system in the interval between $q$ and $q+dq$

In the following we shall be interested only in the stationary solution, in which case the time derivative $\dot{f}$ vanishes. Equation (4.54) can then easily be integrated

$$f_{\mathrm{st}}(q) = N\exp\left(-\frac{2V(q)}{Q}\right) , \tag{4.55}$$

where the potential function $V$ is related to the force $K$ by

$$K(q) = -\frac{\partial V}{\partial q} . \tag{4.56}$$

Let us now try to generalize these results to the case of several variables $q_j$. They obey equations of the form

$$\dot{q}_j = K_j(\boldsymbol{q}) + F_j(t) , \tag{4.57}$$

where, in general, $K_j$ depends on all the components of the vector $\boldsymbol{q}$. We shall assume that the fluctuating forces obey the relationships

$$\langle F_j(t)\rangle = 0 \tag{4.58}$$

and

$$\langle F_j(t)F_k(t')\rangle = Q_{jk}\delta(t-t') . \tag{4.59}$$

The Fokker-Planck equation corresponding to (4.57) reads

$$\dot{f}(\boldsymbol{q},t) = -\sum_j \frac{\partial}{\partial q_j}(K_j f) + \frac{1}{2}\sum_{jk} Q_{jk}\frac{\partial^2}{\partial q_j \partial q_k} f . \tag{4.60}$$

In general it is not possible to find even the stationary solution in closed form. However, if the forces $K$ obey the potential condition

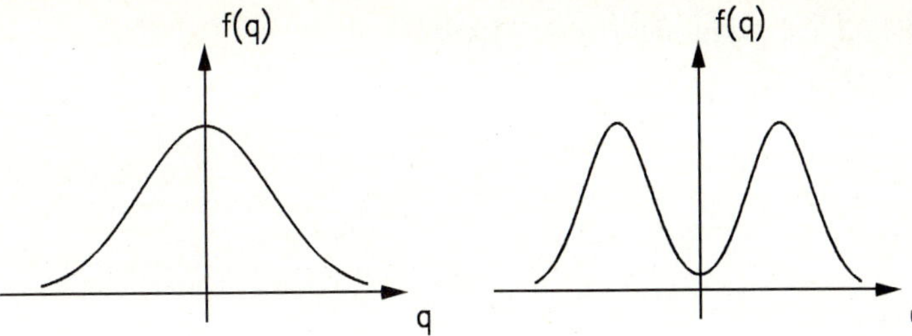


**Fig. 4.13.** The probability distribution for a particle which moves in the potentials of Fig. 4.6. The left- and right-hand sides of the two figures correspond to one another

$$K_j = -\frac{\partial V}{\partial q_j} \tag{4.61}$$

and the strengths of the fluctuating forces are given by

$$Q_{jk} = Q\delta_{jk} \ , \tag{4.62}$$

then the stationary solution can be constructed in the form

$$f_{\mathrm{st}} = N \exp\left(-\frac{2V(q)}{Q}\right) \ . \tag{4.63}$$

The meaning of (4.63) can easily be visualized when we think of the interpretation of $V$ as a potential landscape. The minima of $V$, where the particle will be found most frequently, are at the same time the maxima of $f$. For example, the distribution functions corresponding to the one-dimensional potentials of Fig. 4.6 are given in Fig. 4.13. $N$ in (4.63) is a normalization constant.

# 5. The Standard Model of Synergetics for Pattern Recognition

## 5.1 Prototype Pattern Vectors and Test Pattern Vectors

In order to construct our model, we use three ingredients:

a) The concept of associative memory discussed in Chap. 3. When an incomplete set of data is given, the associative memory must be able to complement it.

b) We construct a dynamical process by which pattern recognition is performed. To this end we invent a potential landscape in which a fictitious particle, which describes the patterns, moves. An example is provided by the ambivalent patterns of Fig. 5.1. Later on we shall see that ambiguous patterns require a specific treatment, but for the time being we shall stick to the idea that the system is pulled into one of its attracting states provided an initial condition is set such that the symmetry is broken. In other words, the pattern that is recognized first is the one for which a certain bias was given, or, expressed in yet another way, the pattern is recognized once it is within its basin of attraction.

c) We treat the system as a synergetic system according to the following idea: In Chap. 4 we saw that a partially ordered system, e.g. a fluid in which some of the rolls have been formed, may generate its order parameter, which then competes with the other order parameters of the system. Because of the special preparation of the initial state involving partially ordered subsystems, the order parameter belonging to that specific order wins the competition and, eventually, enslaves the whole system such that it enters a particular ordered state. In pattern recognition we shall take advantage of the same mechanism. Once a set of features is given, they can form their order parameter which will compete with other order-parameters. Eventually the order parameter that had the strongest initial support will win, and will force the system to exhibit the features that were lacking with respect to the special pattern (Fig. 5.2). Thus we see that there is a complete correspondence between the complementation process during pattern formation and the associative memory during pattern recognition.

In order to show how these ideas can be cast into a mathematical form, we first briefly discuss the selection of features. Actually, there exists a whole literature on how to select features. For our present purposes it is sufficient to illustrate our procedure by means of a specific example. When we have a photograph of a face, we may put a grid over it in order to digitize the whole image. We label the individual cells or pixels by numbers $j = 1, 2, \ldots N$ as shown by the symbol $Z$ in Fig. 5.3. To each pixel we attribute a further number $v_j$ indicating its tone of grey. We then form the vector

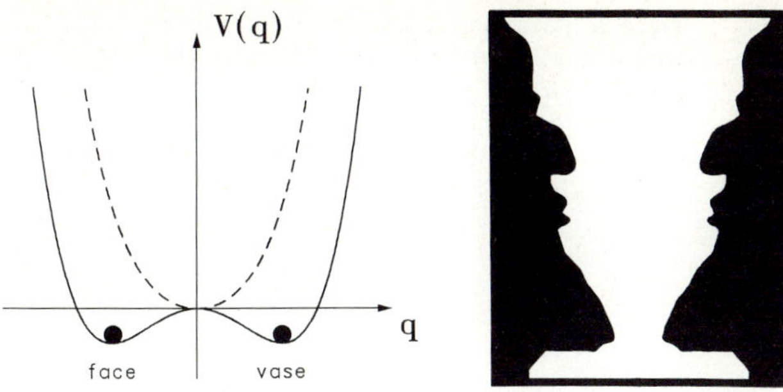


**Fig. 5.1.** Interpretation of pattern recognition by means of an order parameter moving in a potential landscape with two attractors, vase and face, respectively (left). The right-hand side shows the ambiguous pattern vase/face. This interpretation of pattern recognition was given by Haken (1977)

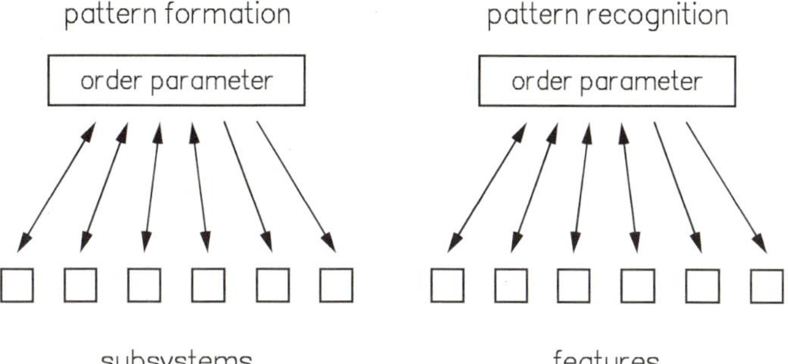


**Fig. 5.2.** Analogy between pattern formation (*left*) and pattern recognition (*right*). In pattern formation the subsystems are enslaved by the order parameters; in the case of pattern recognition it is the features that are enslaved by order parameters. See text for more details. This analogy was established by Haken (1979)

$$v = \begin{pmatrix} v_1 \\ v_2 \\ \vdots \\ v_N \end{pmatrix} . \tag{5.1}$$

Because we wish to store a whole set of different faces in the computer, we distinguish them by a label $k$ so that $v$ is now replaced by the prototype vectors

$$v_k = \begin{pmatrix} v_{k1} \\ v_{k2} \\ \vdots \\ v_{kN} \end{pmatrix} . \tag{5.2}$$

We shall assume that $v_{jk}$ is real. The label $k$ may adopt the values

$$k = 1, \ldots, M \tag{5.3}$$

where $M$ is the number of stored patterns. We shall assume that the number of patterns is smaller than or equal to the number of features

**Fig. 5.3.** Illustration of the way in which the prototype patterns are encoded as vectors. The photographed face is decomposed into pixels, the grey value at each pixel corresponds to a component of the prototype pattern vector

$$M \leq N \ . \tag{5.4}$$

If not stated otherwise, we subject the vectors $\boldsymbol{v}_k$ to the condition

$$\sum_l v_{kl} = 0 \tag{5.5}$$

which can always be achieved by forming

$$\boldsymbol{v}_k = \tilde{\boldsymbol{v}}_k - \frac{1}{N} \sum_j \tilde{v}_{jk} \tag{5.6}$$

where $\tilde{\boldsymbol{v}}_k$ are the "raw vectors" and $N$ is the number of features per pattern.

We shall also need the transposed vector which is defined by

$$\bar{\boldsymbol{v}}_k = (v_{k1}, v_{k2}, \dots v_{kN}) \ . \tag{5.7}$$

We shall assume throughout this book that the normalization

$$(\bar{\boldsymbol{v}}_k \boldsymbol{v}_k) \equiv \sum_{j=1}^{N} v_{kj}^2 = 1 \tag{5.8}$$

holds. This can always be achieved by dividing a "raw vector" $\tilde{\boldsymbol{v}}_k$ by $(\bar{\tilde{\boldsymbol{v}}}_k \tilde{\boldsymbol{v}}_k)^{1/2}$. Because the vectors $\boldsymbol{v}_k$ are not necessarily orthogonal to each other, we shall need the adjoint vectors

$$\boldsymbol{v}_k^+ = (v_{k1}^+, v_{k2}^+, \dots v_{kN}^+) \ , \tag{5.9}$$

which obey the orthonormality relations

$$(\boldsymbol{v}_k^+ \boldsymbol{v}_{k'}) = \delta_{kk'} \ . \tag{5.10}$$

We shall represent the adjoint vectors $\boldsymbol{v}_k^+$ as a superposition of the prototype vectors $\boldsymbol{v}_k$

$$v_k^+ = \sum_{k'} a_{kk'} \bar{v}_{k'} \ , \tag{5.11}$$

where $a_{kk'}$ are constants and $\bar{v}_{k'}$ denotes the transpose of $v_{k'}$. As we shall see later on, (5.11) will help us considerably in doing the numerical calculations.

## 5.2 Construction of the Dynamics

As indicated at the beginning of this chapter, our goal is this: Let a test pattern, which we denote by the vector $q$, be given. We then wish to construct a dynamics which pulls the test pattern via intermediate states $q(t)$ into one of the prototype patterns $v_{k_0}$, namely the one to which $q(0)$ was closest, i.e. in whose basin of attraction it was lying:

$$q(0) \rightarrow q(t) \rightarrow v_{k_0} \ . \tag{5.12}$$

A glance at the main results of the previous chapters immediately provides us with such a dynamics: We construct the equation of motion for $q$ in such a way that it resembles (4.37) or, more specifically (4.45), and has the property that it eventually leads to an order parameter equation of the kind (4.49) which allows a discrimination of the roll patterns in fluids. Here, of course, the patterns may be far more complicated and the required equation reads

$$\dot{q} = \sum_k \lambda_k v_k (v_k^+ q) - B \sum_{k' \neq k} (v_{k'}^+ q)^2 (v_k^+ q) v_k - C(q^+ q) q + F(t) \ . \tag{5.13}$$

Note that the constant $B$ can be made dependent on $k$ and $k'$,

$$B \rightarrow B_{kk'} \ , \tag{5.14}$$

and then has to be taken into the sum. But for the time being such a generalization is not needed.

Let us briefly discuss the meaning of the individual terms on the right-hand side of (5.13). This meaning will become more transparent during the course of the book. $\lambda_k$ are called attention parameters. We shall see that a pattern can be recognized only if the corresponding attention parameters are positive; otherwise it will not be recognized. The expression $v_k \cdot v_k^+$ acts as a matrix. As one can see, first $v_k^+$ is multiplied by a column vector $q$ so that a scalar is generated. Finally, the vector $v_k$ becomes effective which again acts as a column vector. Thus by the whole process, a column vector is transformed into a new column vector or, in other words, $v_k \cdot v_k^+$ acts as a matrix. This matrix occurred in a number of early publications by various authors and is called the learning matrix. The second term serves to discriminate between patterns as we shall demonstrate by both an explicit example (Fig. 5.4) and a general proof below. Because the first term, at least when $\lambda$ is positive, will lead to an exponential growth of $q$, we need a factor which limits that growth. This is achieved by the third term on the right-hand side. Finally $F$ are the fluctuating forces that we shall use occasionally, but which we shall drop when not otherwise noted.

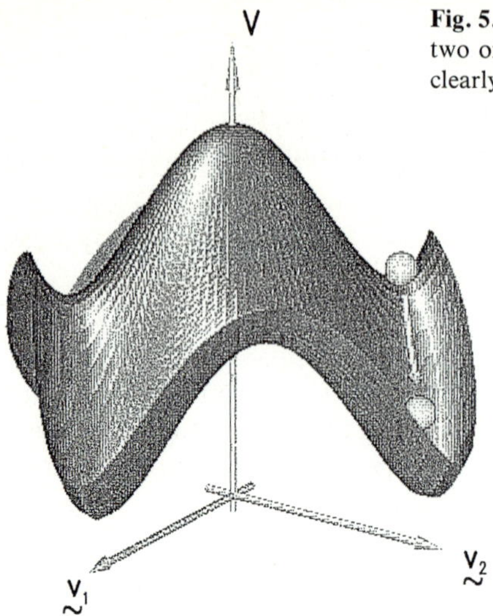


**Fig. 5.4.** Representation of the potential $V$ in the space of two order parameters (or two features). The attractors are clearly visible

We shall decompose the vector $\boldsymbol{q}$ into the prototype vectors (5.2) and a residual vector $\boldsymbol{w}$

$$\boldsymbol{q} = \sum_{k=1}^{M} \xi_k \boldsymbol{v}_k + \boldsymbol{w} \tag{5.15}$$

and require that

$$(\boldsymbol{v}_k^+ \boldsymbol{w}) = 0 \quad \text{for all} \quad k = 1, \ldots, M \ . \tag{5.16}$$

We now define $\boldsymbol{q}^+$ which appears in $C(\boldsymbol{q}^+ \boldsymbol{q})\boldsymbol{q}$ in (5.13), by means of the relations

$$\boldsymbol{q}^+ = \sum_{k=1}^{M} \xi_k \boldsymbol{v}_k^+ + \boldsymbol{w}^+ \tag{5.17}$$

where $\boldsymbol{w}^+$ obeys the orthogonality relations

$$(\boldsymbol{w}^+ \boldsymbol{v}_k) = 0 \quad \text{for all} \quad k = 1, \ldots, M \ . \tag{5.18}$$

One can readily convince oneself that

$$(\boldsymbol{v}_k^+ \boldsymbol{q}) = (\boldsymbol{q}^+ \boldsymbol{v}_k) \ . \tag{5.19}$$

This follows by inserting (5.15) into the left-hand side of (5.19) to yield

$$(\boldsymbol{v}_k^+ \boldsymbol{q}) = \left[ \boldsymbol{v}_k^+ \left( \sum_{k'=1}^{M} \xi_{k'} \boldsymbol{v}_{k'} + \boldsymbol{w} \right) \right] , \tag{5.20}$$

which, by means of the orthogonality relations (5.10, 16), can be written as

$$(v_k^+ q) = \xi_k \ . \tag{5.21}$$

The same result is obtained when we insert (5.17) on the right-hand side of (5.19) and utilize the orthogonality relations (5.10, 18). Equation (5.19) allows us to express the right-hand side of (5.13) either by means of the left-hand side of (5.19) everywhere or by the right-hand side of (5.19) everywhere so that only the variables $q$ or $q^+$ are involved. One can then readily show that the formal equations

$$\dot{q} = -\frac{\partial V}{\partial q^+} \ , \tag{5.22}$$

$$\dot{q}^+ = -\frac{\partial V}{\partial q} \tag{5.23}$$

hold, in which $V$ plays the role of a potential function explicitly given by

$$V = -\tfrac{1}{2} \sum_{k=1}^{M} \lambda_k (v_k^+ q)^2 + \tfrac{1}{4} B \sum_{k \neq k'} (v_k^+ q)^2 (v_{k'}^+ q)^2 + \tfrac{1}{4} C (q^+ q)^2 \ . \tag{5.24}$$

Thus a rather far reaching analogy is revealed with the Eqs. (4.37) and (4.45) of Chap. 4.

We now wish to derive the order parameter equations belonging to (5.13). To this end we multiply (5.13) from the left by $v_k^+$. Using the orthogonality relations between $v_k^+, v_k$, $w$, and $w^+$, and the definition (5.21), we obtain

$$\dot{\xi}_k = \lambda_k \xi_k - B \sum_{k' \neq k} \xi_{k'}^2 \xi_k - C \left[ \sum_{k'=1}^{M} \xi_{k'}^2 + (w^+ w) \right] \xi_k \ . \tag{5.25}$$

Note that the sum over $k' \neq k$ runs over all values $k' = 1 \dots M$ except for the value $k$ which appears as the coefficient of $\dot{\xi}_k$ on the left-hand side of (5.25). When we multiply (5.13) by vectors $u_l^+$ belonging to the space orthogonal to the prototype pattern vectors $v_k$ and sum up over the individual components, we obtain the equations

$$\dot{w} = -C \left[ \sum_{k'=1}^{M} \xi_{k'}^2 + (w^+ w) \right] w \ . \tag{5.26}$$

In the derivation of (5.26), the following relations have been used:

$$w = \sum_{l=M+1}^{N} f_l(t) u_l \ , \tag{5.27}$$

$$w^+ = \sum_{l=M+1}^{N} f_l(t) u_l^+ \ , \tag{5.28}$$

$$(u_l^+ u_{l'}) = \delta_{ll'} \ , \tag{5.29}$$

$$(\boldsymbol{u}_l^+ \boldsymbol{v}_k) = (\boldsymbol{v}_k^+ \boldsymbol{u}_l) = 0 \ . \tag{5.30}$$

Because the factor multiplying $\boldsymbol{w}$ on the right-hand side of (5.26) is negative everywhere, we find

$$|\boldsymbol{w}| \rightarrow 0 \quad \text{for} \quad t \rightarrow \infty \ , \tag{5.31}$$

where the norm $|\boldsymbol{w}|$ is defined by

$$|\boldsymbol{w}| = (\boldsymbol{w}^+ \boldsymbol{w})^{1/2} \ . \tag{5.32}$$

Thus the dynamics reduces the problem to the prototype vector space

$$\dot{\xi}_k = \lambda_k \xi_k - B \sum_{k' \neq k} \xi_{k'}^2 \xi_k - C \left( \sum_{k'=1}^{M} \xi_{k'}^2 \right) \xi_k \ . \tag{5.33}$$

The order parameters obey the initial condition

$$\xi_k(0) = (\boldsymbol{v}_k^+ \boldsymbol{q}(0)) \tag{5.34}$$

which follows directly from (5.21). Quite clearly, the right-hand side of (5.33) can be derived from a potential function

$$\dot{\xi}_k = -\frac{\partial \tilde{V}}{\partial \xi_k} \ , \tag{5.35}$$

where $\tilde{V}$ is given by

$$\tilde{V} = -\tfrac{1}{2} \sum_{k=1}^{M} \lambda_k \xi_k^2 + \tfrac{1}{4} B \sum_{k' \neq k} \xi_{k'}^2 \xi_k^2 + \tfrac{1}{4} C \left( \sum_{k'=1}^{M} \xi_{k'}^2 \right)^2 \ . \tag{5.36}$$

Note that the sum over $k' \neq k$ is now a double sum where $k'$ and $k$ each run from $1 \ldots M$, but with the terms $k' = k$ omitted. The role played by the individual terms in (5.24) or in (5.36) can be easily visualized by considering a plot of the potential $V$ in a two-dimensional feature space, where the two axes are spanned by the two prototype vectors $\boldsymbol{v}_1$ and $\boldsymbol{v}_2$ (Fig. 5.4). Close to the origin, the terms quadratic in $\boldsymbol{q}$ dominate and we see that the first sum in (5.24) has a negative sign provided the attention parameters $\lambda_k$ are positive. This decrease in the potential ceases when $\boldsymbol{q}$ increases further because then the last term in (5.24) takes over and, eventually, increases much more quickly than the first term decreases. This interplay between the first and last terms generates the valleys indicated in Fig. 5.4. The middle term on the right-hand side of (5.24) finally generates the ridges that define the basins of attraction and thus enables discrimination between different patterns.

## 5.3 Important Properties of $V(\xi_k)$

In this section we shall assume that all attention parameters are equal and positive

$$\lambda_k = \lambda > 0 \tag{5.37}$$

and we put $\lambda = C$.

Since this section is rather technical, we first summarize the results.

### 5.3.1 Summary of the Results

The stable fixed points are at $\boldsymbol{q} = \boldsymbol{v}_k$, i.e. at the prototype patterns, and there are no other stable fixed points. The stable fixed points are equivalently characterized by $\xi_k = 1$, all other $\xi$'s $= 0$. The only unstable fixed point is at $\boldsymbol{q} = 0$. There are saddle points situated at $\xi_{k_1} = \xi_{k_2} = \ldots = \xi_{k_m} = 1$, all other $\xi$'s $= 0$. Here $k_1, k_2, \ldots k_m$ may be any selection out of $1, \ldots, M$. If $|\xi_{k_0}|$ is initially bigger than any other $|\xi|$, the dynamics pulls the system to the stable fixed point $\xi_{k_0} = 1$, all other $\xi$'s $= 0$. If $|\xi_{k_1}| = |\xi_{k_2}| = \ldots = |\xi_m|$ are initially bigger than any other $\xi_k$, the dynamics terminates at the corresponding saddle point, from which only a fluctuation can drive the system into any of the fixed points belonging to $k_1, k_2, \ldots, k_m$. In the following we shall prove these assertions. Readers not interested in these details may skip the rest of this section without any loss of understanding of the remainder of this book.

### 5.3.2 Where Are the Deepest Minima of $V$?

Since, in the nomenclature of synergetics, we are dealing with unstable modes only, we shall replace the index $k$ by u. The order parameters obey the equations

$$\dot{\xi}_{\mathrm{u}} = -\frac{\partial V}{\partial \xi_{\mathrm{u}}}, \tag{5.38}$$

where $V$ is given by

$$V = -\frac{\lambda}{2} \sum_{\mathrm{u}=1}^{M} \xi_{\mathrm{u}}^2 + \frac{1}{4}(B+C)\Big(\sum_{\mathrm{u}'} \xi_{\mathrm{u}'}^2\Big)^2 - \frac{1}{4} B \sum_{\mathrm{u}} \xi_{\mathrm{u}}^4, \tag{5.39}$$

which follows from (5.36) by a slight rearrangement of the sums. We first study the steady state where

$$\dot{\xi}_{\mathrm{u}} = 0. \tag{5.40}$$

Equation (5.38) reads explicitly

$$\xi_{\mathrm{u}}\Big[\lambda - (B+C) \sum_{\mathrm{u}'} \xi_{\mathrm{u}'}^2 + B\xi_{\mathrm{u}}^2\Big] = 0. \tag{5.41}$$

In the following we shall use the abbreviation

$$(B+C)\sum_{u'}\xi_{u'}^2 = D \ . \tag{5.42}$$

Equation (5.41) yields the solutions

$$\xi_u = 0 \tag{5.43}$$

or

$$\xi_u^2 = \frac{D-\lambda}{B} \ . \tag{5.44}$$

As a result of (5.44) all solutions $\xi_u \neq 0$ are equal

$$\xi_u^2 = \xi_0^2 \ . \tag{5.45}$$

Let us denote the number of nonvanishing $\xi_u$ by $\alpha$. Then

$$D = (B+C)\alpha\xi_0^2 \ . \tag{5.46}$$

Inserting (5.46) into (5.44) and solving this equation for $\xi_0^2$, we obtain

$$\xi_0^2 = \lambda[\alpha C + B(\alpha-1)]^{-1} \ . \tag{5.47}$$

We now wish to determine the number $\alpha$ of nonvanishing $\xi_u$ for which the potential acquires its deepest value. To this end we insert (5.47) into (5.39). Using the explicit form of $\xi_0^2$ we obtain, after a number of simple intermediate manipulations,

$$V = -\frac{\alpha\lambda^2}{4}[\alpha C + (\alpha-1)B]^{-1} \ . \tag{5.48}$$

This function is plotted in Fig. 5.5. As is evident from (5.48), $V$ has a singularity at a value for $\alpha$ for which the denominator vanishes:

$$\alpha C + (\alpha-1)B = 0 \ . \tag{5.49}$$

Denoting this $\alpha$ by $\alpha_0$ we have

$$\alpha_0 = \frac{B}{B+C} \ . \tag{5.50}$$

Clearly $\alpha_0$ lies between 0 and 1 provided $B>0$ and $C>0$. Since $\alpha$ can adopt only integer values, we have the result that the potential $V$ has its absolute minimum when $\alpha = 1$, i.e. when only one $\xi_u \neq 0$. Because we had assumed $C=\lambda$, we obtain from (5.47):

$$\xi_0^2 = 1 \ . \tag{5.51}$$

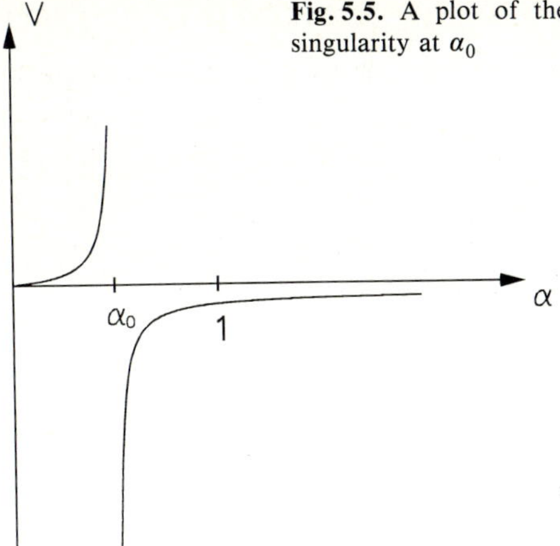


**Fig. 5.5.** A plot of the function $V(\alpha)$ according to (5.48). Note the singularity at $\alpha_0$

We thus find that only one pattern can be recognized at a time. However, it is conceivably possible that there are spurious states of the potential where it has a local minimum at several nonvanishing $\xi_u$. In order to show that this case is excluded, we study the stationary and stable points more closely by investigating the potential $V$.

### 5.3.3 Where Are the Stationary and Stable Points of $V$?

We expand $V$ into power series around the stationary points $\xi_0$

$$V(\xi) = V(\xi_0) + \text{grad}\, V\,\delta\xi + \frac{1}{2}\sum_{u,u'} \frac{\partial^2 V}{\partial\xi_u\,\partial\xi_{u'}}\,\delta\xi_u\,\delta\xi_{u'} \ . \tag{5.52}$$

Because the gradient of $V$ vanishes at the stationary points,

$$\text{grad}\, V = 0 \ , \tag{5.53}$$

we may confine our analysis to the last term in (5.52). Using the form (5.39) for $V$, the second derivative reads

$$\frac{\partial^2 V}{\partial\xi_u^2} = [-\lambda + (B+C)\sum_{u'} \xi_{u'}^2 - B\xi_u^2] + 2C\xi_u^2 \tag{5.54}$$

and the second derivative with respect to $\xi_u$ and $\xi_{u'}$ is

$$\frac{\partial^2 V}{\partial\xi_u\partial\xi_{u'}} = 2(B+C)\xi_u\xi_{u'} \ , \quad u \neq u' \ . \tag{5.55}$$

According to the above discussion, there are only two types of stationary points, namely, at $\xi_u = 0$ or at $\xi_u^2 = \xi_0^2$.

Let us consider the different cases.

1) All $\xi_u = 0$. In this case, from (5.54, 55), we readily obtain the equations

$$\frac{\partial^2 V}{\partial \xi_u^2} = -\lambda \tag{5.56}$$

and

$$\frac{\partial^2 V}{\partial \xi_u \partial \xi_{u'}} = 0 \ , \quad u \neq u' \ . \tag{5.57}$$

Inserting these results into the last term of (5.52) yields

$$\delta^2 V(\xi) = -\frac{\lambda}{2} \sum_u (\delta \xi_u)^2 \ , \tag{5.58}$$

which clearly indicates that the point $\xi_u = 0$ for all u represents a maximum, or, in other words, an unstable fixed point.

2) Now let assume that we are at a stationary point where a number $L$ of $\xi_u$ are nonvanishing, whereas all other $\xi_u$ are zero. Because of the symmetry of the problem, we may assume for simplicity that the nonvanishing $\xi_u$ carry labels $u = 1 \dots L$. We distinguish the following cases:

a) The indices u and u′ run both from $1 \dots L$. Then, by means of (5.54, 55), we obtain the results

$$\frac{\partial^2 V}{\partial \xi_u^2} = 2C\xi_0^2 > 0 \ , \tag{5.59}$$

$$\frac{\partial^2 V}{\partial \xi_u \partial \xi_{u'}} = \pm 2(B+C)\xi_0^2 \ , \quad u \neq u' \ . \tag{5.60}$$

The corresponding part of the last term of (5.52) reads

$$\sum_{uu'=1}^{L} \pm (B+C)\xi_u \xi_{u'} \delta\xi_u \delta\xi_{u'} - \delta_{uu'} B(\delta\xi_u)^2 \ . \tag{5.61}$$

In order to get rid of the ambiguity with respect to the sign in front of $(B+C)$, we choose $\delta\xi$ in such a way that $\delta\xi_u$ is retained if $\xi_u > 0$ but is replaced by $-\delta\xi_u$ if $\xi_u < 0$. Therefore it becomes admissibly to keep only the positive sign.

b) Let the index u be $L+1, \dots, M$ and $u' = 1, \dots, L$ so that

$$\begin{aligned} \xi_u &= 0 \qquad u = L+1, \dots M \\ \xi_{u'} &= \pm \xi_0 \qquad u' = 1, \dots L \ . \end{aligned} \tag{5.62}$$

We readily obtain

$$\frac{\partial^2 V}{\partial \xi_u^2} = B\xi_0^2 \tag{5.63}$$

and

$$\frac{\partial^2 V}{\partial \xi_u \partial \xi_{u'}} = 0, \quad u \neq u' . \tag{5.64}$$

c) We now make the following choices

$$\begin{aligned} \xi_u &= 0 \quad u = L+1, \dots M \\ \xi_{u'} &= 0 \quad u' = L+1, \dots M . \end{aligned} \tag{5.65}$$

We readily obtain

$$\frac{\partial^2 V}{\partial \xi_u^2} = B\xi_0^2 \tag{5.66}$$

and

$$\frac{\partial^2 V}{\partial \xi_u \partial \xi_{u'}} = 0 , \quad u \neq u' . \tag{5.67}$$

The results (5.59) – (5.67) can be summed by the left-hand side of (5.69) below, but with $\kappa = 0$. It represents the matrix with the elements

$$\frac{1}{2} \frac{\partial^2 V}{\partial \xi_u \partial \xi'_u} . \tag{5.68}$$

In order to discuss the definiteness of this matrix we require that the following determinant vanishes

$$\begin{vmatrix} C-\kappa & B+C & B+C \dots B+C \\ B+C & C-\kappa & B+C \dots B+C \\ B+C & B+C & C-\kappa \dots B+C \\ \vdots & & \\ B+C & B+C & B+C \dots C-\kappa \end{vmatrix} = 0 \tag{5.69}$$

where $\kappa$ are the eigenvalues of the matrix with the elements (5.68). Instead of studying the matrix (5.69) directly, we consider instead the corresponding eigenvector equations (5.71). Dividing each row by $(B+C)$, introducing the abbreviation

$$\frac{C-\kappa}{B+C} = \delta , \tag{5.70}$$

and denoting the components of the unknown eigenvectors by $x_j$, we obtain the equations

$$x_1\delta + x_2 + \ldots + x_M = 0 \ ,$$
$$x_1 + x_2\delta + \ldots + x_M = 0 \ ,$$
$$x_1 + \ldots \qquad + \delta x_M = 0 \ . \tag{5.71}$$

In order to solve them, we make the hypothesis

$$x_j = \mathrm{e}^{\mathrm{i}kj} \ , \tag{5.72}$$

where we impose the periodicity condition

$$\mathrm{e}^{\mathrm{i}kM} = 1 \tag{5.73}$$

whence

$$k = 2\pi \frac{n}{M} \ , \tag{5.74}$$

where $n$ is an integer. Inserting the hypothesis (5.72) into (5.71), we obtain the equation

$$\delta \mathrm{e}^{\mathrm{i}k} + \sum_{\nu=2}^{M} \mathrm{e}^{\mathrm{i}\nu k} = 0, \quad M \geq 2 \ . \tag{5.75}$$

For $k \neq 0$ the sum can be easily performed and we obtain via some intermediate steps the result

$$k \neq 0: \quad \delta - 1 = 0 \ . \tag{5.76}$$

In the case $k = 0$ we obtain

$$k = 0: \quad \delta + (M-1) = 0 \ . \tag{5.77}$$

Inserting (5.70) into (5.77) and solving for $\kappa$ yields

$$\kappa = C + (M-1)(B+C) > 0 \ , \tag{5.78}$$

i.e. a positive eigenvalue indicating stability. On the other hand, for all $k \neq 0$ we obtain $(N-1)$-fold degenerate eigenvalues

$$\kappa = -B \ , \tag{5.79}$$

which are negative, indicating instability. Thus we may conclude that provided $M > 2$ all points are unstable. Because one eigenvalue is positive and the others negative, we are dealing with a saddle point. We may summarize our results as follows:

1) If there is only one order parameter $\xi_u \neq 0$, and all others vanish, we have

$$M = 1 \ , \quad \kappa = C \ .$$

Therefore there is one and only one stable state which is at a global minimum of the potential $V$.

2) If there are several stationary states with $\xi_u \neq 0$, while all other vanish, we have

$$M \geq 2 \ , \quad \text{and at least one } \kappa < 0 \ .$$

This is a saddle point. Therefore there are no minima (i.e. fixed points), global or local, other than found under 1).

### 5.3.4 How Are Stable Fixed Points and Saddle Points Reached?

In the aforegoing we have already seen that the lowest state of the potential is given by a combination of $\xi$'s in which one of them is equal to 1 whereas all others are equal to 0. In this section we wish to prove that it is the initially biggest $\xi_k$ which survives, i.e. $\xi_k \to 1$, and all others die out, i.e. $\xi_k \to 0$. We start from (5.38, 39) with (5.42)

$$\dot{\xi}_k = \xi_k(\lambda - D + B\xi_k^2) \tag{5.80}$$

which is invariant with respect to a replacement of $\xi_l$ by $-\xi_l$. For this reason we may always choose

$$\xi_l \geq 0 \ . \tag{5.81}$$

For sake of simplicity (and without loss of generality) we put $\lambda = B = C = 1$ and choose $D$ accordingly to be

$$D = 2 \sum_{k'} \xi_{k'}^2 \ . \tag{5.82}$$

Since all $\xi$'s play the same role, we may assume that $\xi_1$ is the biggest, i.e. that

$$\xi_1 > \xi_l \ , \quad l = 2, \ldots, M \ . \tag{5.83}$$

As a consequence of (5.83), we obviously have

$$(\lambda - D + \xi_1^2) > (\lambda - D + \xi_l^2) \quad \text{for} \quad l = 2, \ldots M \ , \tag{5.84}$$

i.e., of all Eqs. (5.80), the one for $\xi_1$ has the largest right-hand side. Consequently $\xi_1$ grows fastest (or decays slowest) even if

$$(\lambda - D + \xi_1^2) \to 0 \ . \tag{5.85}$$

(In this case $\xi_1$ approaches a steady state value as required by the gradient dynamics, while all other modes die out.) As a consequence of (5.84), we find always that

$$\xi_1 > \xi_l \ , \quad l = 2, \ldots N \ . \tag{5.86}$$

As we know, the lowest value of the potential occurs for

$$\xi_{l_0} = 1 \ , \quad \xi_{l'} = 0 \quad \text{for all other } l' \ . \tag{5.87}$$

As we have shown above, there are no stable fixed points other than (5.87) besides the saddle points, which violate (5.86). The relations (5.86) and (5.87) are compatible only if we make the choice

$$\begin{aligned} &l_0 = 1 \ , \\ &l' = 2, \dots, M \end{aligned} \tag{5.88}$$

which indeed was our original assertion.

Let us briefly discuss the (most unlikely) case in which some of the $\xi$'s initially coincide. In this event we may replace the inequality (5.83) by

$$\xi_1 = \xi_2 = \dots = \xi_K > \xi_{l'} \ , \quad l' = K+1, \dots, M \ . \tag{5.89}$$

Again one may show that all $\xi_{l'}$ die out and only the set of the first $K$ $\xi$'s survives. As we have shown above, this solution belongs to a saddle point which is unstable in at least one direction so that any, even minute, fluctuation will drive the system into the final state given by (5.87) where $l_0$ is now one of the values $1, \dots, K$.

# 6. Examples: Recognition of Faces and of City Maps

It is not our intention here to treat toy problems, but rather problems of real life in order to demonstrate the applicability of the concepts developed in Chap. 5. To this end we shall consider pattern recognition of faces. A number of persons, say ten, were photographed and the photographs were digitized, usually with 60 by 60 pixels. The background was processed so as to yield a uniform background. The resulting pictures are then supplied with labels A, B, C, ..., to identify the names. As described in Chap. 5 we attribute a vector $\boldsymbol{v}_k$ (5.2) to each face with its name, where the components are the grey values of each pixel. In our calculations we used four bits to characterize the grey values. Once $\boldsymbol{v}_k$ is given, we have to construct the adjoint vectors which we represent as superpositions of the transposed vectors $\bar{\boldsymbol{v}}_k$:

$$\boldsymbol{v}_k^+ = \sum_{k'} a_{kk'} \bar{\boldsymbol{v}}_{k'} \ . \tag{6.1}$$

The coefficients $a_{kk'}$ must be determined in such a way that the orthogonality relations

$$(\boldsymbol{v}_k^+ \boldsymbol{v}_{k'}) = \delta_{kk'} \tag{6.2}$$

are satisfied. We briefly indicate how the coefficients $a_{kk'}$ can be determined: We multiply equations (6.1) by $\boldsymbol{v}_{k'}$ from the right-hand side and use the relation (6.2). This yields

$$\delta_{kk'} = \sum_{k''} a_{kk''} (\bar{\boldsymbol{v}}_{k''} \boldsymbol{v}_{k'}) \ . \tag{6.3}$$

We interpret the coefficients $a_{kk''}$ and the scalar products on the right-hand side of (6.3) as elements of the corresponding matrices $A$ and $W$

$$A = (a_{kk''}) \tag{6.4}$$

$$W = [(\bar{\boldsymbol{v}}_{k''} \boldsymbol{v}_{k'})] \ . \tag{6.5}$$

Equation (6.3) can thus be written in the form ($I$ is the unit matrix)

$$I = AW \tag{6.6}$$

and can be solved formally by

$$A = W^{-1} \ . \tag{6.7}$$

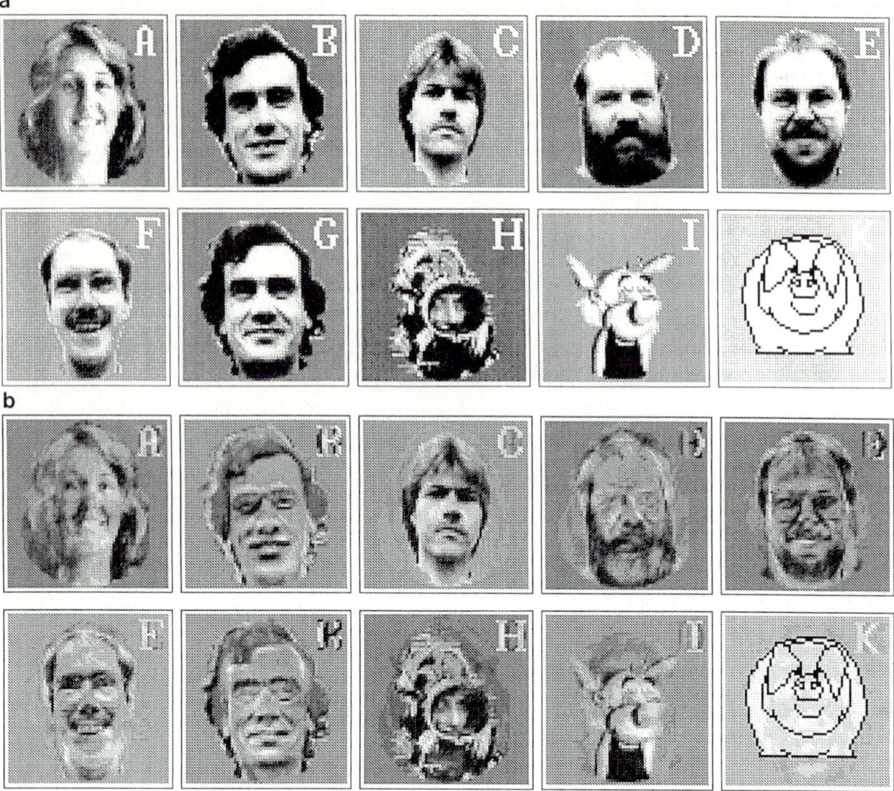


**Fig. 6.1.** **(a)** The faces that are stored as the prototype patterns used in this book. The letters encode the names or identify the figures. In addition to the faces other figures were also included to check how the synergetic computer responds and what properties it displays when recognizing these patterns. From Fuchs and Haken (1988a). **(b)** The prototype patterns corresponding to the adjoint vectors $\boldsymbol{v}^+$. From Fuchs and Haken (1988a)

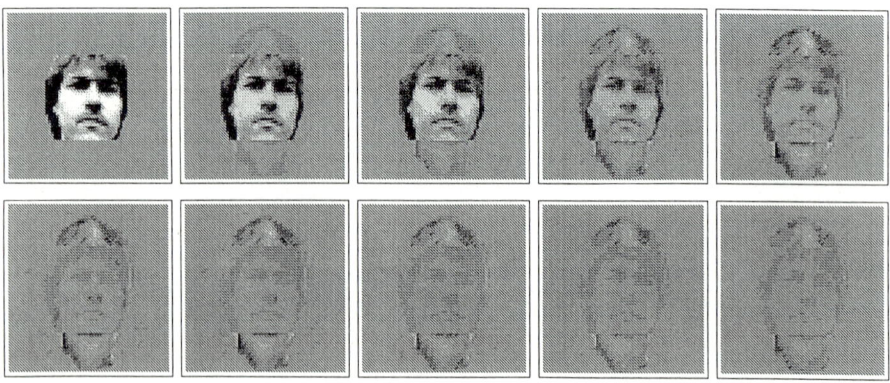

**Fig. 6.2.** When part of a face is presented to the computer, whose attention parameter is set to a negative value, the face eventually disappears from the computer screen. From Fuchs and Haken (1988)

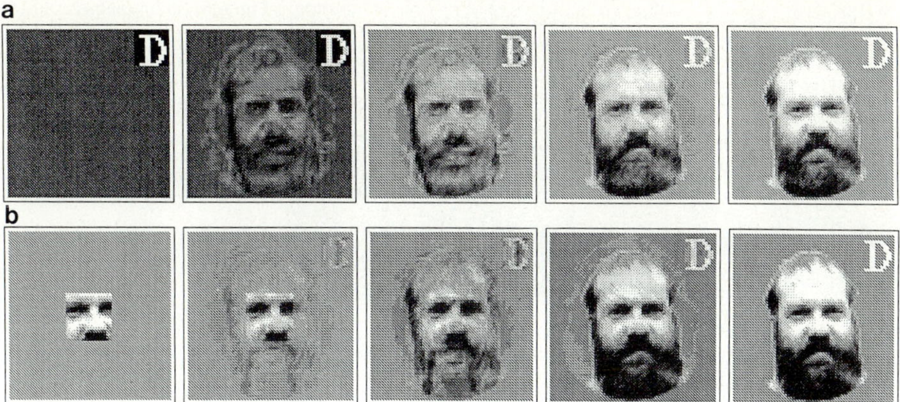


**Fig. 6.3** (**a**) When a letter from one of the patterns of Fig. 6.1a is presented, the synergetic computer can restore the whole pattern – face plus letter. (**b**) When part of a face is offered, the computer can restore the whole face together with the letter encoding the name. From Fuchs and Haken (1988a)

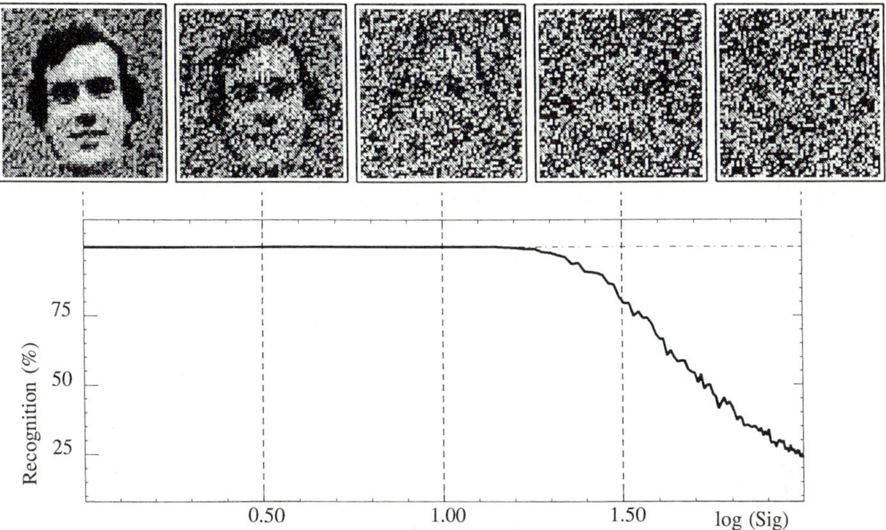


**Fig. 6.4.** Recognition of noisy patterns. For a given width of the Gaussian noise intensity, a noisy face is offered again and again to the computer and its percentage success rate in recognizing the face is recorded. This figure shows how the results of these trials vary when the noise increases (abscissa). The ordinate shows the percentage of successful recognition. From Fuchs and Haken (1989)

The vectors $\boldsymbol{v}_k^+$ are occasionally also called the pseudo-inverse. Later we shall demonstrate how they can be determined in a variety of ways (Sects. 10.2 and 10.6). This will be particularly important when we consider the problem of learning Chap. 10.

We now represent some of our results. Figure 6.1a shows a series of the stored faces together with their labels and also some other images. Figure 6.1b displays the adjoint vectors $\boldsymbol{v}_k^+$. In order to demonstrate that we are dealing

**Fig. 6.5.** Some examples of city maps together with their letters coding for the city (Fuchs and Haken, unpublished)

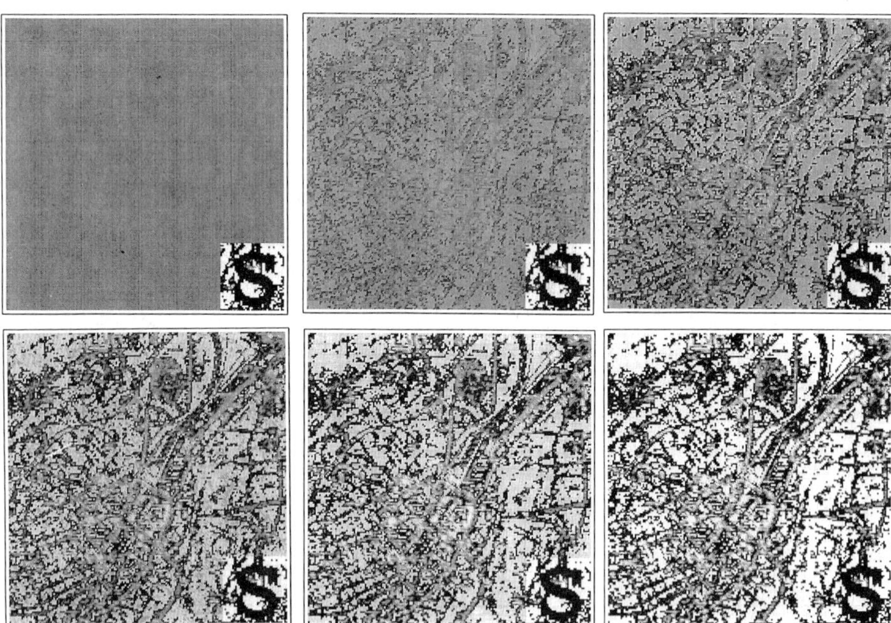


**Fig. 6.6.** When a letter is offered, the computer can complete it to produce the whole city map plus letter (Fuchs and Haken, unpublished)

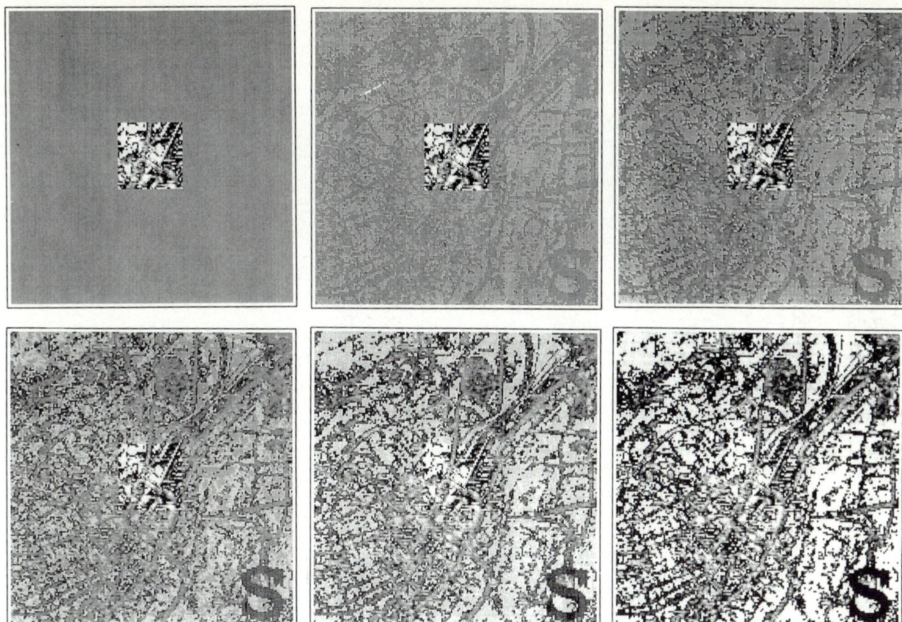

**Fig. 6.7.** When part of the map is shown, the computer can complement it to recreate the total map plus letter (Fuchs and Haken, unpublished)

with some kind of nonequilibrium phase transition, we first set all the attention parameters $\lambda < 0$. An example is given in Fig. 6.2. Here part of a face is offered to the computer as an initial state $\boldsymbol{q}_0$. As the figure shows, the face disappears in the course of time, i.e. as $\boldsymbol{q}(t)$ evolves. Thus the (partly) ordered structure, namely part of the face, decays and leads to microscopic disorder. In the next step of our analysis we put $\lambda > 0$ and offer one of the letters, i.e. the name of the person. Then by the power of the associative memory, which is realized by the dynamics described in Chap. 5, the system can restore the whole face (Fig. 6.3 a). Figure 6.3 b shows how a part of a face is supplemented and also equipped with the corresponding name. As a more recent study by Haken, Hönlinger and Vanger showed, our procedure can also identify facial expressions.

We have also checked the robustness of this approach by offering noisy patterns. We first generated a number of test patterns, with random noise superimposed on them, and increased the noise level. Because of the randomness of the process, we repeated this numerical experiment several times. Figure 6.4 shows the outcome of the experiment. Quite evidently the computer still recognizes the face, even in cases where humans would already have difficulties. In order to demonstrate how this procedure works in other cases, we present the recognition and restoration of city maps in Figs. 6.5 – 7.

# 7. Possible Realizations by Networks

In Chaps. 5 und 6 we presented our general algorithm for the recognition of patterns. This algorithm exploited strong analogies between pattern formation and pattern recognition as unearthed by synergetics. In this chapter we wish to show how this algorithm can be also implemented on a network which acts in a highly parallel manner. To do this, we write the basic equations of our algorithm (5.13) for the vector components of $\boldsymbol{q}$ in the form

$$\dot{q}_j = \sum_l \lambda_{jl} q_l + \sum \lambda_{jll'l''} q_l q_{l'} q_{l''} + F_j(t) \ . \tag{7.1}$$

The coefficients $\lambda$ and $\lambda_{jll'l''}$ are connected with the components of the adjoint vectors $v^+_{ki}$. For instance $\lambda_{jl}$ can be expressed in the form

$$\lambda_{jl} = \sum_k \lambda_k v_{kj} v^+_{kl} \tag{7.2}$$

and a similar relationship can be established for $\lambda_{jll'l''}$. To exploit the meaning of (7.1), we replace the time derivative on the left-hand side by

$$\frac{1}{\tau}\,[q_j(t+\tau) - q_j(t)] \tag{7.3}$$

where $\tau$ is a small time interval. In this way we may replace (7.1) by

$$q_j(t+\tau) = q_j(t) + \tau\Big(\sum_l \lambda_{jl} q_l + \sum \lambda_{jll'l''} q_l q_{l'} q_{l''}\Big) \ . \tag{7.4}$$

Now let us interpret the index $j$ as that of a cell (or element, or neurone). Equation (7.4) tells us that at time $t+\tau$ the cell $j$ receives inputs not only from its own cell but also from all other cells $q_l, q_{l'}, \dots$ . These inputs stem from the earlier time $t$. Equation (7.4) can be represented as a network of cells in one layer, in which each single cell receives inputs from all other cells via connective strengths which are given by $\lambda_{jl}$ and $\lambda_{jll'l''}$. The first term tells us that the cell $j$ receives inputs from just one other cell with index $l$, whereas the last term in (7.4) tells us that the cell $j$ receives inputs from triplets of cells (Fig. 7.1). In this way, the network can be interpreted as a network of formal neurones, each of which has the capability of multiplying inputs and summing up over them.

The properties of this network are significantly different from those usually considered in neural networks where threshold elements are used. In our case the network is operating as follows: Once an initial state is given, the initial values

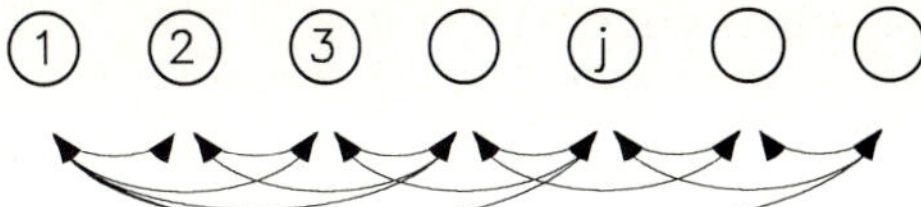


**Fig. 7.1.** Visualization of a one-layer network

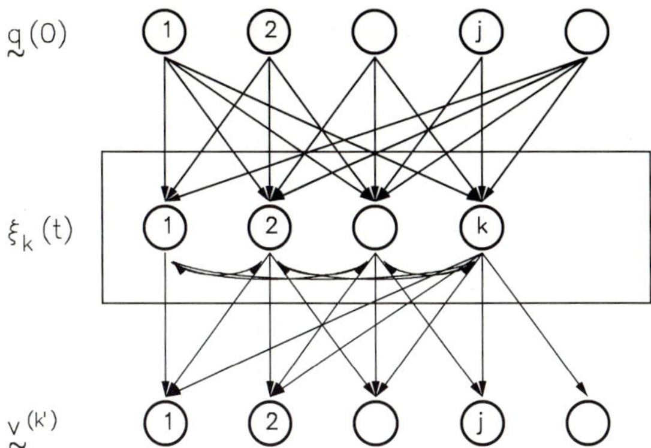


**Fig. 7.2.** A three-layer network. The upper layer is the input layer with initial values $q_j(0)$, the second layer represents the order parameter cells (or grandmother cells). The third layer is the output layer in which the totally restored pattern occurs in the case of auto-associative memory or a new pattern occurs in the case of hetero-associative memory. From Haken (1987)

of the individual neurones are set to $q_j(0)$. The network then operates according to equations (7.4). In the course of time a final state is reached from which the $q_j$ may be read off. In this way the net acts as associative memory. For instance, in the initial state, some of the $q_j$ may be put equal to 0 but then via the process of associative memory, the $q_j$ acquire final values which fill in the gaps in the state vector describing the specific pattern.

By using the concept of the order parameter, the network can be considerably simplified: As we have seen, the order parameters are defined by

$$\xi_k = (\boldsymbol{v}_k^+ \boldsymbol{q}) \tag{7.5}$$

and obey equations of the form

$$\dot{\xi}_k = \xi_k(\lambda - D + B\xi_k^2) \ , \tag{7.6}$$

where we have used the abbreviation

$$D = (B + C) \sum_{k'} \xi_{k'}^2 \ . \tag{7.7}$$

This leads us to construct the following network (Fig. 7.2): There is an input layer of cells, each of which receives the necessary input, i.e. the cell $j$ receives the input $q_j(0)$. Each incoming value $q_j(0)$ is multiplied by a connectivity $v_{kj}^+$ and the sum of these values is taken over all indices $j$. This summation takes place

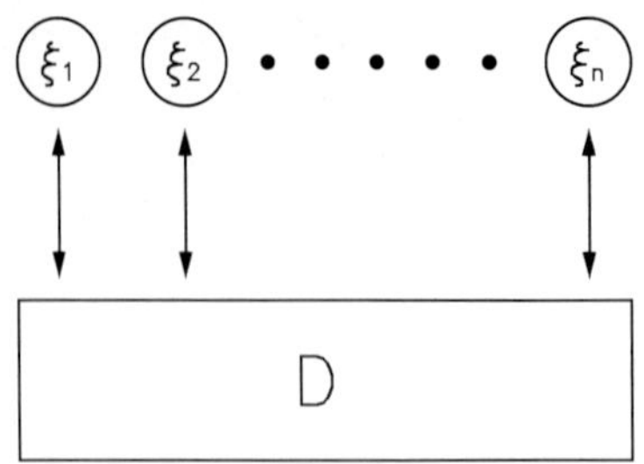


**Fig. 7.3.** Representation of the indirect interaction between the order parameter cells via a reservoir $D$. From Haken (1987)

in cells of a second layer with indices $k$ which have activities $\xi_k$. Thus the order parameters possess a direct representation as neurones in this second layer. Since the label $k$ refers to the specific prototype patterns, we may say that the cells with activities $\xi_k$ recognize the specific pattern. In this sense they act like the so-called "grandmother" cells discussed in neurobiology. But in contrast to the concept of grandmother cells, the cells here interact with each other via the term $D$ in (7.6). This interaction causes a competition in which only the activity of one grandmother cell survives, namely the one which was originally most strongly excited. If the network has to act as an associative memory, one has to add a third layer, the output layer, on which the patterns are represented by the formula

$$q_j(t) = \sum_k \xi_k(t) v_{kj} \ , \tag{7.8}$$

where $q_j$ is the activity of the cell $j$ at the output layer, $\xi_k$ the final state of the grandmother cell layer with $\xi_k = 1$ for $k = k_0$, and $\xi_k = 0$ otherwise. $v_{kj}$ are the $j$th components of the originally stored prototype vectors $k$. In this sense the network acts as an auto-associative memory. It can easily be made to act as a hetero-associative memory by replacing the vector components $v_{kj}$ by $u_{kj}$ where $u_{kj}$ describes a new pattern belonging to the index $k$. Note that the index $j$ need not run over $1 \ldots N$ but may run over other indices. Quite clearly, this formalism can easily be used to describe the transformation of qualities of one kind into those of another kind, e.g. the input layer may consist of optical signals, originating for example from letters, whereas the output layer may consist of specific sounds like vowels and consonants. Such a network may constitute a reading machine.

Our network can still be considerably simplified when we study the structure of (7.6) more closely. According to (7.6) and (7.7), the grandmother cells with activities $\xi_u$ interact with each other only by the common expression (7.7). In other words, we don't need any direct connections between the grandmother cells, but can replace these connections by the cells' individual interactions with the common reservoir $D$ (Fig. 7.3). In this way, the number of connections can be further reduced.

For practical applications the number of connections is a limiting factor. It is thus important to construct networks in which the number of connections is a small as possible. Let us therefore discuss the number of connections in the various models. We begin with the network of Fig. 7.1. Here each cell receives inputs from the other $N-1$ cells. Because there are $N$ cells, there are $N \cdot (N-1)$

connections. In the case of the two or three layer network of Fig. 7.2 there are $N$ input cells, each of which connects to $M$ grandmother cells. Therefore we have $N \cdot M$ connections. The $M$ grandmother cells are also connected with each other, which leads to $M \cdot (M-1)$ connections. Finally the output layer requires a further $N \cdot M$ connections. Therefore we have a total of

$$2N \cdot M + M(M-1) \tag{7.9}$$

connections. Finally in the case of the network of Fig. 7.3 there are $N \cdot M$ connections projecting from the input layer to the middle layer. In the middle layer we have one connection per cell with the reservoir $D$, i.e. $M$ connections. Finally to project onto an output layer, there are (as in Fig. 7.2) a further $M \cdot N$ connections in the case of an auto-associative memory. Thus we have $2NM + M$ connections.

In this reasoning we have assumed that the connections $\lambda_{jl}$ are not necessarily symmetric in $j$ and $l$. In the case where $M$ is much smaller than the number of input cells $N$, the network of type 3, corresponding to Fig. 7.3, evidently has the minimum number of connections. Networks of types 2 and 3 have a further great advantage over serial computers which solve equations (7.1). Namely, in these networks, one may form (7.5) in parallel for all different $k$'s. Then the whole dynamics of the network is described by (7.6) and (7.7), solution of which is a relatively simple task. In particular, it is interesting to note that equations (7.6) and (7.7) are of a universal nature, i.e. they are entirely independent of the kind of patterns originally offered and of the output patterns that are to be eventually produced. The only quantity that enters (7.6) and (7.7) is the number of possible prototype patterns that can be detected. These results may have an impact on our understanding of brains in various ways. We see that the concept of grandmother cells comes in here in a natural fashion via the order parameter concept, and we see that grandmother cells can lead to a considerable reduction in the number of connections or synapses.

# 8. Simultaneous Invariance with Respect to Translation, Rotation and Scaling

## 8.1 An Approach Based on Fourier Transforms and Logarithmic Maps

In this chapter we wish to show how pattern recognition can be made invariant with respect to the above-mentioned transformations. To this end we write the test pattern vectors $\boldsymbol{q}$ and prototype pattern vectors $\boldsymbol{v}_k$ by means of their components and replace the discrete index $j$ by the Cartesian coordinates $x$ and $y$

$$q_j \rightarrow q(x,y) \ , \qquad v_{kj} \rightarrow v_k(x,y) \ , \tag{8.1}$$

where $q$ and $v$ represent for instance the value of grey tones at the position $x, y$.

In the first step we Fourier analyze $q(x,y)$ and correspondingly $v_k(x,y)$ (Fig. 8.1). In the following we shall describe our procedure by means of the functions $q$, but the same can be done in each case with respect to the functions $v_k$. We shall denote the Fourier transform of $q$ by $c$:

$$c(k_x, k_y) = \frac{1}{(2\pi)^2} \iint dx\, dy\, q(x,y) \exp\left[-\mathrm{i}(k_x x + k_y y)\right] \ . \tag{8.2}$$

We shall study the behavior of the Fourier transform $c$ when the pattern $q(x,y)$ is displaced by a vector with components $x_0, y_0$ (Fig. 8.2)

$$q(x,y) \rightarrow q(x+x_0, y+y_0) \ . \tag{8.3}$$

Instead of $x, y$ we introduce new integration variables in (8.2) by means of

$$x' = x + x_0 \ , \qquad y' = y + y_0 \ . \tag{8.4}$$

We then readily obtain for the Fourier coefficients $c'$ of the displaced pattern

$$c'(k_x, k_y) = \frac{1}{(2\pi)^2} \iint dx'\, dy'\, q(x', y') \times \exp\left[-\mathrm{i}(k_x x' + k_y y')\right] \exp\left[+\mathrm{i}(k_x x_0 + k_y y_0)\right] \ . \tag{8.5}$$

The result tells us that the Fourier coefficients of the displaced pattern is identical with that of the undisplaced pattern except for the phase factor depending on $x_0$ and $y_0$. In order to get rid of this exponential function, we take the absolute values of (8.2) or (8.5). In this way we obtain the relationship

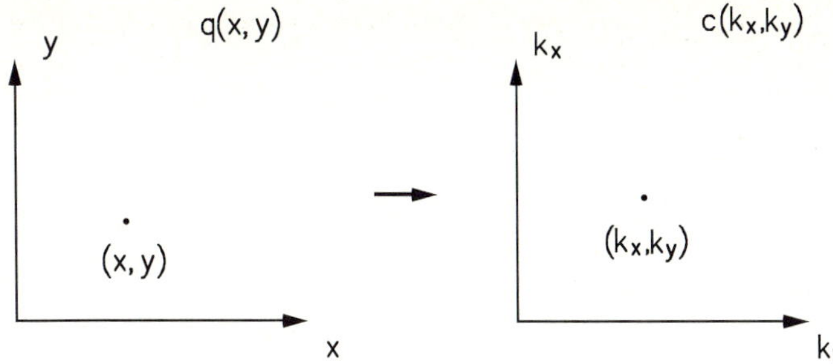


**Fig. 8.1.** Left: The real space (plane) for the representation of the grey values of a pattern. Right: The $(k_x, k_y)$-plane of the Fourier transform $c(k_x, k_y)$

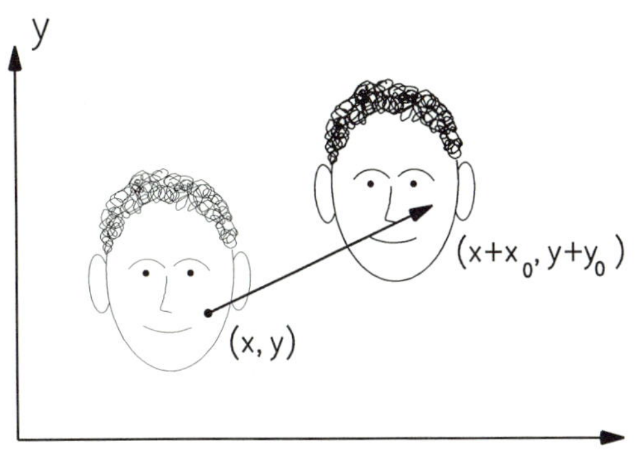


**Fig. 8.2.** Example of the displacement of a figure in real space

$$|c'(k_x, k_y)|^2 = |c(k_x, k_y)|^2 \; . \tag{8.6}$$

By taking the absolute value, we throw away the relative phases. There are general theorems that tell us that the patterns can be reconstructed without a knowledge of the relative phases under conditions which are fulfilled in the case of the faces treated here. [For more details see A. Fuchs (1989).]

In order to recognize faces irrespective of their position in space, we proceed as follows: We first Fourier analyze the prototype vectors $v_k$ and the test pattern vectors $q$ according to (8.2) and take the absolute values. These new functions then serve as new prototypes or test pattern vectors which are now subjected to the algorithm described in Chap. 5, especially (5.13). Before representing our numerical results, we shall discuss how one can introduce, in addition to translational invariance, an invariance with respect to rotation in the plane and also scale invariance. We first investigate the effect of a rotation through an angle $\phi_0$ in the $x-y$ plane on the Fourier coefficients (Fig. 8.3). Such a rotation transforms the pattern $q(x,y)$ into a new pattern $q(x',y')$,

$$q(x,y) \rightarrow q(x',y') \; , \tag{8.7}$$

where the new coordinates $x',y'$ are related to the original coordinates $x,y$ by

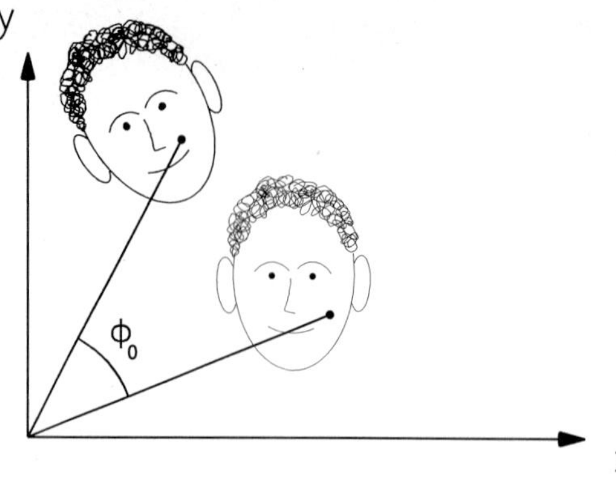


**Fig. 8.3.** Rotation of a figure in real space

$$\begin{aligned} x' &= x\cos\phi_0 \quad + y\sin\phi_0 \\ y' &= -x\sin\phi_0 + y\cos\phi_0 \ . \end{aligned} \tag{8.8}$$

Let us now introduce the two-dimensional vectors

$$\boldsymbol{x} = \begin{pmatrix} x \\ y \end{pmatrix} \tag{8.9}$$

and

$$\boldsymbol{x}' = \begin{pmatrix} x' \\ y' \end{pmatrix} \tag{8.10}$$

so that the coordinate transformation (8.8) can be written in the form

$$\boldsymbol{x}' = D\boldsymbol{x} \ , \tag{8.11}$$

where the matrix $D$ can be directly read off from the right-hand side of (8.8). We also use the notation $q(\boldsymbol{x}) \equiv q(x,y)$. We introduce the vector

$$\boldsymbol{k} = \begin{pmatrix} k_x \\ k_y \end{pmatrix} \tag{8.12}$$

and denote the Fourier coefficients of the rotated pattern by $\tilde{c}(\boldsymbol{k}) \equiv \tilde{c}(k_x, k_y)$ where we again use a vector notation. The equation for $\tilde{c}(\boldsymbol{k})$ reads

$$\tilde{c}(\boldsymbol{k}) = \frac{1}{(2\pi)^2} \iint dx\,dy\,q(D\boldsymbol{x}) \exp(-\mathrm{i}\boldsymbol{k}\cdot\boldsymbol{x}) \ . \tag{8.13}$$

To make contact with the unrotated pattern $q(\boldsymbol{x})$, we introduce the new integration variables $x', y'$ by means of (8.8) or (8.11). Since the determinant of $D$ is unity, and $\boldsymbol{x} = D^{-1}\boldsymbol{x}'$, we may transform the integral on the r.h.s. of (8.13) in the following way

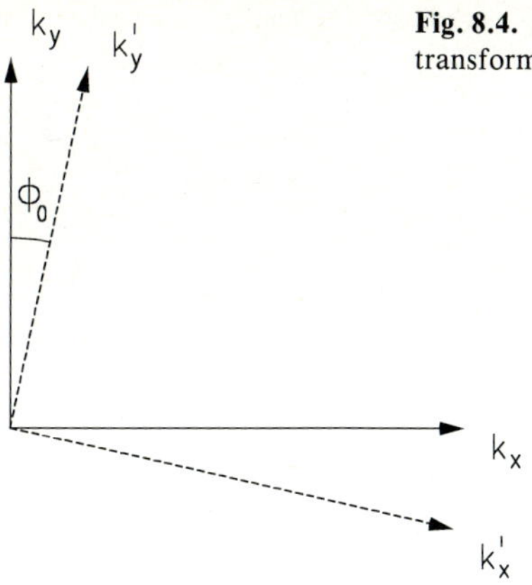


**Fig. 8.4.** Rotation of the coordinate system of the Fourier transform belonging to the rotated pattern of Fig. 8.3

$$\tilde{c}(\boldsymbol{k}) = \frac{1}{(2\pi)^2} \iint dx' dy' q(\boldsymbol{x}') \exp(-\mathrm{i}\boldsymbol{k}D^{-1}\boldsymbol{x}') \ . \tag{8.14}$$

A comparison of (8.14) with the corresponding relation for the unrotated pattern (8.13), where $D = 1$, reveals that $\boldsymbol{k}$ in (8.13) is replaced by $\boldsymbol{k}' = \boldsymbol{k}D^{-1}$. Thus a rotation in $\boldsymbol{x}$-space induces a rotation in $\boldsymbol{k}$-space. As a consequence we obtain

$$\tilde{c}(\boldsymbol{k}) = c(\boldsymbol{k}D^{-1}) \ . \tag{8.15}$$

Thus the Fourier transform $\tilde{c}(\boldsymbol{k})$ of the rotated pattern $q(D\boldsymbol{x})$ is just the Fourier transform $c$ of the unrotated pattern $q(\boldsymbol{x})$ but in a rotated $\boldsymbol{k}$-space (Fig. 8.4). In a completely analogous fashion we may show that the change of the length scale by a factor $r_0$ in $\boldsymbol{x}$-space changes the scale in $\boldsymbol{k}$-space by a factor $1/r_0$ and we find the relation

$$\tilde{c}(\boldsymbol{k}) = \frac{1}{r_0^2} c \left(\frac{\boldsymbol{k}}{r_0}\right) \ . \tag{8.16}$$

One may easily convince oneself that rotation and scaling may be applied jointly. If a general invertible linear transformation $L$ between $\boldsymbol{x}$ and $\boldsymbol{x}'$ is applied in the form

$$\boldsymbol{x}' = L\boldsymbol{x} \tag{8.17}$$

the general result reads as follows. When $q(\boldsymbol{x})$ is transformed into $q(L\boldsymbol{x})$, the Fourier transform $\tilde{c}(\boldsymbol{k})$ of $q(L\boldsymbol{x})$ is related to the transform $c(\boldsymbol{k})$ of $q(\boldsymbol{x})$ by

$$\tilde{c}(\boldsymbol{k}) = \frac{1}{\det L} c(\boldsymbol{k}L^{-1}) \ . \tag{8.18}$$

In the remainder of this chapter we shall be concerned with rotation and scaling. To implicitly include translation invariance we shall study $|c(\boldsymbol{k})|^2$. To make

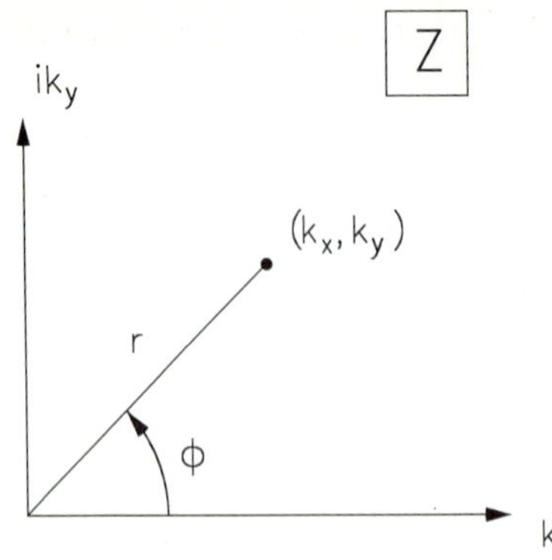


**Fig. 8.5.** Polar coordinates in Fourier space which is also interpreted here as the complex plane

pattern recognition invariant with respect to rotation and scaling, we proceed in several steps. We first interpret $\boldsymbol{k}$ as a vector in a complex $z$-plane ($z = k_x + \mathrm{i} k_y$) (Fig. 8.5) and introduce polar coordinates $r, \phi$.

$$z \equiv k_x + \mathrm{i} k_y = r \mathrm{e}^{\mathrm{i}\phi} \; . \tag{8.19}$$

We map the complex $z$-plane to a complex $\tilde{z}$-plane via the logarithmic function

$$\tilde{z} = \ln z = \ln r + \mathrm{i}\phi \; . \tag{8.20}$$

Since we know that a rotation through an angle $\phi_0$ in $\boldsymbol{x}$-space corresponds to a rotation through $-\phi_0$ in $\boldsymbol{k}$-space, and that scaling by a factor $r_0$ in $\boldsymbol{x}$-space corresponds to a scale factor $1/r_0$ in $\boldsymbol{k}$-space, we obtain

$$\tilde{z}' = \ln z' = \ln r' + \mathrm{i}\phi' = \ln (r/r_0) + \mathrm{i}(\phi - \phi_0) \tag{8.21}$$

or, finally

$$z' = \ln r + \mathrm{i}\phi - \ln r_0 - \mathrm{i}\phi_0 \; . \tag{8.22}$$

But this result may be written as

$$\tilde{z}' = \tilde{z} - \ln r_0 - \mathrm{i}\phi_0 \; . \tag{8.23}$$

We may thus draw the important conclusion that a rotation and scaling in $\boldsymbol{x}$- or $z$-space becomes a *translation* in $\tilde{z}$-space.

We saw at the beginning of this chapter how to make a representation invariant with respect to translation. Thus, here too, we must Fourier analyze and then take the absolute value. Putting the steps together, we find

$$q(\boldsymbol{x}) \to c(\boldsymbol{k}) \to |c(\boldsymbol{k})|^2 \quad \text{Fourier transform} \tag{8.24a}$$

$$|c(\boldsymbol{k})|^2 \to w(z) \quad \text{complex variable } z \tag{8.24b}$$

$$z \to \tilde{z} = \ln z \tag{8.24c}$$

$$w(z) \to \hat{w}(\tilde{k}) \to |\hat{w}(\tilde{k})|^2 \quad \text{Fourier transform} \; . \tag{8.24d}$$

To perform pattern recognition $q(\boldsymbol{x})$ and $v_k(\boldsymbol{x})$ are subjected to the sequence of transformations shown above and then the formalism of Chap. 5 is applied to the resulting $|\hat{w}(\hat{k})|^2$ corresponding to $\boldsymbol{q}$ and $\boldsymbol{v}_k$. Our procedure is simultaneously invariant with respect to translation, rotation and scaling.

## 8.2 Numerical Calculations

In a first example we apply the above procedure to a pattern (Fig. 8.6, left) which is part of a face. It is displaced from its normal location but is neither rotated nor scaled. This means that we only have to apply the first step of the invariance transformations, i.e. the first Fourier-transform, to the test pattern and to the prototypes.

In order to explain Fig. 8.6 as a whole, the initial values of $\xi_k$ and those of the vector $\boldsymbol{w}$ were calculated, and the dynamics of $\xi_k$ was started. The behavior in time of the $\xi_k$ and the exponential decay of the absolute value $|\boldsymbol{w}|$ are also shown in Fig. 8.6 where the curve corresponding to the "correct" $\xi_k$ is plotted as a solid line, and the other curves are dotted. After a transient behavior, the dynamics reaches a stationary state with only one of the $\xi_k$ not equal to zero – the pattern has been selected. Now, as the pattern is identified as the prototype $\boldsymbol{v}_j$, we can derive the shift of the former test pattern $\boldsymbol{q}(0)$ from the original location. To this end we calculate the correlation function

$$G(x_0,y_0) = \int_{-\infty}^{\infty} dx \int_{-\infty}^{\infty} dy\, v_j(x-x_0,y-y_0)\,q(x,y,t=\infty) \ , \tag{8.25}$$

where $q(x,y,t=\infty)$ is the pattern in real-space when the dynamics has reached its stationary state. Using the Fourier transforms of $v_j$ and $q$, which we denote by $\tilde{v}_j(k_x,k_y)$ and $\tilde{q}(k_x,k_y,t=\infty)$, respectively, the correlation function can be cast into the form

$$\begin{aligned} G(x_0,y_0) = \int_{-\infty}^{\infty} dk_x \int_{-\infty}^{\infty} dk_y\, \tilde{v}_j^*(k_x,k_y) \\ \times \tilde{q}(k_x,k_y,t=\infty)\,\mathrm{e}^{\mathrm{i}(k_x x_0+k_y y_0)} \end{aligned} \tag{8.26}$$

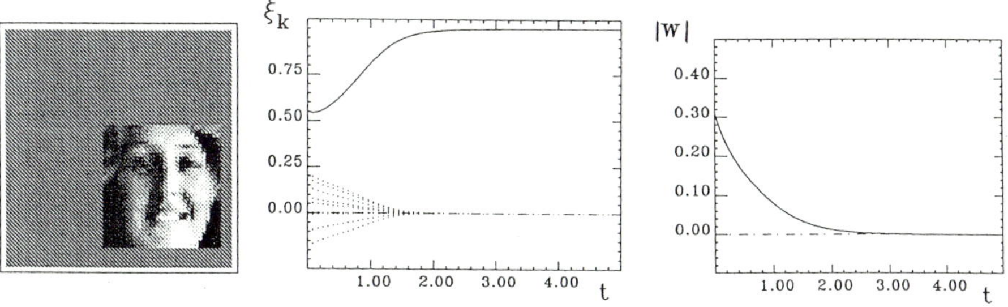


**Fig. 8.6.** Left: Test pattern that is shifted in the $(x,y)$ plane. Middle: time evolution of the order parameters $\xi_k$. Right: time evolution of the length of the residual vector $|\boldsymbol{w}|$. From Fuchs and Haken (1988)

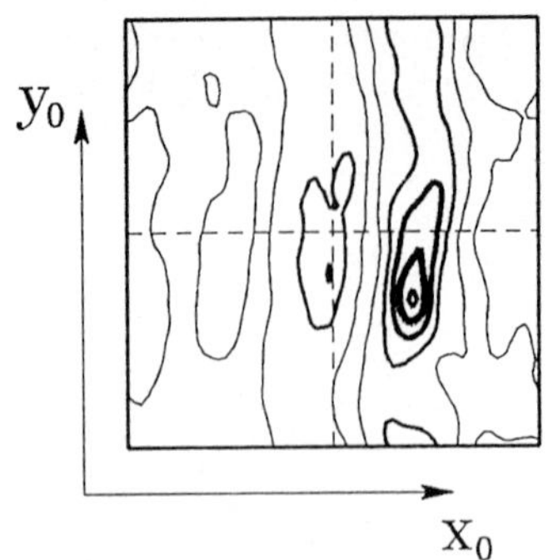


**Fig. 8.7.** Contour plot of the correlation function (8.26) for the example of Fig. 8.6, left. Abscissa: $x_0$, ordinate: $y_0$

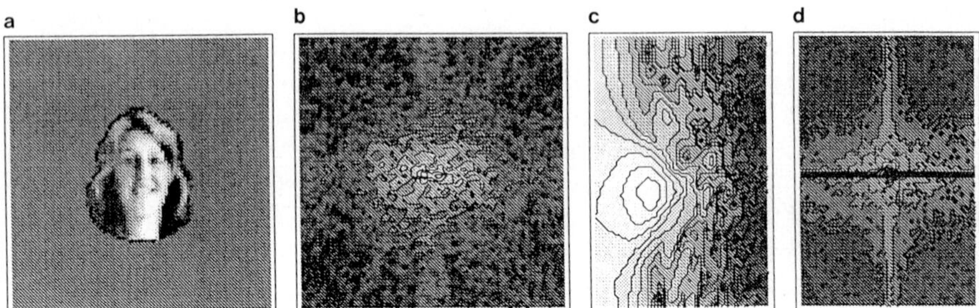


**Fig. 8.8a–d.** The various transformations applied to a face. From left to right: (**a**) the original pattern in the $(x,y)$ plane; (**b**) the absolute value of its Fourier transform in the $(k_x, ik_y)$ plane. Light shading corresponds to large values of $|c(k_z, k_y)|$; (**c**) the logarithmic map; (**d**) the absolute square of the Fourier transform of pattern (c), i.e. $\hat{w}(\hat{k})$. From Fuchs and Haken (1988b)

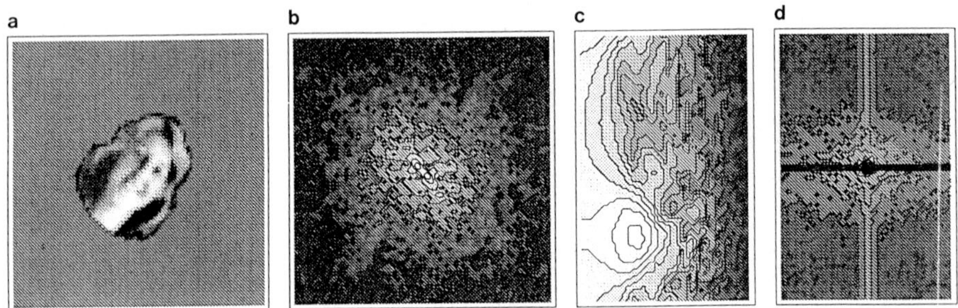


**Fig. 8.9a–d.** As in Fig. 8.6 but for a rotated face. Note that part (**d**) of Fig. 8.9 is identical to that of Fig. 8.8. From Fuchs and Haken (1988b)

which is the inverse Fourier transform of the product $v_j^* q$ in Fourier-space. The asterisk denotes the complex conjugate. The values of $x_0$ and $y_0$ at which $G(x_0, y_0)$ reaches its absolute maximum give the spatial shift of the test pattern against the prototype. With the relation (8.26) the advantages of the Fast Fourier transform can be used for the explicit calculation of $G(x_0, y_0)$. A contour plot of the correlation function for the example given above is shown in Fig. 8.7. Some examples are shown in Figs. 8.8–11. As our computer calculations dem-

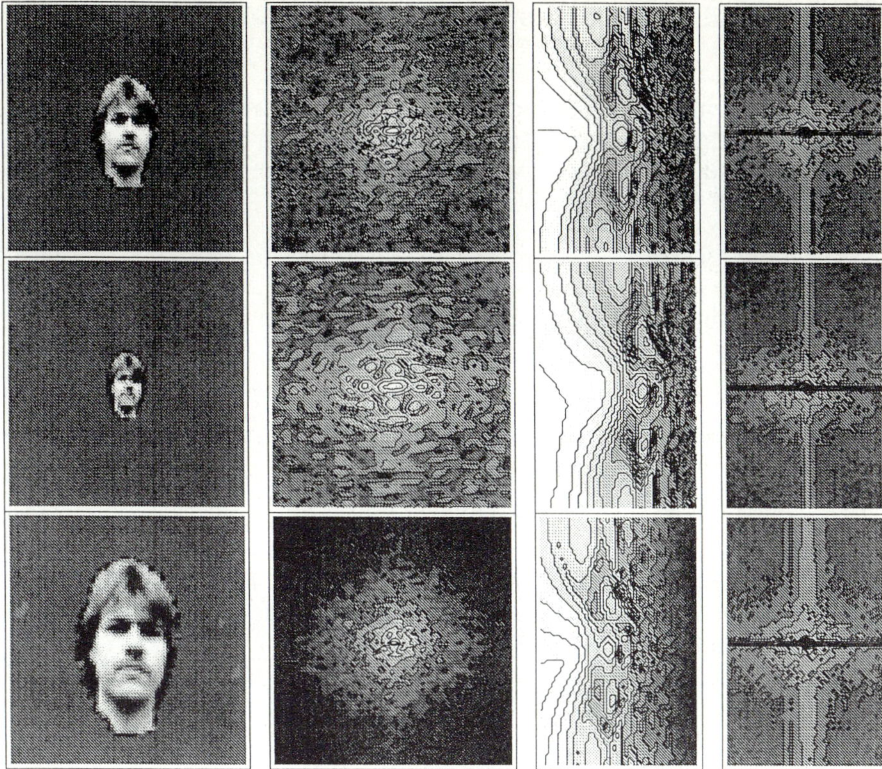

**Fig. 8.10.** As in Fig. 8.8 but for reduced and magnified faces. From Fuchs and Haken (1988b)

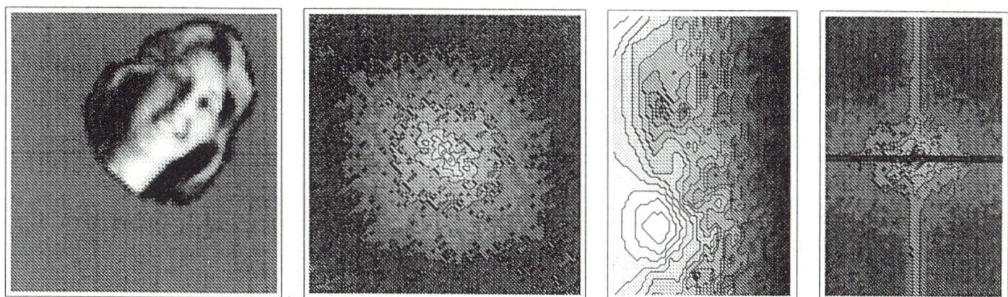

**Fig. 8.11.** As in Fig. 8.8 but with all transformations performed simultaneously. From Fuchs and Haken (1988b)

onstrate, this procedure facilitates for instance the recognition of faces. Some further applications are described in Chap. 9.

## 8.3 A Second Approach to the Invariance Problem

In this section we develop an alternative approach which avoids both the Fourier transformation and the logarithmic map. As we shall see in Chap. 12, this approach comes closer to the process of human perception than the procedure described in the preceding section. Again we assume that the prototype and test pattern vectors are replaced by continuous functions

$$v \rightarrow v(\boldsymbol{x}) \ . \tag{8.27}$$

The scalar product between $\boldsymbol{v}^+$ and $\boldsymbol{q}$ then becomes an integral

$$(\boldsymbol{v}^+ \boldsymbol{q}) = \int v^+(\boldsymbol{x}) q(\boldsymbol{x}) d^2x \ , \tag{8.28}$$

where the integration range extends over the whole pattern. We again assume the normalization condition, which now reads

$$\int v(\boldsymbol{x})^2 d^2x = 1 \ . \tag{8.29}$$

The basic idea is as follows: Let a test pattern be given and let us permit this to be shifted by a vector $\boldsymbol{f}$ with respect to any of the prototype patterns and to be rotated and dilated in addition. This leads to the idea of considering a transformation

$$S(\boldsymbol{x}) = S'\boldsymbol{x} + \boldsymbol{f} \tag{8.30}$$

where $\boldsymbol{x}$ is defined by (8.9) and the matrix $S'$ by

$$S' = \begin{pmatrix} a & b \\ c & d \end{pmatrix} \ . \tag{8.31}$$

We wish to adjust the matrix $S'$ and the displacement $\boldsymbol{f}$ in such a way that one of the prototype patterns gives the best match to the test pattern. To achieve this we first introduce a set of new prototype pattern vectors by making the substitution

$$v_k(\boldsymbol{x}) \rightarrow \hat{v}_k(\boldsymbol{x}) = (\det S')^{1/2} v_k[S(\boldsymbol{x})] \tag{8.32}$$

$$v_k^+(\boldsymbol{x}) \rightarrow \hat{v}_k^+(\boldsymbol{x}) = (\det S')^{1/2} v_k^+[S(\boldsymbol{x})] \ , \tag{8.33}$$

for every index $k$, where det $S'$ is the determinant of (8.31). One can readily convince oneself that the normalization condition (8.29) is also fulfilled for $\hat{v}$. Using the definition (8.32) we obtain

$$\int \hat{v}(\boldsymbol{x})^2 d^2x = (\det S') \int v[S(\boldsymbol{x})]^2 d^2x \ . \tag{8.34}$$

Making the replacement

$$S(\boldsymbol{x}) = \boldsymbol{x}' \tag{8.35}$$

and making use of its inverse

$$x = S^{-1}(x') \ , \tag{8.36}$$

one can change the integration variables in (8.34) to yield

$$\det S' \int v(x')^2 d^2x' \, \frac{1}{\det S'} \ . \tag{8.37}$$

Because $v$ was normalized in (8.29), so is $\hat{v}$ in (8.34). Similarly, one can readily check that the relation

$$(\hat{v}_k^+ \hat{v}_{k'}) = \delta_{kk'} \tag{8.38}$$

holds. We now introduce a potential function

$$V = -\tfrac{1}{2} \sum_k \lambda_k (\hat{v}_k^+ q)^2 + \tfrac{1}{4} B \sum_{k \neq k'} (\hat{v}_k^+ q)^2 (\hat{v}_{k'}^+ q)^2 + \tfrac{1}{4} C \left(\int q(x)^2 d^2x\right)^2 \tag{8.39}$$

which is constructed in complete analogy to that of (5.24) where, however, the prototype patterns have been replaced by $\hat{v}^+$. In this way $V$ is not only a function of the test pattern $q$ but also a function of the matrix $S'$ and of the displacement $f$. The idea is to minimize $V$ as a function of $q, S'$, and $f$. In other words, we have to supplement the dynamics of Chap. 5 with respect to $q$ by one in which the matrix $S'$ and the displacement vector $f$ are varied; this may again be achieved by a gradient dynamics. We will discuss below how this idea works in practice. Before that we wish to demonstrate some simple relationships. We may again introduce order parameters $\xi_k$ by means of

$$\xi_k = (\hat{v}_k^+ q) \ . \tag{8.40}$$

Because of the definition of $\hat{v}_k^+$, $\xi_k$ becomes a function of $S'$ and $f$. So far, our approach implies that a test pattern vector is given and that the prototype pattern vectors are adjusted by means of appropriate transformations $S'$ and $f$. The procedure becomes still more symmetric when we use the transformation of the test pattern vectors instead of the prototype pattern vectors. To this end let us consider the scalar product between $\hat{v}_k^+$ and $q$. Using the definition (8.33) of $\hat{v}^+$ we obtain

$$\int \hat{v}_k^+ (x) q(x) d^2x = \int (\det S')^{1/2} v_k^+ [S(x)] q(x) d^2x \ . \tag{8.41}$$

Changing variables according to (8.35) and (8.36), we can express (8.41) as

$$\int (\det S')^{-1/2} v_k^+ (x') q[S^{-1}(x')] d^2x' \ . \tag{8.42}$$

This suggests that one introduces the definition

$$\hat{q}(x) = (\det S')^{-1/2} q[S^{-1}(x)] \tag{8.43}$$

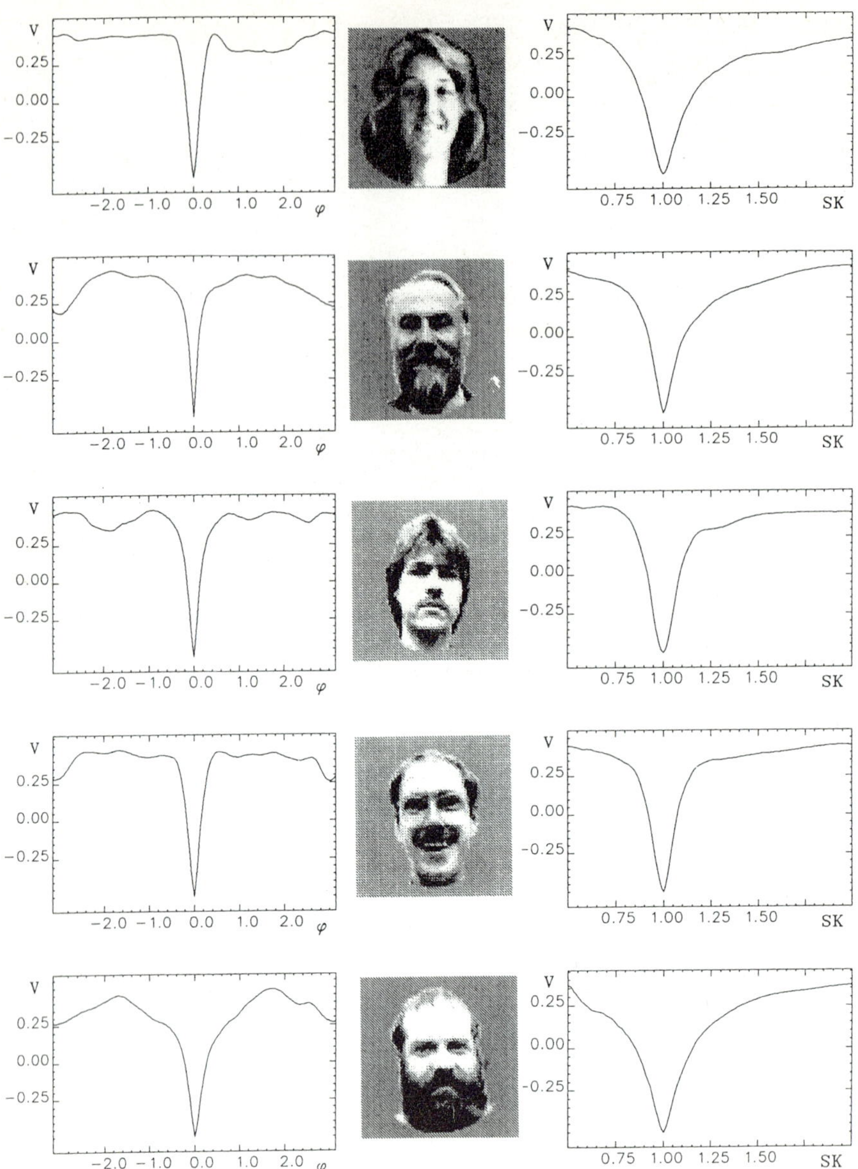

Fig. 8.12. Middle column: test patterns. Left-hand column: potential $V$ versus angle of rotation. Right-hand column: potential $V$ versus scaling factor $s \equiv SK$. From Fuchs and Haken (1988c)

for the shifted $\hat{q}$ so that we eventually obtain the relation

$$(\hat{v}_k^+ q) = (v_k^+ \hat{q}) \ . \tag{8.44}$$

Let us now consider some typical examples. We first treat test patterns taken from a set of prototype patterns (Fig. 6.1 a) but without letters. The test patterns

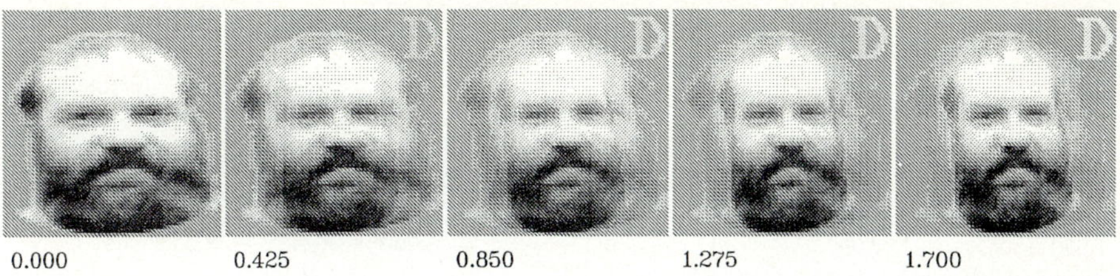


**Fig. 8.13.** A broadened face without a letter is offered as the test pattern. The stored prototype patterns are those of Fig. 6.1 a. The algorithm of Chap. 5 suffices to restore the face and to supplement it with the corresponding letter. Thus the broadened face is recognized. The numbers refer to the time steps. From Hönlinger (1989)

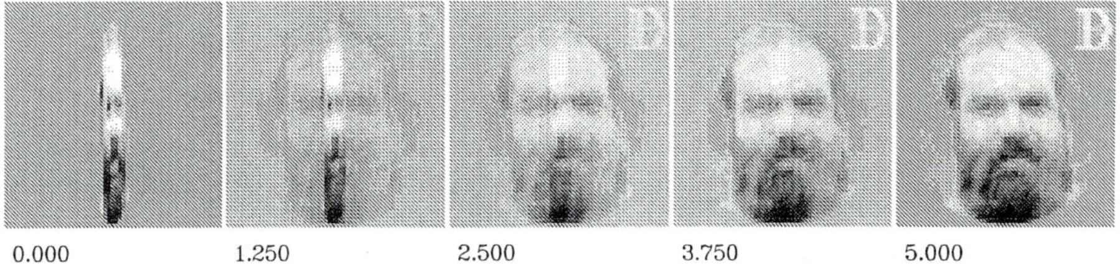


**Fig. 8.14.** As in Fig. 8.13, but with a squeezed face offered as the test pattern. From Hönlinger (1989)

are rotated with respect to the prototype patterns by an angle $\alpha$. Thus the transformation $S'$ is described

$$S' = \begin{pmatrix} \cos\alpha & \sin\alpha \\ -\sin\alpha & \cos\alpha \end{pmatrix} , \quad f = 0 \; . \tag{8.45}$$

Figure 8.12 shows some typical examples of the test patterns (middle part) and the corresponding potential curves (l.h.s.). Our next example refers to a uniform scaling where $S' = \begin{pmatrix} s & 0 \\ 0 & s \end{pmatrix}$.

Results are shown on the right-hand side of Fig. 8.12. In the case of a dilation in the $x$-direction, we have

$$S' = \begin{pmatrix} s & 0 \\ 0 & 1 \end{pmatrix} \; . \tag{8.46}$$

Figure 8.13 shows how the computer restores a stretched face in the course of time and supplements it with the correct label, while Fig. 8.14 presents analogous results for an initially squeezed face. Note that these calculations are based on the conventional dynamics of Chap. 5, where the potential $V$ depends on all stored prototype patterns. Let us now consider the potential as a function of the "stretching" factor $s$ in (8.46). To get an impression of how we perceive a stretched face for a specific $s$, look at Fig. 8.15. Its upper part corresponds to $s > 1$,

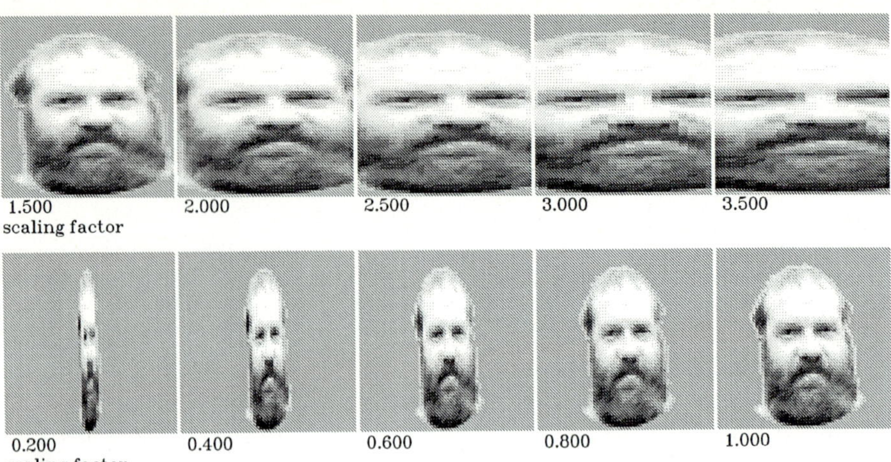


**Fig. 8.15.** Distorted faces for a variety of scaling ("stretching") factors $s$. From Hönlinger (1989)

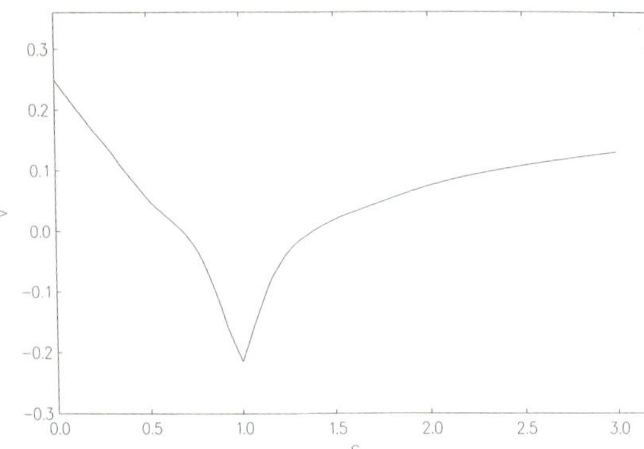


**Fig. 8.16.** Potential $V$ versus scaling factor for a test pattern corresponding to pattern $D$ of Fig. 6.1a in the presence of the prototype patterns of Fig. 6.1a. From Hönlinger (1989)

whereas its lower part refers to $s<1$. The individual stretching factor is indicated in each case. (Note that the letter in the upper right corner has been dropped.) The potential curve corresponding to the deformed faces of Fig. 8.15 (in the presence of all other prototype patterns) is shown as a function of $s$ in Fig. 8.16. When a two-dimensional dilation,

$$S'_{\bullet} = \begin{pmatrix} s_1 & 0 \\ 0 & s_2 \end{pmatrix}, \tag{8.47}$$

is present, the potential has to be plotted above the $s_1$, $s_2$ plane. In this case it is convenient to plot equipotential lines as shown in Fig. 8.17. When a gradient dynamics is used, the trajectories followed by $s_1, s_2$ are those shown in Fig. 8.18. These results indicate that the concept of a potential dynamics can be successfully applied in a good many cases. There are some cases, however, in which local minima occur, such that the dynamics gets trapped there without reaching the

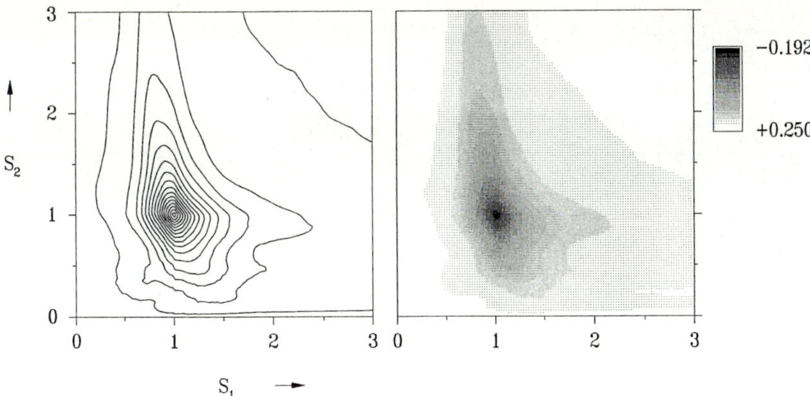


**Fig. 8.17.** Left: Equipotential lines for the potential belonging to the test pattern $A$ of Fig. 6.1 a versus the scaling parameters $s_1, s_2$. Right: Magnitude of the potential $V$ encoded by grey values. The potential is calculated in the presence of the prototype patterns of Fig. 6.1 a. From Hönlinger (1989)

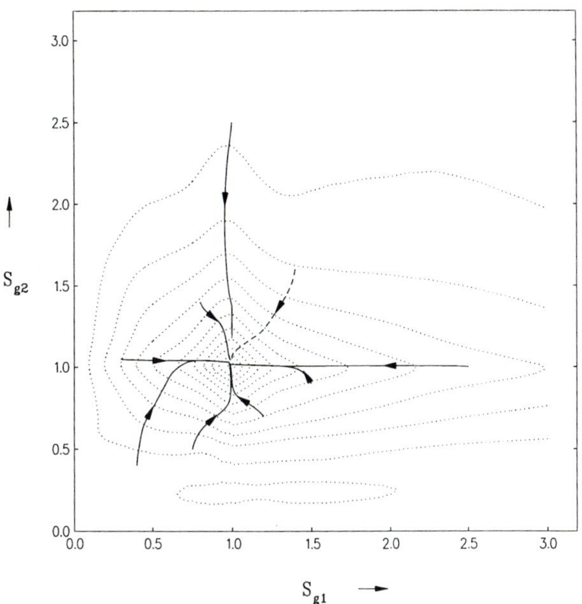


**Fig. 8.18.** Trajectories in the potential of the test pattern $D$ of Fig. 6.1 a in the presence of all the prototype patterns of Fig. 6.1 a. From Hönlinger (1989)

global minimum located at the correct position. There are at least two ways to overcome this difficulty. The first is the inclusion of fluctuating forces which may drive the system out of local minima. The second approach, which we believe to be still more promising, is to smooth the slopes around the deepest minimum or at least to expand the basin of attraction of the deepest minimum. This can be achieved by expanding the test pattern vector into a set of suitable orthonormal functions. For the case of rotation we introduce polar coordinates with their origin located at the center of gravity of the pattern and use Bessel

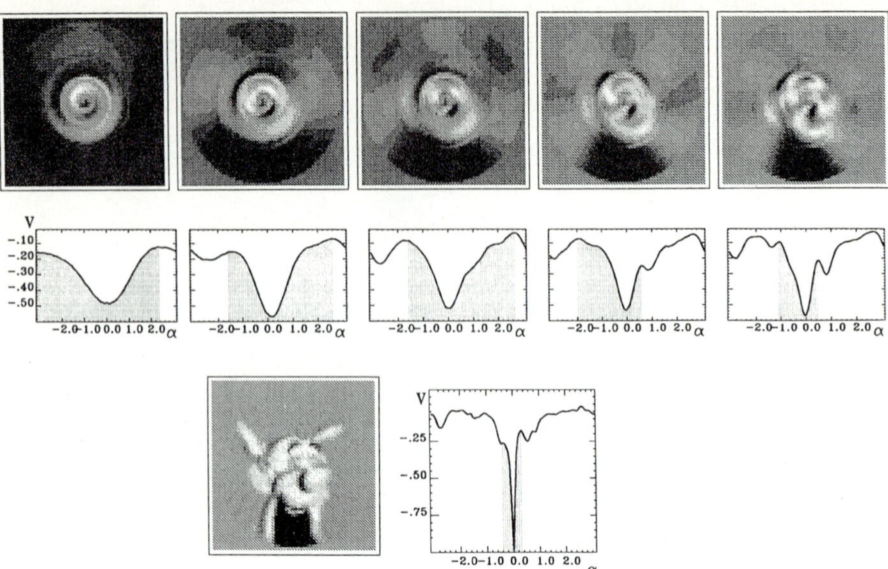


**Fig. 8.19.** Lower part: test pattern (*left*) and potential $V$ versus rotation angle $\alpha$ (*right*). Middle part: the potential $V$ is calculated by means of the expansion (8.49) for (*from left to right*) $m_{\max} = 1, \ldots, 5$ and plotted versus the rotation angle $\alpha$. Upper part: $w(x,t)$ (8.49) for (*from left to right*) $m_{\max} = 1, \ldots, 5$. From Fuchs and Haken (1988c)

functions $J_k^m(r)$ of the first kind in the radial direction and the functions $e^{im\phi}$ in the azimuthal direction.

The expansion then reads

$$q(\boldsymbol{x},t) = \sum_{k,m} \xi_{km}(t) J_k^m(r) e^{im\phi} \quad \text{with} \quad \boldsymbol{x} = \begin{pmatrix} r \\ l \end{pmatrix} . \tag{8.48}$$

We now construct a new function $w(\boldsymbol{x},t)$ where the sum over $|m|$ runs only up to a given value $m_{\max}$

$$w(\boldsymbol{x},t) = \sum_{m=-m_{\max}}^{m_{\max}} \sum_k \xi_{km}(t) J_k^m(r) e^{im\phi} . \tag{8.49}$$

Figure 8.19 shows the result of this treatment where the individual figures show the test patterns processed by means of (8.49) and the potential $V$ for increasing $m_{\max}$ in the range $m_{\max} = 1-5$. The smoothing effect can easily be seen.

## 8.4 General Transformations of Patterns

In Sect. 8.2 we studied some specific transformations with the aim of maximizing the overlap between the test pattern vector $q$ and one of the prototype vectors

$v_k$. There we considered rotations, dilations, and translations. As humans we are capable of recognizing patterns even if they are inhomogeneously deformed. Thus we wish to devise an algorithm which allows for inhomogeneous deformations. We describe the deformations by the transformation

$$\boldsymbol{x}' = \boldsymbol{S}(\boldsymbol{x}) \tag{8.50}$$

and, if not otherwise stated, we assume that this transformation (8.50) possesses an inverse which we describe formally by

$$\boldsymbol{x} = \boldsymbol{S}^{-1}(\boldsymbol{x}') \ . \tag{8.51}$$

We then introduce the deformed test pattern vectors $\hat{v}_k$ by means of

$$\hat{v}_k(\boldsymbol{x}) = N(\boldsymbol{x})\, v_k[S(\boldsymbol{x})] \ . \tag{8.52}$$

Here the normalization factor $N(\boldsymbol{x})$ is given by

$$N(\boldsymbol{x}) = |\det \boldsymbol{S}'|^{1/2} \ , \tag{8.53}$$

where

$$\det \boldsymbol{S}' = \begin{vmatrix} \partial S_x/\partial x & \partial S_x/\partial y \\ \partial S_y/\partial x & \partial S_y/\partial y \end{vmatrix} \tag{8.54}$$

is the functional determinant which occurs when we proceed from the volume element $dx'dy'$ to $dxdy$. The form (8.52) with (8.53) guarantees in particular that the normalization condition

$$\int \hat{v}_k^2 d^2x = 1 \tag{8.55}$$

is fulfilled. When we choose the adjoint vector $\hat{v}_k^+$ in the form

$$\hat{v}_k^+(\boldsymbol{x}) = N(\boldsymbol{x})\, v_k^+[S(\boldsymbol{x})] \ , \tag{8.56}$$

the orthogonality relation

$$\int \hat{v}_k^+ \hat{v}_{k'} d^2x = \delta_{kk'} \tag{8.57}$$

is also fulfilled, provided is was fulfilled for $v_k^+, v_k$.

The order parameters related to $\hat{v}_k$ are defined by

$$\hat{\xi}_k = \int \hat{v}_k^+(\boldsymbol{x}) q(\boldsymbol{x}) d^2x \ . \tag{8.58}$$

Note that because $q$ will depend on time $t$, and because $\hat{v}$ depends on the transformation $S$, the order parameters become a function of both $S$ and $t$. We define $q^+$ by means of the relation

$$\int \hat{v}_k^+ q d^2x = \int q^+ \hat{v}_k d^2x \ . \tag{8.59}$$

As we have seen in Chap. 5, the potential $V$ can be expressed as a function of the order parameters $\xi_k$. Because of (8.58), this potential function now becomes a function of the new order parameters $\hat{\xi}_k$, i.e.,

$$V(\xi_k) \rightarrow V(\hat{\xi}_k) \ . \tag{8.60}$$

We may now formulate a gradient dynamics with respect to the test pattern vector $q(\boldsymbol{x},t)$ in analogy to (5.13). In order to exhibit the possibility of varying the relaxation time constants, we shall introduce a decay constant $\gamma_1$ as a factor in (8.61) below. Because $q$ is a continuously varying function of the spatial coordinate $\boldsymbol{x}$, the ordinary derivative must be replaced by the so-called variational derivative so that we obtain

$$\dot{q}(\boldsymbol{x},t) = -\gamma_1 \frac{\delta V}{\delta q^+(\boldsymbol{x},t)} = -\gamma_1 \sum_k \frac{\partial V}{\partial \hat{\xi}_k} \frac{\delta \hat{\xi}_k}{\delta q^+(\boldsymbol{x},t)} \ , \tag{8.61}$$

where the right-hand side of this equation stems from the fact that $V$ is a function of $\hat{\xi}_k$ which in turns depends on $q^+$ via (8.58, 59). The variational derivative then means that we drop the integral in (8.59) and differentiate the integrand locally with respect to $q^+(\boldsymbol{x})$. Thus the last factor in (8.61) reduces to $\hat{v}_k(\boldsymbol{x})$ and the equation is transformed into

$$\dot{q}(\boldsymbol{x},t) = -\gamma_1 \sum_k \frac{\partial V}{\partial \hat{\xi}_k} \hat{v}_k(\boldsymbol{x}) \ . \tag{8.62}$$

In the present context, a central question is how we may determine the transformation $\boldsymbol{S}$. As the explicit examples of Sect. 8.2 have shown, in a number of important cases the potential $V$ has a global minimum for a specific transformation $\boldsymbol{S}$. This suggests that we might attempt a gradient dynamics with respect to $\boldsymbol{S}$.

Again introducing a decay constant $\gamma_2$, we formulate this gradient dynamics as

$$\dot{S}_x(\boldsymbol{x},t) = -\gamma_2 \frac{\delta V}{\delta S_x(\boldsymbol{x},t)} + C_x \ , \tag{8.63}$$

with a corresponding equation for $\dot{S}_y$.

We shall discuss the additional term $C_x$, which stems from a so-called cost function, below. The variational derivative of $V$ with respect to $S_x$ can be taken in analogy to the procedure which led us to (8.61). We obtain

$$\dot{S}_x = -\gamma_2 \sum_k \frac{\partial V}{\partial \hat{\xi}_k} \frac{\delta \hat{\xi}_k}{\delta S_x(\boldsymbol{x},t)} + C_x \ . \tag{8.64}$$

The variational derivative of $\hat{\xi}_k$ can be found by using the chain rule of differential calculus which yields

$$\frac{\delta \xi_k}{\delta S_x(x,t)} = q(x) \frac{\partial}{\partial S_x} \{N(x) v_k[S(x)]\} . \tag{8.65}$$

Note that $N$ depends implicitly on $S$ [cf. (8.53)] so that the derivative with respect to $S_x$ applies to the whole bracket in (8.65).

In practice one may proceed in two ways: Either we allow formally for all kinds of transformations $S$ and introduce a cost function in order to constrain these transformations to a specific class of allowed transformations or, alternatively, we assume the transformations to have a specific form, e.g. those that were studied in Sect. 8.2. Let us consider the example in which $S_x$ is given by

$$S_x = sx \ , \quad S_y = y \ . \tag{8.66}$$

Insertion of (8.66) into (8.63) leads to

$$x\dot{s} = -\gamma_2 \sum_k \frac{\partial V}{\partial \xi_k} q(x) \frac{\partial}{\partial (sx)} [s v_k(sx, y)] \ . \tag{8.67}$$

A typical difficulty now arises because the equation (8.67) should be an equation for $s$ which depends only on time and is independent of space. On the other hand, both the left- and right-hand sides of (8.67) depend on the spatial variables $x, y$. Because the derivative occurring in (8.67) can be written in the form

$$\frac{\partial}{\partial (sx)} = \frac{1}{x} \frac{\partial}{\partial s} , \tag{8.68}$$

this suggests that we multiply both sides of (8.67) by $x$. We then integrate both sides over the coordinates $x$ and $y$ and obtain

$$\int x^2 d^2x \cdot \dot{s} = -\gamma_2 \sum_k \frac{\partial V}{\partial \xi_k} \frac{\partial}{\partial s} \int s v_k(sx, y) q(x) d^2x \ , \tag{8.69}$$

where $d^2x \equiv dx dy$. Using the abbreviation

$$\overline{x^2} = \int x^2 d^2x \tag{8.70}$$

and going one step backwards, namely from (8.64) to (8.63), we may cast the result in the form

$$\dot{s} = -(\gamma_2/\overline{x^2}) \frac{\partial V}{\partial s} \ . \tag{8.71}$$

Here $V$ is the potential function which we calculated for the example of faces in Sect. 8.2.

So far, we have studied transformations which act on the argument of $v$, i.e. on the spatial coordinates $x, y$. This procedure can be generalized still further. Let us imagine that we transform not only the argument of the function $v$, but also its shape. To this end we introduce the transformed prototype patterns, $\hat{v}$, by means of

$$\hat{v}(x) = Tv(x) \; . \tag{8.72}$$

We write the adjoint $\hat{v}^+$ in the form

$$\hat{v}^+(x) = v^+(x)T^{-1} \; , \tag{8.73}$$

where we assume that $T$ possesses an inverse $T^{-1}$, which acts on all the factors preceding it (i.e. the factors to its right). If no such inverse exists, we shall use the form

$$\hat{v}^+(x) = Tv^+(x) \; . \tag{8.74}$$

Our former set of transformations is included as a special case, in which we may define the action of $T$ by means of

$$Tv(x) = N(x)v[S(x)] \; . \tag{8.75}$$

But $T$ may be more general than that; for instance, it may imply a band pass filter which we shall study in Sect. 12.3. $T$ may also describe any other kind of convolution in the form

$$\hat{v}(x) = \int K(x,x')v(x')d^2x' \; . \tag{8.76}$$

In order to convince ourselves that (8.76) contains (8.75) as a special case, we put

$$K(x,x') = N(x)\delta[x' - S(x)] \tag{8.77}$$

and insert this into (8.76). Because of the $\delta$-function we immediately obtain the result (8.75). The dynamics with respect to the test pattern $q$ is found directly in analogy to (8.61) and has precisely the same form as (8.61) and (8.62).

We now want to demonstrate that the transformation $T$ can be shifted from the prototype patterns $\hat{v}$ to the test pattern $q$. This is achieved by the individual steps in

$$\begin{aligned} \xi_k &= \int \hat{v}_k^+(x)q(x)d^2x = \int v_k^+(x)T^{-1}q(x)d^2x \\ &= \int v_k(x)\hat{q}(x)d^2x \end{aligned} \tag{8.78}$$

which are self-explanatory. In the last step we have used the definition of the transformed test pattern $\hat{q}$. Now consider equation (8.62) in which we insert the definition (8.77) of $\hat{v}$. We may multiply both sides of (8.62) by $T^{-1}$ to yield

$$T^{-1}\dot{q} \equiv \frac{d}{dt}\hat{q}(x,t) = -\gamma_1 \sum_k \frac{\partial V}{\partial \xi_k} v_k(x) \; . \tag{8.79}$$

On account of the relations (8.78), the potential function $V$ can be considered not only as a functional of $\hat{v}_k^+$ and $q$, but equally well as a functional of the transformed test pattern $\hat{q}$ and of the original, i.e. untransformed, prototype vectors $v_k$. If the transformation $T$ is time-independent or varies much more slowly than $q$, we may replace $T^{-1}\dot{q}$ by $d/dt\,(T^{-1}q) \equiv (d/dt)\hat{q}$ on the left-hand side of (8.79). Thus (8.79) can be understood equally well as an equation for $\hat{q}$.

Finally we observe that (8.62) (which applies also to $\hat{v}_k$'s of the form (8.72)!) can be transformed into an equation for the order parameters $\hat{\xi}_k$ (8.58). To show this we multiply (8.62) by $\hat{v}_k^+(\boldsymbol{x})$, use the definition (8.58), the property (8.57), and the fact that $V$ is a function of $\hat{\xi}_{k'}$, $k' = 1, \ldots, M$ only. We obtain

$$\dot{\hat{\xi}}_k = -\gamma_1 \frac{\partial V}{\partial \hat{\xi}_k} \, . \tag{8.80}$$

Note that in this representation $\hat{\xi}_k$ is an independent variable depending on time, $t$, but not on $S$. In principle, it is possible to define equations for the transformation $T$ by means of a gradient dynamics and by the introduction of adequate definitions for derivatives with respect to the transformation $T$. For practical purposes, however, it is advantageous to consider more explicit transformations $T$ which then depend on specific parameters, such as the deformation parameters of Sect. 8.2, or on cut off frequencies of band pass filters as will be discussed in Sect. 12.3. The differentiation of the potential must then be done with respect to these parameters. It may prove useful in the recognition process to change the approach in such a way that one starts with the gross features and then proceeds to finer details. An example of this type of approach was presented in the last part of Sect. 8.2 (expansion of $v$ in terms of Bessel functions).

Here we want to make a few general remarks. There may be set of basic transformations $T_1, T_2 \ldots, T_N$; they can be considered as the generators of a semigroup in which $T_l T_m$ is again an element and where the associative law

$$(T_l T_m) T_n = T_l (T_m T_n) \tag{8.81}$$

is obeyed. If an inverse of each generator exists, then $T_1, \ldots, T_M$ form a group. This leads us to the definition of an invariance group with respect to pattern recognition. We must remember, however, that the group elements act in the presence of a cost function which we will discuss now. We know that human beings can recognize deformed patterns up to a certain degree of deformation. Thus, when we wish to construct a machine which performs pattern recognition, this maximum allowed degree of deformation must be implemented into the recognition system. This can be done by means of a cost function. For instance, let us study a case in which we imagine that patterns are drawn on a rubber sheet and that this sheet may be deformed according to the laws of elasticity. This leads us to the formulation of a number of cost functions, e.g. in the form

$$C = \alpha \int [\boldsymbol{x} - S(\boldsymbol{x})]^2 d^2x \tag{8.82}$$

which means that only small deviations will be permitted. Alternatively, we many stipulate

$$C = \alpha \int [\nabla S(\boldsymbol{x})]^2 d^2x \; , \tag{8.83}$$

which means that the deviations change only little on a local scale. To the best of our knowledge the study of such cost functions is still in its infancy. When we consider the recognition of faces (or of letters), we realize that the cost functions must depend on the prototype patterns. For instance noses and foreheads are practically rigid while other parts like the mouth can be more easily deformed, or in letters, some lines or angles are less deformable than others. This of course must be taken care of in the formulation of cost functions.

Let us conclude this section with a general remark on the possible implementation of these procedures in a synergetic computer. As we have seen in Chap. 7, there is a realization by means of order parameter (or grandmother) cells in which $v_k(\boldsymbol{x})$ is the synaptic strength between the space point $(x,y)$ of the input pattern and the order parameter cell with index $k$. Quite clearly, $T$ acts on the synaptic strengths. This leads us to the hypothesis that in humans these synaptic strengths can learn specific classes of transformations $T$ and then perform these transformations when required. The question of how to implement this kind of learning and performance of transformations by means of the synaptic strengths in a synergetic computer remains to by solved by further research.

# 9. Recognition of Complex Scenes. Scene-Selective Attention

In this brief chapter we deal with the recognition of prototype patterns within complex scenes. To be most explicit, we consider test patterns such as that shown in Fig. 9.1. The prototype patterns to be identified are those of Fig. 6.1 a. Since the patterns corresponding to the prototype patterns are spatially shifted with respect to each other, we first make the process invariant with respect to translation by means of the procedure described in Sect. 8.1. In addition, we let the attention parameter $\lambda$ in (5.13) and (5.33) depend on the index $k$ which labels the specific prototype pattern. For instance $k = 1$ corresponds to a particular face in Fig. 6.1 a, $k = 2$ to a second one, and so on.

In the first step of our analysis we set all $\lambda_k = \lambda$ and offer the test pattern of Fig. 9.1 (or more precisely, its translation-invariant version) to the computer. The resulting time evolution of the order parameters $\xi_k$ is shown in panel I of Fig. 9.2. The order parameter $\xi$ belonging for instance to the woman with the label $k = 1$, reaches its fixed point $\xi_1 = 1$, while the other order parameters $\xi$ decay to zero. At this moment (or even somewhat earlier) we or the computer set the attention parameter, $\lambda_1$, which belongs to the pattern just recognized equal to zero, whereas all other $\lambda$'s remain unchanged. Then the test pattern (in its translation-invariant form) is offered to the computer again. The results are shown in panels II and III of Fig. 9.2. $\xi_1$ decays and finally crosses the growing $\xi_2$-curve. $\xi_2$ eventually reaches its fixed point, indicating that the partly hidden face in Fig. 9.1 has been recognized.

This procedure can be generalized to the recognition of several prototype patterns in composite scenes. For instance Fig. 9.3 has been analyzed in this way. The temporal evolution of the order parameters is shown in the left column of Fig. 9.4 where from top to bottom the $\lambda$'s of the patterns already recognized were successively put equal to zero. We have applied the same procedure to the case in which the complex test pattern and the prototype patterns were made simultaneously invariant with respect to translation, rotation and scaling.

In most cases this procedure worked, though in some exceptional cases it failed and gave a wrong pattern identification. We shall discuss this failure in Chap. 10 where we will compare it with a similar failure in human perception.

**Fig. 9.1.** A complex scene to be recognized by the synergetic computer. From Fuchs and Haken (1988a)

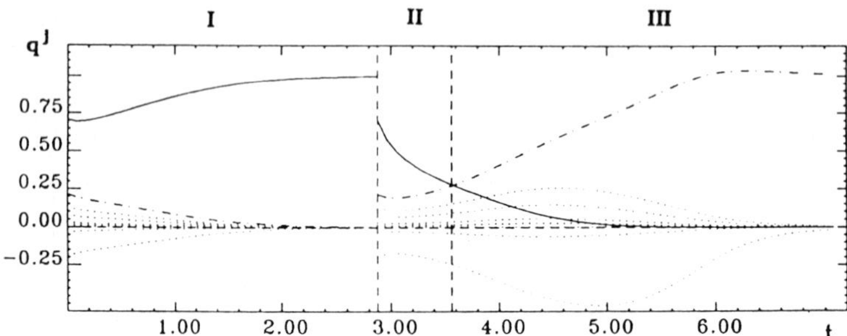


**Fig. 9.2.** Time evolution of the order parameters $\xi_1$ (woman), $\xi_2$ (man) corresponding to Fig. 9.1. When $\xi_1$ has come close to unity, the attention parameter for the woman is switched to zero and then a new time evolution sets in as shown, eventually indicating that the man has been recognized. From Fuchs and Haken (1988a)

**Fig. 9.3.** Example of a scene composed of five faces recognized by the computer using the procedure described in the text. From Fuchs and Haken (1988a)

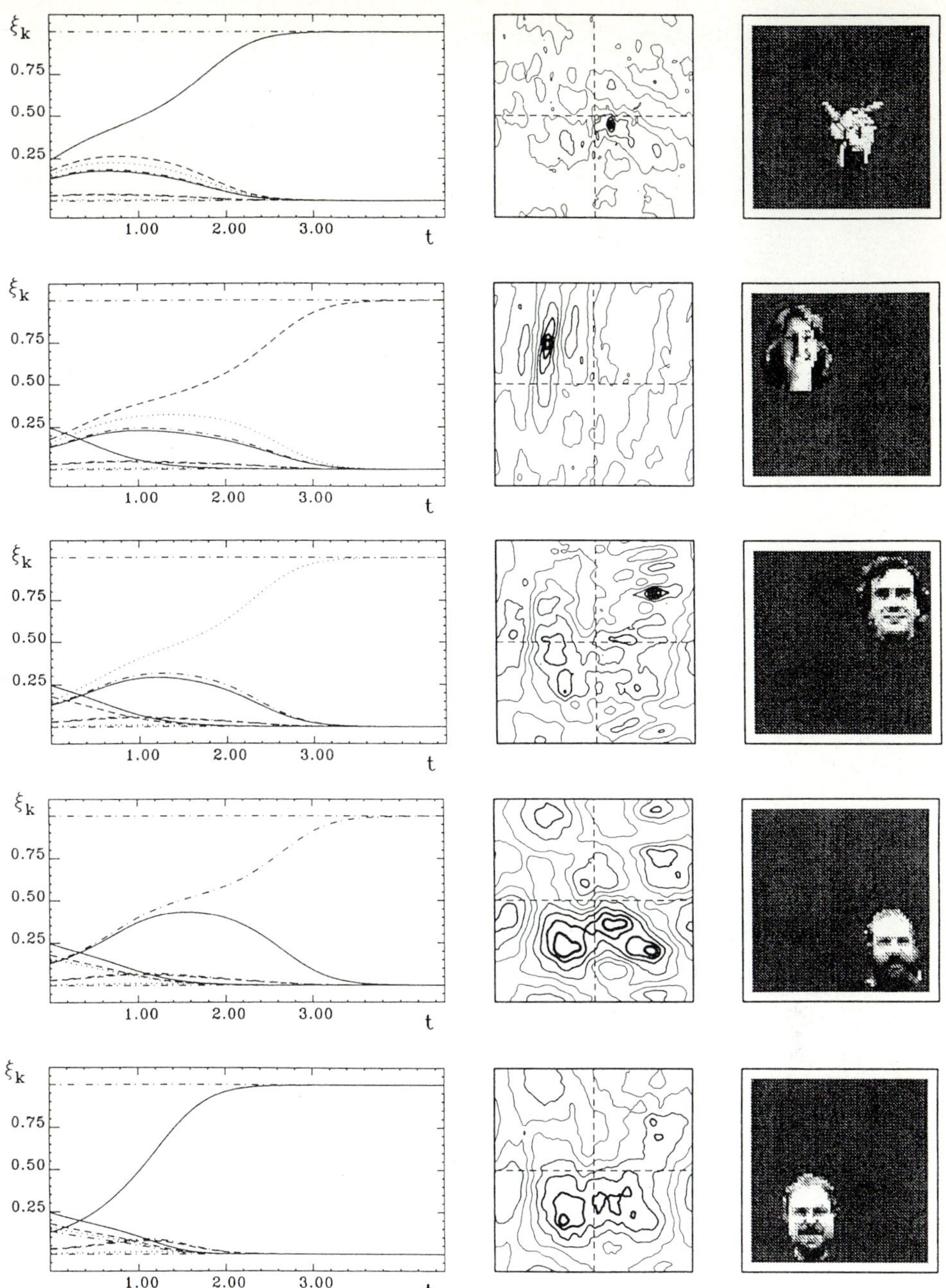


**Fig. 9.4.** Time evolution of the order parameters. From Fuchs and Haken (1988b)

# 10. Learning Algorithms

## 10.1 Survey; Several Lines of Approach

Learning is a central problem for neural and synergetic computers and in this chapter we shall present a number of learning algorithms. As we have seen in previous chapters, patterns are stored in the form of vectors $\boldsymbol{v}_k$. In order to perform pattern recognition, the formalism requires that the adjoint vectors $\boldsymbol{v}_k^+$ are known. These $\boldsymbol{v}_k^+$ occur in different ways depending on whether the formalism is realized on a serial computer or on a network. In a serial computer we have to form the scalar products $(\boldsymbol{v}_k^+ \boldsymbol{q})$ as is evident from the basic equation (5.11). The same projection is needed when the computer consists of a parallel network with three layers, as shown in Figs. 7.2 and 7.3. When we use a one-layer network, the $\boldsymbol{v}_k^+$ and $\boldsymbol{v}_k$ are related to the synaptic strengths $\lambda_{ij}$ and $\lambda_{ijlm}$ in the following way, as may be shown by a comparison between (5.11) and (7.1):

$$\lambda_{ij} = \sum_k v_{ki} v_{kj}^+ \ , \tag{10.1}$$

$$\lambda_{ijlm} = \sum_{kk'} (B + C - B\delta_{kk'}) v_{ki} v_{kj}^+ v_{k'l}^+ v_{k'm}^+ \ . \tag{10.2}$$

In the following we shall discuss several possible approaches. In the first of these (Sect. 10.2) we shall show how the vectors $\boldsymbol{v}_k^+$ can be constructed by an iterative procedure once a set of prototype patterns $\boldsymbol{v}_k$ is provided. In Sects. 10.3 – 5 we shall present a formalism based on information and information gain which tells us how the $\lambda_{ij}$ and $\lambda_{ijkl}$ can be determined directly. Finally, in Sect. 10.6 we shall show how the potential function introduced in Sect. 5.1 can be utilized to determine the $\boldsymbol{v}_k$ and $\boldsymbol{v}_k^+$ simultaneously, even in the presence of noise. Sections 10.2 – 5 are somewhat technical. According to our experience, however, the approach of Sect. 10.6 is the most elegant and efficient method.

## 10.2 Learning of the Synaptic Strengths

### 10.2.1 An Iterative Procedure for Determining the Adjoint Vectors $\boldsymbol{v}_k^+$

Let us assume that the first $n$ pattern vectors have been stored in the computer and that their adjoint vectors have been determined so that the following quantities are known

$$v_k, v_k^+ \ , \quad k=1,\ldots,n \ . \tag{10.3}$$

They obey the relations

$$(v_k^+ v_{k'}) = \delta_{kk'} \ . \tag{10.4}$$

In the following we assume, as everywhere in this book, that

$$(\bar{v}_k v_k) = 1 \ , \tag{10.5}$$

where $\bar{v}$ is the transposed vector belonging to $v$. We now assume that an additional pattern vector $v_{n+1}$ is added so that all the vectors

$$v_k \ , \quad k=1,\ldots,n+1 \tag{10.6}$$

are known to the computer. As we shall see, the old vectors $v_k^+$ no longer obey the orthogonality relations (10.4). Instead, we have to construct a new set of such vectors, which we shall denote by

$$u_k^+ \ , \quad k=1,\ldots,n+1 \ . \tag{10.7}$$

We shall demand that the additional pattern vector for $n+1$ is normalized

$$(\bar{v}_{n+1} v_{n+1}) = 1 \ . \tag{10.8}$$

We then require that the relations (10.4) hold for $u_k$, i.e.,

$$(u_k^+ v_{k'}) = \delta_{kk'} \ , \quad k,k' = 1 \ ,\ldots,n+1 \ . \tag{10.9}$$

In order to construct the vectors $u_j^+$, we assume for $j=1,\ldots,n$ the relationships

$$u_j^+ = \sum_{k=1}^{n} a_{jk} v_k^+ + a_{j,n+1} \bar{v}_{n+1} \ , \tag{10.10}$$

and for $j=n+1$

$$u_{n+1}^+ = \sum_{k=1}^{n} a_{n+1,k} u_k^+ + a_{n+1,n+1} \bar{v}_{n+1} \tag{10.11}$$

where the coefficients $a_{jk} (j=1,\ldots,n+1; k=1,\ldots,n+1)$ are as yet unknown. In order to derive equations for these coefficients, we multiply (10.10) from the right-hand side by

$$v_{k'} \ , \quad k'=1,\ldots,n \ , \tag{10.12}$$

with the indices as indicated. We then obtain

$$(u_j^+ v_{k'}) = \sum_{k=1}^{n} a_{jk} (v_k^+ v_{k'}) + a_{j,n+1} (\bar{v}_{n+1} v_{k'}) \ , \quad j=1,\ldots,n \ , \tag{10.13}$$

which, because of the orthogonality relations (10.4) and (10.9), can be cast into the form

$$\delta_{jk'} = \sum_{k=1}^{n} a_{jk}\delta_{kk'} + a_{j,n+1}Q_{n+1,k'} \ , \tag{10.14}$$

where we have used the abbreviation

$$(\bar{v}_{n+1}v_{k'}) = Q_{n+1,k'} \ . \tag{10.15}$$

Using the properties of the Kronecker symbol $\delta$, we obtain

$$\delta_{jk'} = a_{jk'} + a_{j,n+1}Q_{n+1,k'} \tag{10.16}$$

which we shall utilize later.

We now multiply (10.10) from the right-hand side by

$$v_{n+1} \tag{10.17}$$

which yields

$$(u_j^+ v_{n+1}) = \sum_{k=1}^{n} a_{jk}(v_k^+ v_{n+1}) + a_{j,n+1}Q_{n+1,n+1}, \quad j = 1, \ldots, n \ , \tag{10.18}$$

which, by means of the orthogonality relations (10.4) and (10.9), can be re-expressed as

$$\delta_{j,n+1} = \sum_{k=1}^{n} a_{jk}Q_{k,n+1} + a_{j,n+1}Q_{n+1,n+1} \ . \tag{10.19}$$

Note that, because of (10.8), we have

$$Q_{n+1,n+1} = 1 \ . \tag{10.20}$$

Solving (10.16) for $a_{jk}$, we obtain

$$a_{jk} = \delta_{jk} - a_{j,n+1}Q_{n+1,k} \ , \tag{10.21}$$

which we insert into (10.19) for $j = 1, \ldots, n$ to obtain

$$0 = \sum_{k=1}^{n} \delta_{jk}Q_{k,n+1} - \sum_{k=1}^{n} a_{j,n+1}Q_{n+1,k}Q_{k,n+1} + a_{j,n+1}Q_{n+1,n+1} \ . \tag{10.22}$$

We make use of the property of the Kronecker symbol $\delta_{jk}$ and rearrange the last two expressions on the right-hand side to yield

$$0 = Q_{j,n+1} + a_{j,n+1}\left(Q_{n+1,n+1} - \sum_{k=1}^{n} Q_{n+1,k}Q_{k,n+1}\right) \tag{10.23}$$

which can be solved with respect to $a_{j,n+1}$:

$$a_{j,n+1} = Q_{j,n+1}\left(\sum_{k=1}^{n} Q_{n+1,k}Q_{k,n+1} - 1\right)^{-1} . \tag{10.24}$$

This result enables us to express $a_{jk}$ in (10.21) by the quantities $Q$ which themselves can be directly calculated from the already known $\boldsymbol{v}_k$ and their transposed vectors. We thus obtain our final result

$$a_{jk} = \delta_{jk} - Q_{n+1,k}Q_{j,n+1}\left(\sum_{k=1}^{n} Q_{n+1,k}Q_{k,n+1} - 1\right)^{-1} \tag{10.25}$$

for

$$j = 1,\dots,n \tag{10.26}$$

$$k = 1,\dots,n .$$

We now have to establish equations for $a_{n+1,k}$, $k = 1,\dots,n+1$. To achieve this we multiply (10.11) from the right-hand side by $\boldsymbol{v}_{k'}$ and obtain

$$(\overset{+}{\boldsymbol{u}}_{n+1}\boldsymbol{v}_{k'}) = \sum_{k=1}^{n} a_{n+1,k}(\overset{+}{\boldsymbol{u}}_k\, \boldsymbol{v}_{k'}) + a_{n+1,n+1}(\bar{\boldsymbol{v}}_{n+1}\boldsymbol{v}_{k'}) . \tag{10.27}$$

We first treat the case

$$k' = 1,\dots,n \tag{10.28}$$

and find, with reasoning analogous to that above,

$$\delta_{n+1,k'} = \sum_{k=1}^{n} a_{n+1,k}\delta_{kk'} + a_{n+1,n+1}Q_{n+1,k'} , \tag{10.29}$$

which can be simplified to

$$0 = a_{n+1,k} + a_{n+1,n+1}Q_{n+1,k} \tag{10.30}$$

where we have replaced $k'$ by $k$. In the least step of our analysis we multiply (10.11) from the right-hand side by $\boldsymbol{v}_{n+1}$ to obtain

$$(\overset{+}{\boldsymbol{u}}_{n+1}\boldsymbol{v}_{n+1}) = \sum_{k=1}^{n} a_{n+1,k}(\overset{+}{\boldsymbol{u}}_k\, \boldsymbol{v}_{n+1}) + a_{n+1,n+1}Q_{n+1,n+1} . \tag{10.31}$$

As a result of (10.9) we have

$$R_{k,n+1} \equiv (\overset{+}{\boldsymbol{u}}_k\, \boldsymbol{v}_{n+1}) = 0 \quad \text{for} \quad k = 1,\dots,n , \tag{10.32}$$

In the next step of our analysis we study equation (10.27) for $k' = n+1$. Using the now familiar orthogonality relations and the relations (10.30, 32) and

$$Q_{n+1,n+1} = 1 , \tag{10.33}$$

we obtain

$$a_{n+1,n+1} = 1 \ . \tag{10.34}$$

We may now summarize our results as follows: For

$$j = 1, \ldots, n \tag{10.35}$$

we obtain the relations

$$\boldsymbol{u}_j^+ = \boldsymbol{v}_j^+ - Q_{j,n+1} N \left( \sum_{k=1}^{n} Q_{n+1,k} \boldsymbol{v}_k^+ - \bar{\boldsymbol{v}}_{n+1} \right) , \tag{10.36}$$

where $N$ is defined by

$$N = \left( \sum_{k=1}^{n} Q_{n+1,k} Q_{k,n+1} - 1 \right)^{-1} \ . \tag{10.37}$$

For $k = n+1$, on the other hand, we find

$$\boldsymbol{u}_{n+1}^+ = - \sum_{k=1}^{n} Q_{n+1,k} \, \boldsymbol{u}_k^+ + \bar{\boldsymbol{v}}_{n+1} \ . \tag{10.38}$$

### 10.2.2 A Special Case

Let us now consider the special case in which the transposed vector $\bar{\boldsymbol{v}}_{n+1}$ is orthogonal to the originally stored pattern vectors, i.e.,

$$Q_{n+1,k} \equiv (\bar{\boldsymbol{v}}_{n+1} \boldsymbol{v}_k) = 0 \quad \text{for} \quad k = 1, \ldots, n \ . \tag{10.39}$$

It follows immediately from the above formulas (10.37, 38) that the adjoint pattern vector $\boldsymbol{u}_{n+1}^+$ is given by

$$\boldsymbol{u}_{n+1}^+ = \bar{\boldsymbol{v}}_{n+1} \ , \tag{10.40}$$

and that the corresponding pattern vectors for the indices $j = 1, \ldots, n$ are

$$\boldsymbol{u}_j^+ = \boldsymbol{v}_j^+ - Q_{j,n+1} \bar{\boldsymbol{v}}_{n+1} \ . \tag{10.41}$$

If, in addition, the adjoint vectors for $j = 1, \ldots, n$ are orthogonal to the newly given pattern vector $\boldsymbol{v}_{n+1}$

$$Q_{j,n+1} \equiv (\boldsymbol{v}_j^+ \boldsymbol{v}_{n+1}) = 0 \ , \tag{10.42}$$

we obtain

$$\boldsymbol{u}_j = \boldsymbol{v}_j^+ \ . \tag{10.43}$$

### 10.2.3 Implementation in a Three-Layer (Two-Layer) Network

Let us now discuss the individual steps by which the newly offered pattern

$$v_{n+1} \tag{10.44}$$

can be implemented in the network of Fig. 10.1. As is evident from the above formulas, the synaptic strengths must be changed from $v_{kl}$ to $u_{kl}$.

This study is of particular interest because in most parallel networks (neurocomputers) the "synaptic strengths" are fixed from the outside. Here we shall discover what is necessary for a network to perform this function itself. It will turn out that each "neuron" must have specific storage and arithmetic properties.

We shall be concerned with the connections between the cells $l$ of the input layer and the cells $j$ of the middle layer consisting of order parameter cells (or grandmother cells). Before the pattern $n+1$ is offered, the network looks like that of Fig. 10.1, where only the synaptic connections given by $v_{jl}^{+}$ are realized, and where $j = 1, \ldots, n$. When a new pattern $n+1$ is offered, the system has to generate a new cell in the middle layer with index $j = n+1$. In a first step, it also establishes connections between the cells $l$ of the input layer and the cell $n+1$ in the middle layer with synaptic strengths $\bar{v}_{n+1,l}$ (Fig. 10.2). Since the incoming pattern is given by its individual components with index $l$, $\bar{v}_{n+1,l}$ is known. In order to establish the new synaptic strengths given by (10.36 – 38), the network has first to form these quantities whereby it utilizes the already existing connections realized by $v_{jl}^{+}$ and $\bar{v}_{n+1,l}$. When we offer the system the prototype patterns $k = 1, \ldots, n$ again, the network may transmit the individual components via $\bar{v}_{n+1,l}$ to the cell $n+1$. We shall assume that in this way the cell $n+1$ calculates the quantities

$$Q_{n+1,k} = (\bar{v}_{n+1} v_k) \tag{10.45}$$

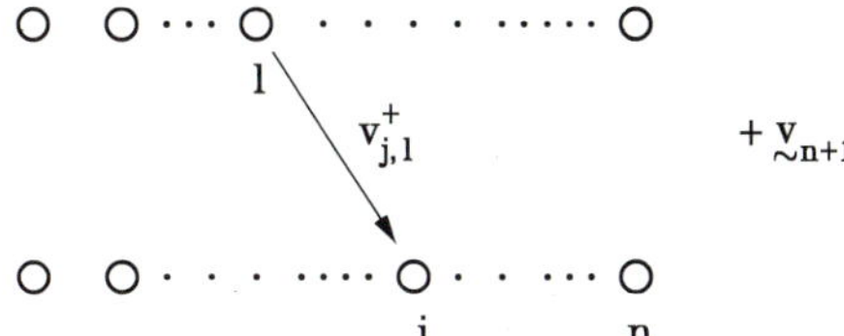


**Fig. 10.1.** Typical part of a network showing the input and middle layers. The input cell with index $l$ is connected to the order parameter cell $j$ by $v_{jl}^{+}$ so that a signal strength $v_{jl}^{+} q_l$ results. The pattern $v_{n+1}$ must be learnt by this network

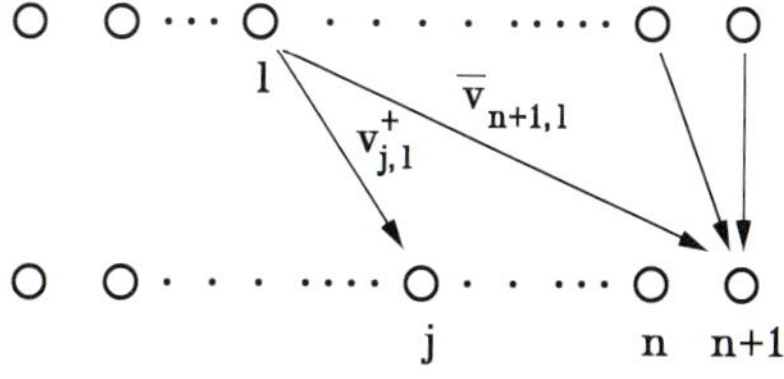


**Fig. 10.2.** In the first step, a new order parameter cell $n+1$ is established and is connected with the input layer by means of $\bar{v}_{n+1,l}$

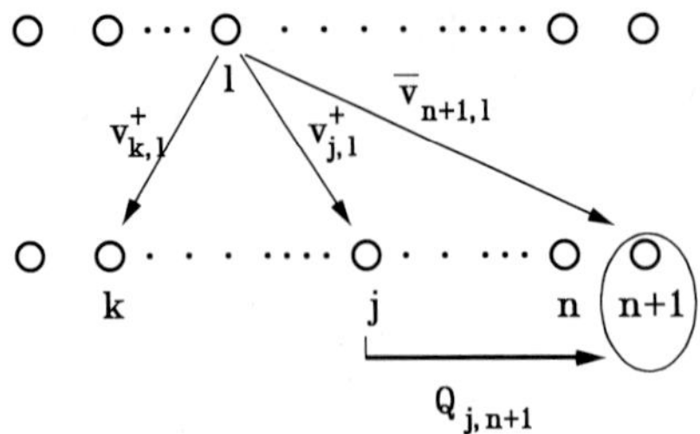


**Fig. 10.3.** The quantity $Q_{jn+1}$ is transferred to the cell $n+1$. See text for details

and stores them under the labels $k = 1, \ldots, n$. In the next step the network communicates the pattern $n+1$ from the cell $l$ to the specific cell $j$. The corresponding quantities

$$Q_{j,n+1} \tag{10.46}$$

are then stored in the cell $j$. In the following step the cells of the middle layer establish connections to the cell $n+1$ of this same layer and communicate their values $Q_{j,n+1}$ to the cell $n+1$ (Fig. 10.3). They communicate these values in a channel $j$ of the cell $n+1$ where $Q_{n+1,j}$ is stored. Cell $n+1$ can now form $N$ according to

$$N = \left( \sum_{j=1}^{n} Q_{n+1,j} Q_{j,n+1} - 1 \right)^{-1} \tag{10.47}$$

and subsequently the quantity

$$Q_{n+1,j} N \ . \tag{10.48}$$

This quantity is now sent from cell $n+1$ of the middle layer to the cells $j$ of the same layer with the corresponding index $j$. We thus arrive at the scheme of Fig. 10.4 where the old connections are still present but the cells of the middle layer have now stored the quantities indicated in the figure. In the next step (Fig. 10.5) the cell $l$ receives an input

$$N Q_{n+1,k} \overset{+}{v}_{kl} \tag{10.49}$$

from each of the cells $k$ of the middle layer and performs the summation

$$\sum_{k=1}^{n} Q_{n+1,k} \overset{+}{v}_{kl} \ . \tag{10.50}$$

This quantity is now stored in the cell $l$ of the input layer. The final steps can now be taken to alter the strengths of the connections between the cells of the input layer and the cells $k = 1, \ldots, n$ of the middle layer. To this end the cell $l$ of the input layer emits the signal (10.50) while the cell $j$ of the middle layer emits the signal $NQ_{j,n+1}$. The corresponding product defines the alteration of the synaptic strength (Fig. 10.6).

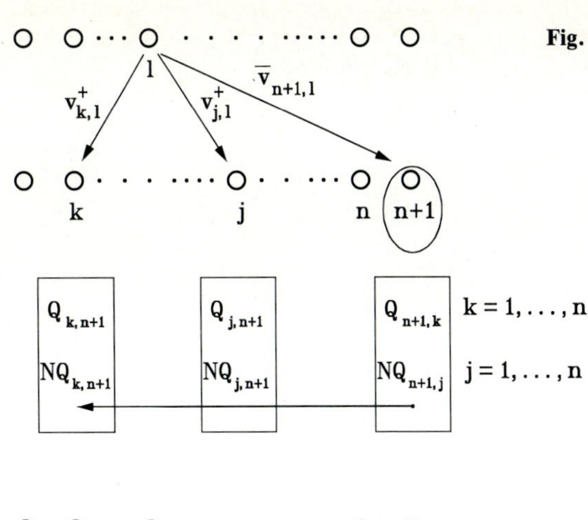


**Fig. 10.4.** See text

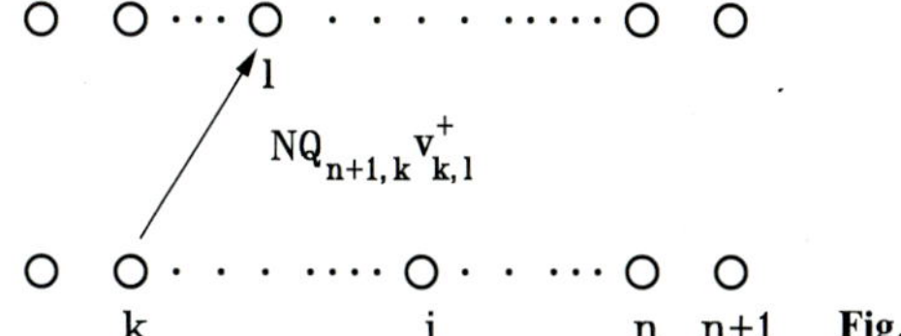


**Fig. 10.5.** See text

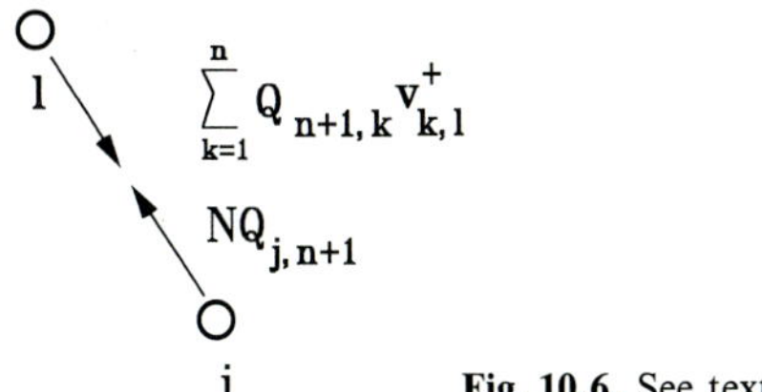


**Fig. 10.6.** See text

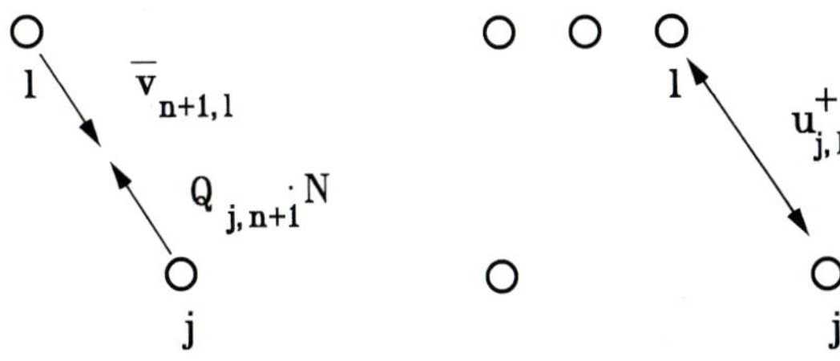


**Fig. 10.7.** See text

**Fig. 10.8.** See text

In order to take care of the last term in (10.36), the cell $l$ emits the signal $\bar{v}_{n+1,l}$ which is then multiplied in the synaptic connection by the signal $Q_{j,n+1}N$ emitted from the cell $j$ of the middle layer (Fig. 10.7). Taking all these effects together, the network has now established the new synaptic strengths $u^+_{jl}$ (Fig. 10.8).

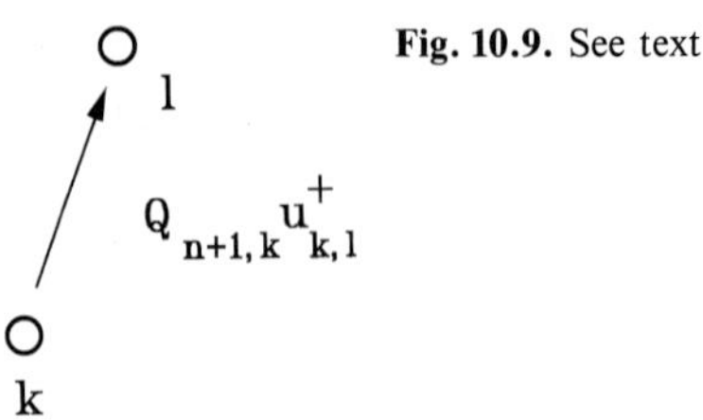


**Fig. 10.9.** See text

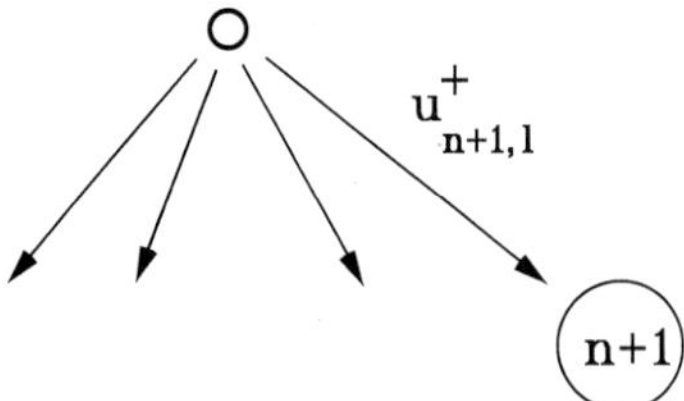


**Fig. 10.10.** See text

Now let us turn to the last step, namely how the network may establish the new connections between the input layer cell $l$ and the middle layer cell $n+1$. To achieve this, the cell $l$ first has to collect the quantities $Q_{n+1,k} \cdot u_{kl}^{+}$ from the middle layer cell $k$ and to perform the sum (Fig. 10.9)

$$\sum_{k=1}^{n} Q_{n+1,k} u_{kl}^{+} \ . \tag{10.51}$$

With these quantities available, the cell $l$ can alter the strength of its synaptic connection to cell $n+1$ of the middle layer by means of the prescription (10.38) (Fig. 10.10). Thus the procedure by which the network internalizes the different steps is completed.

## 10.3 Information and Information Gain

The learning algorithms that we shall present in Sects. 10.4, 5 and in Chap. 11 are based on the concepts of information and information gain. Here information is meant in the sense of Shannon and we shall briefly remind the reader of this concept. Let us consider the example of throwing dice. When we throw a single die there are $R_1 = 6$ possible outcomes. When, on the other hand, we are throwing two dice, then the number of outcomes is

$$R = R_1 R_2 \tag{10.52}$$

because we assume that the outcomes are independent of each other. We now wish to define a quantity, $I$, which depends on the number of outcomes $R$ and which has an additive property so that

$$I(R) = I(R_1) + I(R_2) \ . \tag{10.53}$$

Since (10.53) must hold for any choice of $R_1$, $R_2$, this is a functional relationship which possesses the unique solution

$$I = K \ln R \ . \tag{10.54}$$

The as yet arbitrary constant $K$ is usually fixed in such a way that when $R$ is given by

$$R = 2^n \tag{10.55}$$

the quantity $I$ is equal to $n$:

$$I \equiv K \ln R = K n \ln 2 = n \ . \tag{10.56}$$

This yields a value of the constant $K$

$$K = \frac{1}{\ln 2} = \log_2 \mathrm{e} \tag{10.57}$$

Inserting (10.57) into (10.56) and using the properties of the logarithm, we can write $I$ in the form

$$I = \log_2 R \ . \tag{10.58}$$

With this definition, $I$ is measured in "bits". In many practical applications, instead of the information $I$ a somewhat different type of definition is used, which can nonetheless be derived from that of (10.58). We will study this alternative definition for the case of a simplified Morse alphabet consisting of dots and dashes (but no intervals). Let us consider a message which contains altogether $N_1$ dots and $N_2$ dashes where

$$N_1 + N_2 = N \tag{10.59}$$

is the total number of symbols. When $N_1$ and $N_2$ are fixed, a variety of messages can be sent because the dashes and dots can be arranged in different orders. As is shown in combinatorics, the number $R$ of possible realizations is then given by

$$R = \frac{N!}{N_1! N_2!} \ . \tag{10.60}$$

We wish to evaluate $I$ [as defined in (10.58)] for the case where $N$ is a large number. Inserting (10.60) into (10.54) and using Stirling's formula

$$\ln Q! \approx Q(\ln Q - 1) \tag{10.61}$$

for larger numbers $Q$, we may cast $I$ into the form

$$I \approx K[N(\ln N - 1) - N_1(\ln N_1 - 1) - N_2(\ln N_2 - 1)] \ . \tag{10.62}$$

We now divide both sides by $N$, i.e. the total number of symbols, and define the information $i$ by

$$i \equiv \frac{I}{N} = -K\left(\frac{N_1}{N}\ln\frac{N_1}{N}+\frac{N_2}{N}\ln\frac{N_2}{N}\right) . \tag{10.63}$$

Defining the relative frequencies of dots and dashes by

$$p_j = \frac{N_j}{N}, \quad j=1,2 , \tag{10.64}$$

we may rewrite (10.63) in the form

$$i = \frac{I}{N} = -K(p_1 \ln p_1 + p_2 \ln p_2) . \tag{10.65}$$

This form can be easily generalized to a larger set of symbols which are labelled by an index $j$. In this case one readily obtains

$$i = -K \sum_j p_j \ln p_j . \tag{10.66}$$

Our brief considerations reveal the following: The definition of information (10.66), which is given here according to Shannon, has nothing to do with the information content of a message in the ordinary sense of this word. Rather, $i$ is a quantitative measure of possible realizations of events $j$ which possess a given probability distribution $p_j$. In fact, the transition from relative frequency to probability distribution is a nontrivial step because relative frequency refers, at least in principle, to a set of measurements whereas probability distributions $p_j$ refer to predictions about the relative frequency of events. We shall not enter a more profound discussion here because the reader will see by means of the explicit examples how to use the concept of information in the present context of pattern recognition.

So far, we have introduced the information $i$ (10.66) for given $p_j$. This relationship can also be used, however, to make so-called unbiased guesses. Such guesses are required if the information (in the usual sense of the word) about a system is incomplete and only a limited set of data is available. In the following we shall assume that these data are given in the form of average values which define constraints

$$\sum p_j f_j^{(k)} = f_k . \tag{10.67}$$

To illustrate the meaning of (10.67), let us consider the example of a gas composed of individual non-interacting molecules. Then we may measure the total energy of the gas and divide this by the number of molecules, $N$. It is assumed that the total energy $E \equiv f_E$ (cf. 10.67) is a sum over the energies of the individual particles $E_j \equiv f_j^{(E)}$, which just possess the specific energy $E_j$. For sake of simplicity we assume that $E$ and $E_j$ are discrete quantities, as is actually the case in quantum mechanics. The total energy of a system divided by $N$ can then be represented by the energies $E_j$ multiplied by their relative frequencies $p_j$. The problem to be addressed is how to make an unbiased guess about $p_j$ so that the value $f_E$ is obtained. This is achieved by the "maximum information principle" or "maximum entropy principle" in which (10.66) is maximized under the constraints (10.67) with the additional requirement of normalization

$$\sum_{j=1}^{M} p_j = 1 \ . \tag{10.68}$$

We consider the $p_j$ as variables and take the constraints (10.67) and (10.68) into account by means of the method of Lagrange multipliers. The Lagrange multiplier belonging to (10.68) is denoted $\lambda - 1$, and those corresponding to (10.67) will be denoted $\lambda_k$. We then require that the variation of the resulting expression vanishes:

$$\delta \left[ i - (\lambda - 1) \sum p_j - \sum_k \lambda_k \sum_j p_j f_j^{(k)} \right] = 0 \ . \tag{10.69}$$

The variation $\delta$ can easily be performed because the $p_j$ are now independent variables with respect to which the left-hand side of (10.69) may be differentiated. We then readily obtain

$$-\ln p_j - 1 - (\lambda - 1) - \sum_k \lambda_k f_j^{(k)} = 0 \ , \tag{10.70}$$

which possesses the solution

$$p_j = \exp\left(-\lambda - \sum_k \lambda_k f_j^{(k)}\right) \ . \tag{10.71}$$

The Lagrange parameter $\lambda$ can be determined from the normalization condition (10.68) which now reads

$$\mathrm{e}^{-\lambda} \sum_j \exp\left(-\sum_k \lambda_k f_j^{(k)}\right) = 1 \ . \tag{10.72}$$

The expression

$$\sum_j \exp\left(-\sum_k \lambda_k f_j^{(k)}\right) = Z(\lambda_1, \ldots, \lambda_M) \tag{10.73}$$

is called the partition function. With this definition of $Z$ we have the simple relationship

$$\mathrm{e}^{\lambda} = Z \tag{10.74}$$

or

$$\lambda = \ln Z \ . \tag{10.75}$$

This formalism allows one to derive the basic rules of thermodynamics and statistical mechanics, e.g. the Boltzmann distribution function, but this will not be our concern here.

In order to define the *information gain*, we write the expression (10.66) in the form

$$i = \sum_j p_j(-\ln p_j) \tag{10.76}$$

(where we have put $K = 1$).

The information $i$ appears as a sum over the individual states $j$ of their probability distribution function $p_j$ each time multiplied by $-\ln p_j$. In other words, (10.76) has the form of an average. This leads us to the idea of identifying each individual term $-\ln p_j$ as the information belonging to the state $j$

$$i_j = -\ln p_j \ . \tag{10.77}$$

Let us assume that one first makes a set of measurements which yield a distribution $p_j$ and then a second set of measurements leading to the distribution $p'_j$ so that

$$i'_j = -\ln p'_j \ . \tag{10.78}$$

The difference between (10.77) and (10.78) can be written in the form

$$i'_j - i_j = -\ln p'_j + \ln p_j = \ln\left(\frac{p_j}{p'_j}\right) \ . \tag{10.79}$$

If we now average this expression over the original distribution $p_j$, we obtain a measure of the average information change

$$K = \sum_j p_j \ln\left(\frac{p_j}{p'_j}\right) \ . \tag{10.80}$$

Equation (10.80) is called information gain or Kullback information.

One may show on purely mathematical grounds that

$$K \geq 0 \ . \tag{10.81}$$

It is assumed that both $p_j$ and $p'_j$ are normalized. The equality sign in (10.81) holds if and only if the two probability distributions $p_j$, $p'_j$ are identical,

$$p_j = p'_j \ . \tag{10.82}$$

## 10.4 The Basic Construction Principle of a Synergetic Computer Revisited

In this section we wish to show how the general form of the evolution equation for the test pattern vector $\boldsymbol{q}$ can be derived from an unbiased estimate of the distribution function of a limited set of observed data. This will give us a new access to the construction of a synergetic computer by generalizing (5.12).

Let us assume that a system can receive a set of data that are described by state vectors $\boldsymbol{q}$. We further assume that the detecting system is composed of elements $j$, where element $j$ measures the component (feature) $q_j$ of $\boldsymbol{q}$. In the following we shall study the properties that these elements and their connections must have in order to perform pattern recognition. If we have a stationary process, the incoming signals will obey a probability distribution $f(\boldsymbol{q})$. In the spirit of junior-school teaching we shall assume that some specific patterns are offered again and again so that the maxima of $f(\boldsymbol{q})$,

$$f(\boldsymbol{q}) = \max! \tag{10.83}$$

correspond to these patterns.

How can a system determine $f(\boldsymbol{q})$ from measurements? To answer this we assume that the system can measure the moments

$$\langle q_i \rangle, \langle q_i q_j \rangle, \langle q_i q_j q_k \rangle, \langle q_i q_j q_k q_l \rangle \ . \tag{10.84}$$

[As it will turn out below, see (10.91, 92), this choice will lead to an equation of the type (5.24).]

In order to guess $f(\boldsymbol{q})$ from given moments we employ the maximum information (maximum entropy) principle and discuss the minimum order of moments necessary to arrive at a sensible guess of $f$. If we use only linear moments, then according to the maximum information (entropy) principle $f$ must be of the form $f(\boldsymbol{q}) = N \exp(-\boldsymbol{\lambda} \cdot \boldsymbol{q})$ where $\boldsymbol{\lambda}$ is real.

Quite evidently $f(\boldsymbol{q})$ cannot be normalized in the space of $\boldsymbol{q}$ if the $\boldsymbol{q}$ variables run from minus infinity to plus infinity, so that this approach is not possible. When we employ moments up to second order, the general form of the distribution function will be

$$f(\boldsymbol{q}) = N \exp(\bar{\boldsymbol{a}} \cdot \boldsymbol{q} + \bar{\boldsymbol{q}} \cdot \boldsymbol{a} - \bar{\boldsymbol{q}} B \boldsymbol{q}) \ . \tag{10.85}$$

Introducing the new variable $\xi$ via

$$\boldsymbol{q} = \xi + B^{-1} \boldsymbol{a} \ , \tag{10.86}$$

equation (10.85) can be cast into the form

$$\tilde{f}(\xi) = N' \exp(-\bar{\xi} B \xi) \ . \tag{10.87}$$

Because $B$ must be a positive definite matrix, the maximum of (10.87) can be acquired for one single value of $\xi$ only, namely $\xi = 0$.

By using (10.86) we realize that there is only one maximum, i.e. only one pattern, which is almost invariably incompatible with the fact that a whole set of patterns is actually offered. This leads us to consider moments up to fourth order. For the sake of simplicity we shall assume that the moments of odd order vanish. Then, according to the maximum information (entropy) principle, the distribution function acquires the form

$$f(\boldsymbol{q}) = N\exp\left(-\sum_{ij} \lambda_{ij} q_i q_j - \sum_{ijmn} \lambda_{ijmn} q_i q_j q_m q_n\right) . \tag{10.88}$$

Our next objective is to show how we can construct a network which reproduces (10.88). To this end we assume that (10.88) is the solution (4.63) of the Fokker-Planck equation (4.60) with (4.61) and (4.62) where, in the present case, $V$ is a still unknown potential function. To make contact between (10.88) and the desired quantities $V$ and $Q$ in (4.60) we abbreviate the bracket in (10.88) by

$$\left(-\sum_{ij} \lambda_{ij} q_i q_j - \sum_{ijmn} \lambda_{ijmn} q_i q_j q_m q_n\right) = -\tilde{V}(q, \lambda) \tag{10.89}$$

and require that the stochastic forces $F_j$ of the Langevin equation corresponding to (4.60) obey the relations (4.58, 59, 62). We further set

$$\tilde{V} = \frac{2V}{Q} . \tag{10.90}$$

The Langevin equation belonging to the Fokker-Planck equation (4.60) has the same general form as (4.57) with (4.61), namely

$$\dot{q}_j = -\frac{\partial V}{\partial q_j} + F_j(t) . \tag{10.91}$$

However, $V$ is now determined by (10.89, 90), i.e. by means of measurements. We thus obtain

$$-\frac{\partial V}{\partial q_i} = Q\left(\sum_j \lambda_{ij} q_j + 2 \sum_{jmn} \lambda_{ijmn} q_j q_m q_n\right) . \tag{10.92}$$

We now observe that (10.91) together with (10.92) has a form similar to that of (7.1) describing the network of Fig. 7.1. In other words, we are capable of constructing a network that reproduces the distribution function $f(\boldsymbol{q})$, provided that the second- and fourth-order moments of this function are known. The only role the network must play is to transfer the value of a quantity $q_j$ of the element $j$, multiplied by a "synaptic strength" $\lambda_{ij}$ to the element $i$ [first term in (10.92)], or to transfer the value $q_j q_m q_n$ from elements $j, m, n$, multiplied by $\lambda_{ijmn}$ to the element $i$ [second term in (10.92)]. Then, in the corresponding element $i$, a summation is performed.

There is a further quite general and important conclusion: If the network can measure only a specific set of correlation functions (10.84) (or of higher order), we need only include the corresponding terms in (10.92). Because of the attractor states of the potential dynamics, any initial state will be pulled into any one of the local minima of $V(\boldsymbol{q})$ that are located at the points of the prototype patterns. If the initial state is close enough to one of these minima, then this minimum will be realized and an initially incomplete pattern will thereby be completed, i.e. the whole formalism acts as "associative memory" and thus as a pattern recognizer.

The approach described in this section has led us to the form of the network. In it the "synaptic strengths" $\lambda_{ij}, \lambda_{ijmn}$ are fixed by the requirement that $f(\boldsymbol{q})$ reproduces the experimentally given values of the moments (10.84). In practice, this is a formidable task. For this reason, we shall describe in the next section an iterative procedure which enables the $\lambda$'s to be calculated.

## 10.5 Learning by Means of the Information Gain

We shall deal here with the question of how the "synaptic strengths" $\lambda_{ij}, \lambda_{ijmn}$ can be learnt by the network.

Let us denote the given distribution function of the incoming patterns by $f(\boldsymbol{q})$ and the distribution function generated by the system by $\tilde{f}(\boldsymbol{q})$. We introduce the information gain (Kullback information) as a measure of the distance between these two distribution functions

$$K = \int f \ln \left(\frac{f}{\tilde{f}}\right) d^N q \geq 0 \tag{10.93}$$

where we have to observe the constraints

$$\int f d^N q = 1 \ , \tag{10.94}$$

$$\int \tilde{f} d^N q = 1 \ . \tag{10.95}$$

Because $f$ is a fixed quantity and (10.93) can be written in the form

$$K = \int f \ln f d^N q - \int f \ln \tilde{f} d^N q \ , \tag{10.96}$$

it will suffice to maximize the expression

$$\int f \ln \tilde{f} d^N q = \max! \tag{10.97}$$

To be specific, let us assume that $\tilde{f}$ has the form

$$\tilde{f} = \exp[-\tilde{\lambda} - \sum_j \tilde{\lambda}_j V_j(\boldsymbol{q})] \ , \tag{10.98}$$

where $V_j$ may contain polynomials in $\boldsymbol{q}$ up to an order to be fixed by us. The $\tilde{\lambda}_j$ are parameters which can be varied. The left-hand side of (10.97) (multiplied by $-1$) can be expressed in the form

$$W \equiv -\int f \ln \tilde{f} d^N q = \tilde{\lambda} + \int f \sum_j \tilde{\lambda}_j V_j(\boldsymbol{q}) \, d^N q \ . \tag{10.99}$$

We now assume that the $\tilde{\lambda}_j$ are subject to an evolutionary strategy, e.g. the network may change its connectivities. If this procedure reduces the value of the right-hand side of (10.99), the new value of $\tilde{\lambda}_j$ will be accepted, otherwise it will be rejected. A particularly elegant evolution strategy is that which employs gradients of some potential function. Let us therefore consider (10.99) as a potential function to be minimized. In it we express $\tilde{\lambda}$ by means of (cf. (10.75))

$$\tilde{\lambda} = \ln \int \exp [- \sum_j \tilde{\lambda}_j V_j(\boldsymbol{q})] d^N q \ . \tag{10.100}$$

The gradient strategy now consists of subjecting the Lagrange parameters $\tilde{\lambda}_j$ to the equation

$$\dot{\tilde{\lambda}}_j = -\gamma \frac{\partial W}{\partial \tilde{\lambda}_j} \ . \tag{10.101}$$

In order to evaluate the right-hand side of (10.101), we insert (10.100) into (10.99) and take the derivative

$$\frac{\partial W}{\partial \lambda_j} = -\{(\int \exp [- \sum_j \lambda_j V_j(\boldsymbol{q})] d^N q)^{-1} \int V_j(\boldsymbol{q}) \exp [- \sum_j \lambda_j V_j(\boldsymbol{q})] d^N q\}$$
$$+ \int f(\boldsymbol{q}) V_j(\boldsymbol{q}) d^N q \ . \tag{10.102}$$

Some simple reasoning shows that the expression in the curly bracket in (10.102) can be interpreted as the average value

$$\{\dots\} = \langle V_j(\boldsymbol{q}) \rangle_{\tilde{f}} \ , \tag{10.103}$$

whereas the second term in (10.102) is the average value

$$\langle V_j(\boldsymbol{q}) \rangle_f \ . \tag{10.104}$$

Thus equation (10.101) can now be written in the very concise form

$$\dot{\tilde{\lambda}}_j = \gamma (\langle V_j \rangle_{\tilde{f}} - \langle V_j \rangle_f) \tag{10.105}$$

where the first term in the bracket is the average of $V_j$ over the distribution function $\tilde{f}$, whereas the second term is the same function averaged over the distribution function prescribed from the outer world. Let us now investigate how to evaluate the right-hand side (10.105).

The determination of the average values of $V_j$ for the experimentally given distribution function $f$ is quite simple because the average values are just the corresponding measured moments. In practice one may proceed as follows: We assume that $f$ is the stationary distribution function of the incoming signals, $\boldsymbol{q}$. Let us further assume that these signals arrive at discrete times $\tau$ and that each incoming signal is described by the corresponding vector $\boldsymbol{q}_\tau$. When there are $L$ measurements, $\langle V_j \rangle_f$ can be replaced by

$$\langle V_j \rangle_f = \frac{1}{L} \sum_{\tau=1}^{L} V_j(\boldsymbol{q}_\tau) \ . \tag{10.106}$$

Of course, we may also have continuous registration over a time $T$, in which case we must make the replacement

$$\frac{1}{L}\sum_{\tau=1}^{L} V_j(q_\tau) \rightarrow \frac{1}{T}\int_0^T V_j[q(\tau)]\,d\tau \ . \tag{10.107}$$

The evaluation of $V_j$ averaged over $\tilde{f}$ is more complicated, however. In our experience the most convenient approach is to replace the average values by time averages in the form (10.106) or (10.107) but where the state vector $q(t)$ must be determined by means of the dynamics described by the Langevin equation (10.91) with the right-hand side given explicitly by (10.92) (see below). Here one must use the Lagrange parameters $\lambda_{ij}, \lambda_{ijmn}$ that were determined in the previous time step. In this way (10.105) defines an iterative procedure which we shall illustrate by an explicit example that follows (10.129).

To make contact with the standard computer model presented in this book we specialize $V_j(q)$ and $\lambda_j$ by setting

$$V_{j'}(q) = \begin{cases} q_i q_j & j' = (i,j) \\ q_i q_j q_m q_n & j' = (i,j,m,n) \end{cases} \tag{10.108}$$

where the index $j'$ must be replaced by the index combinations as indicated above. Similarly we put

$$\lambda_{j'} = \begin{cases} \lambda_{ij} \\ \lambda_{ijmn} \ . \end{cases} \tag{10.109}$$

We wish to evaluate (10.105) by means of a dynamics which yields the stationary distribution function

$$\tilde{f}(q) = N\exp\left[\frac{2}{Q}\Big(-\sum_{ij}\lambda_{ij}q_iq_j - \sum_{ijmn}\lambda_{ijmn}q_iq_jq_mq_n\Big)\right] \ . \tag{10.110}$$

(Note that the $\lambda$'s of this equation differ from those in (10.88) by the constant factor $2/Q$.) To proceed further we subject the random variable $q(t)$ to the now familiar Langevin equation

$$\dot{q}_i = -\gamma_1\Big(2\sum_j \lambda_{ij}q_iq_j - 4\sum_{jmn}\lambda_{ijmn}q_jq_mq_n\Big) + F_i(t) \tag{10.111}$$

where we have added a decay constant $\gamma_1$ that will allow us to use two different time scales, as will be necessary later on.

Our goal is to evaluate the averages of the products of $q$ in terms of time averages, i.e.,

$$\langle q_iq_j\rangle_{\tilde{f}} = \lim_{T\rightarrow\infty}\frac{1}{T}\int_0^T q_i(t)q_j(t)\,dt \tag{10.112}$$

$$\langle q_i q_j q_m q_n \rangle_{\bar{f}} = \lim_{T\to\infty} \frac{1}{T} \int_0^T q_i(t) q_j(t) q_m(t) q_n(t) dt \ , \tag{10.113}$$

a procedure that, in general, requires a very long time, $T$. But we can avoid this by using the following trick: We write

$$q_i(t) q_j(t) = \langle q_i(t) q_j(t) \rangle_{\bar{f}} + P_{ij}(t) \tag{10.114}$$

where $P_{ij}(t)$ is a fluctuating variable with

$$\langle P_{ij}(t) \rangle = 0 \tag{10.115}$$

and

$$\langle P_{ij}(t) P_{ij}(t) \rangle = \langle q_i q_j q_i q_j \rangle_{\bar{f}} - \langle q_i q_j \rangle_{\bar{f}}^2 \equiv Q_{ij} \ . \tag{10.116}$$

Similar relations hold for the fluctuating variables $P_{ijmn}$ belonging to the fourth-order moments $\langle q_i q_j q_m q_n \rangle$, where, in particular,

$$\langle P_{ijmn}(t) \rangle = 0 \ . \tag{10.117}$$

If the learning dynamics takes place on a time scale much larger than that of the dynamics of the Langevin equation (10.111), $P_{ij}(t)$ and $P_{ijmn}$ will be approximately equivalent to white noise, i.e.,

$$\langle P_{ij}(t) P_{ij}(t') \rangle = \tilde{Q}_{ij} \delta(t-t') \ , \tag{10.118}$$

with a corresponding equation describing $P_{ijmn}$.

Summing up, we describe the learning dynamics by

$$\dot{q}_i = \gamma_1 [-2 \sum_j \lambda_{ij} q_j - 4 \sum_{jmn} \lambda_{ijmn} q_j q_m q_n] + F_i(t) \tag{10.119}$$

$$\dot{\lambda}_{ij} = \gamma [q_i(t) q_j(t) - \langle q_i q_j \rangle_f] \tag{10.120}$$

$$\dot{\lambda}_{ijmn} = \gamma [q_i(t) q_j(t) q_m(t) q_n(t) - \langle q_i q_j q_m q_n \rangle_f] \ . \tag{10.121}$$

A comparison of (10.120, 121) with (10.105) [cf. (10.108, 109)] shows that because of (10.115, 117) the equations (10.105) may be considered as averaged equations without noise, whereas (10.120, 123) contain noise stemming form $P_{ij}$ and $P_{ijmn}$. For the whole procedure to be valid it is essential that $\gamma_1 \gg \gamma$.

Let us study how the impact of noise changes, when we make $\gamma$ smaller. To this end we write the Langevin equation

$$\dot{\lambda} = \gamma [\langle q_i q_j \rangle_{\bar{f}} - \langle q_i q_j \rangle_f] + P(t)\gamma \tag{10.122}$$

in its differential form by means of the theory of stochastic differential equations (cf. Haken, Advanced Synergetics, Chap. 4)

$$d\lambda = \gamma [\langle q_i q_j \rangle_{\bar{f}} - \langle q_i q_j \rangle_f] dt + P(t)\gamma \sqrt{dt} \ . \tag{10.123}$$

A rescaling of time,

$$t = \frac{t'}{\gamma} \ , \tag{10.124}$$

yields

$$d\lambda = [\langle q_i q_j \rangle_{\tilde{f}} - \langle q_i q_j \rangle_f]\, dt' + P'(t)\sqrt{dt'} \ , \tag{10.125}$$

where we put

$$P'(t) = \sqrt{\gamma} P(t) \ . \tag{10.126}$$

Thus with decreasing time constant $\gamma$, the noise $P'(t)$ decreases, but the time of learning increases correspondingly. To simulate the system of stochastic differential equations numerically, we write the equations (10.119 – 121) in differential form:

$$dq_i = \gamma_1 [\ldots]\, dt + \sqrt{Q \gamma_1 dt} F_i(t) \ , \tag{10.127}$$

$$d\lambda_{ij} = \gamma [\ldots]\, dt \tag{10.128}$$

$$d\lambda_{ijmn} = \gamma [\ldots]\, dt \ . \tag{10.129}$$

The $F_i$'s that appear here are Gaussian distributed fluctuating forces. To illustrate the whole procedure, let us consider a case where the feature space is two-dimensional. We assume a "true" distribution function, $f(\boldsymbol{q})$, which is a superposition of 4 Gaussians located at the positions of the patterns to be learnt. Hereby we assume, as everywhere in this book, that the distribution functions have inversion symmetry, i.e. $f(-\boldsymbol{q}) = f(\boldsymbol{q})$. The function $f(\boldsymbol{q})$ is shown in Fig. 10.11 a. Its form allows us to calculate the moments of $\boldsymbol{q}$ with respect to $f(\boldsymbol{q})$ explicitly. We then integrate equations (10.127 – 129) by means of the Euler forward procedure. The initial conditions are chosen as

$$\boldsymbol{q}(t=0) = 0 \ , \quad \lambda_{ij} = \lambda_{ijmn} = 0 \ . \tag{10.130}$$

The resulting time-dependent $\lambda_{ij}$, $\lambda_{ijmn}$ are inserted into $\tilde{f}$ which is plotted for several times in Figs. 10.11 b, c, d. The important parameters and final values of the $\lambda$'s are summarized in Table 10.1. Figure 10.11 e shows the potential of the Langevin equation. Figure 10.12 a, b shows the results for a more complicated distribution $f$ and $\tilde{f}$, respectively. The learning procedure can also be applied to higher dimensions, but it must be observed that practical limitations soon enter because the number $Z$ of $\lambda$' increases with $N^4$. For instance, for the faces treated in this book, $N = 3600$, so that $Z \approx 10^{13}$, if we use the symmetry of the $\lambda$'s.

One thus requires more efficient learning algorithms. In the next section we shall present an algorithm for which $Z \propto N$.

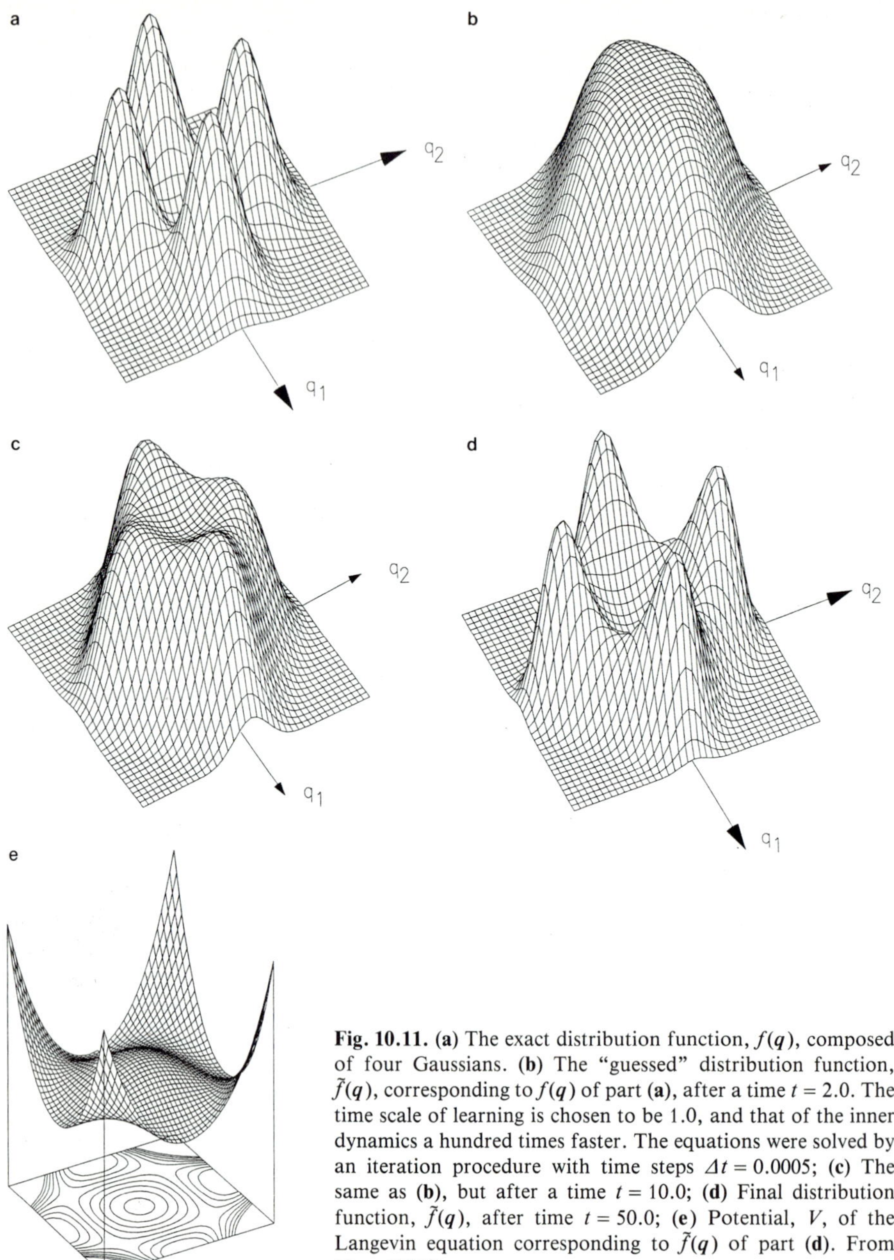


**Fig. 10.11.** (**a**) The exact distribution function, $f(\boldsymbol{q})$, composed of four Gaussians. (**b**) The "guessed" distribution function, $\tilde{f}(\boldsymbol{q})$, corresponding to $f(\boldsymbol{q})$ of part (**a**), after a time $t = 2.0$. The time scale of learning is chosen to be 1.0, and that of the inner dynamics a hundred times faster. The equations were solved by an iteration procedure with time steps $\Delta t = 0.0005$; (**c**) The same as (**b**), but after a time $t = 10.0$; (**d**) Final distribution function, $\tilde{f}(\boldsymbol{q})$, after time $t = 50.0$; (**e**) Potential, $V$, of the Langevin equation corresponding to $\tilde{f}(\boldsymbol{q})$ of part (**d**). From Haas (1989)

Before we proceed to that section, let us briefly comment on the relation between our procedure and Hebb's learning rule which plays an important role in neurology and neurocomputers. According to Hebb's ideas, the synaptic strength between two neurones is enhanced when they are frequently *jointly*

**Table 10.1.** Important parameters and final values of the $\lambda$'s belonging to the model described by (10.127–130)

| | |
|---|---|
| Time constant for internal dynamics | $\gamma_1 = 100$ |
| Time constant for learning dynamics | $\gamma = 1.0$ |
| Time step | $\Delta t = 0.0005$ |
| Time of learning | $t = 50.0$ |
| Strength of fluctuations | $Q = 1.0$ |
| Ranges of coordinates represented | $-2.0 \ldots +2.0$ |

Final values after learning

| Indices | $\lambda$ | $\langle q_i q_j \rangle_{\tilde{f}}$ | $\langle q_i q_j \rangle_f$ |
|---|---|---|---|
| $i,j;\, m,n$ | | | |
| (1, 1) | −1.002 | 0.6121 | 0.625 |
| (1, 2) | −0.001 | −0.0001 | 0.0 |
| (2, 2) | −1.000 | 0.6126 | 0.625 |
| (1, 1, 1, 1) | 0.409 | 0.9203 | 0.9219 |
| (1, 1, 1, 2) | 0.000 | 0.0001 | 0.0 |
| (1, 1, 2, 2) | 2.11 | 0.1943 | 0.1406 |
| (1, 2, 2, 2) | 0.004 | −0.0030 | 0.0 |
| (2, 2, 2, 2) | 0.406 | 0.9132 | 0.9219 |

Here we have used the symmetry of $\lambda_{ij}$ and $\lambda_{ijmn}$ to calculate $V$:

$$V = \sum_{i \le j}^{N} \lambda_{ij} q_i q_j + \sum_{i \le j \le m \le n}^{N} \lambda_{ijmn} q_i q_j q_m q_n$$

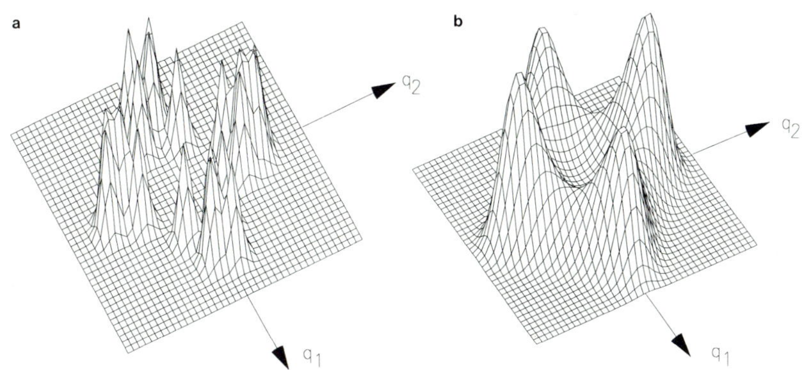


**Fig. 10.12.** **(a)** A more complicated "true" distribution function $f(q)$. **(b)** Final "guessed" distribution function, $\tilde{f}(q)$, corresponding to $f(q)$ in part **(a)**. Note the smoothing effect. From Haas (1989)

active. In our approach the activity of neurones $i$ and $j$ is represented by $q_i$ and $q_j$, respectively, and their joint activity by $q_i q_j$.

According to (10.120), the synaptic strength $\lambda_{ij}$ between neurones $i$ and $j$ changes in time depending on the difference between the actual joint activity

$q_i q_j$ due to the synaptic strengths the net has already formed, and the desired joint activity of this pair. This desired activity is the average of $q_i q_j$ when the neural net mimics the distribution of the input patterns, so that $\langle q_i q_j \rangle_f$ results. Thus (10.120) is a mathematical sharpening of Hebb's rule. Equation (10.121) may be considered as a generalization of this rule to a quartet of neurones.

## 10.6 A Learning Algorithm Based on a Gradient Dynamics

In this section we introduce a Lyapunov function which will allow us, by means of a gradient dynamics, to calculate the vectors $\boldsymbol{v}_k^+$ determining the synaptic strengths. Our approach is applicable to noiseless patterns as well as to sets of noisy patterns defined by their second and fourth order moments.

Here, as practically everywhere in this book, we shall assume that for each acceptable pattern, its negative is also acceptable. Thus the odd-order moments, and in particular the first- and third-order, vanish:

$$\langle v \rangle = 0 \tag{10.131}$$

and

$$\langle v_i v_j v_k \rangle = 0 \ . \tag{10.132}$$

We shall use the adjoint vectors $\boldsymbol{v}_k^+$ which have the property

$$(\boldsymbol{v}_k^+ \boldsymbol{v}_{k'}) = \delta_{kk'} \ , \tag{10.133}$$

and we assume that the adjoint vectors are represented as superpositions of the transposed vectors $\boldsymbol{v}_k$

$$\boldsymbol{v}_k^+ = \sum_{k'} g_{kk'} \bar{\boldsymbol{v}}_k \ . \tag{10.134}$$

In Chap. 5 a dynamics was constructed according to which an initially given test pattern vector $\boldsymbol{q}(0)$ is eventually pulled into the prototype vector $\boldsymbol{v}_k$ to which it was originally nearest

$$\boldsymbol{q}(0) \to \boldsymbol{q}(t) \to \boldsymbol{v}_k \ . \tag{10.135}$$

The dynamics is described by an equation of the form [cf. (5.22)]

$$\dot{\boldsymbol{q}} = -\frac{\partial V}{\partial \boldsymbol{q}^+} \tag{10.136}$$

where $V$ is a potential function defined by

$$V = -\tfrac{1}{2}\sum_{k} \lambda_k (v_k^+ q)^2 + \tfrac{1}{4}B \sum_{k \neq k'} (v_k^+ q)^2 (v_{k'}^+ q)^2$$
$$+ \tfrac{1}{4}C \sum_{kk'} (v_{k'}^+ q)^2 (v_k^+ q)^2 \ . \tag{10.137}$$

We further remind the reader that we have defined the adjoint vector $q^+$ by means of the relations

$$q = \sum_k \xi_k v_k + w \tag{10.138}$$

and

$$q^+ = \sum_k \xi_k v_k^+ + w^+ \ . \tag{10.139}$$

The equations resulting from (10.136, 137) with (10.138, 139) can be written quite generally in the form

$$\dot{q}_i = \sum_j \lambda_{ij} q_j + \sum_{jlm} \lambda_{ijlm} q_j q_l q_m \ . \tag{10.140}$$

As was shown in Sect. 10.1, the coefficients $\lambda_{ij}$, $\lambda_{ijlm}$ can be interpreted as synaptic strengths in a neural net where for instance $\lambda_{ij}$ is given by

$$\lambda_{ij} = \sum_k \lambda_k v_{ki} v_{kj}^+ \tag{10.141}$$

and a similar expression holds for $\lambda_{ijlm}$ [cf. (10.2)]. When our algorithm is realized on a three-layer network, the synaptic strength between cell $i$ of the input layer and cell $k$ of the middle layer is directly given by the vector component $v_{ki}^+$, while the synaptic strength between cell $k$ of the middle layer and cell $l$ of the output layer is given by the vector component $v_{kl}$.

### 10.6.1 Construction of the Lyapunov Function

We now wish to construct a Lyapunov function from which the $v_k$ and $v_k^+$ can be determined by a straightforward minimization procedure. As a first step we introduce a number of patterns to be learned

$$q_j \ , \quad j = 1, \dots, M. \tag{10.142}$$

We also introduce the vectors $v_k$ for $k = 1, \dots, K$

$$v_k \ , \quad k = 1, \dots, K \tag{10.143}$$

where we shall decide later whether $K = M$ or $K < M$. In what follows we consider (10.137) as a function of the vectors $v_k^+$

$$V = V(v_k^+, q_j) \ , \tag{10.144}$$

from which we construct the potential function $V_1$

$$V_1 = \sum_j V(\boldsymbol{v}_k^+, \boldsymbol{q}_j) , \tag{10.145}$$

where the sum runs over all the patterns $\boldsymbol{q}_j$ offered to the system and to be learned by it. If the patterns are noisy, a suitable average has to be taken over the distribution function $f(\boldsymbol{q})$ of these patterns. Denoting the corresponding average by $\langle \ldots \rangle$, we define

$$V_1 = \langle V(\boldsymbol{v}_k^+, \boldsymbol{q}) \rangle . \tag{10.146}$$

We now want to show that $V_1$ is a Lyapunov function with respect to $\boldsymbol{v}_k^+$, at least in the case where the $\boldsymbol{q}_j$'s are noiseless and linearly independent. For the case of noisy patterns, $V_1$ will be used to find optimal vectors $\boldsymbol{v}_k^+$. We shall assume that $\boldsymbol{v}_k$ and $\boldsymbol{v}_k^+$ lie in the $\boldsymbol{q}_j$-space. We wish to determine the set of $\boldsymbol{v}_k^+$ by minimizing
$V_1$.

$$V_1 = \text{min!} \tag{10.147}$$

Let $\boldsymbol{v}_k^+$ be given at an initial time $t_\mathrm{i}$

$$\boldsymbol{v}_k^+(t_\mathrm{i}) . \tag{10.148}$$

We then wish to show that there is a dynamics according to which $\boldsymbol{v}_k^+$ is pulled at a final time $t_\mathrm{f}$ into $\boldsymbol{v}_k^+(t_\mathrm{f})$

$$\boldsymbol{v}_k^+(t_\mathrm{f}) \equiv \boldsymbol{v}_k^+ \tag{10.149}$$

which minimizes (10.147) and belongs to the set of test patterns $\boldsymbol{q}_j$. To demonstrate this, we assume, according to the formalism of the synergetic computer, that the set $\boldsymbol{v}_k^+$ had been fixed so that $V$ (10.137) is minimal for all $\boldsymbol{q}_j$. This presupposes that the prototype pattern vectors $\boldsymbol{v}_k$ and the test pattern vectors $\boldsymbol{q}_j$ in the final state are linearly independent.

Note that $V_1$ (10.145) depends only on the scalar products

$$(\boldsymbol{v}_k^+(t) \boldsymbol{q}_j) . \tag{10.150}$$

We now employ the fact that scalar products are invariant under a change of the basis of the vector space, provided the new basis vectors are linearly independent. Thus instead of using the basis of the time-independent vectors $\boldsymbol{q}_j$, we choose a new time-independent basis $\boldsymbol{v}_k^+$. In this basis, the $\boldsymbol{q}_j$-vectors become time-dependent:

$$\boldsymbol{q}_j \rightarrow \boldsymbol{q}_j(t) . \tag{10.151}$$

Thus the time-dependence of the *set* of $\boldsymbol{v}_k$-vectors is shifted to time-dependence of the *set* of $\boldsymbol{q}_j$-vectors. Let us now study the behavior of an individual term $V[\boldsymbol{v}_k, \boldsymbol{q}_j(t)]$ in (10.145). Such a term contains the set of all *fixed* vectors $\boldsymbol{v}_k$ and a specific vector $q_j(t)$. As we know from Chap. 5, there is a gradient dynamics which pulls $q_j(t)$ into an attractor state whereby $V[v_k, q_j(t)]$ decreases continuously, provided no saddle point is reached. (This special case of a saddle point will be discussed below.) Because $V$ does not contain any spurious minima, it does indeed acquire its lowest value. Thus $V[v_k, q_j(t)]$ is a Lyapunov function. Because $V_1$ (10.145) is a sum over such functions where each $q_j(t)$ undergoes its own dynamics, $V_1$ itself is a Lyapunov function for the full *set* $q_j(t)$. In the final step of our proof we recall that the dynamics of $v_k^+$ induces one of the $q_j$ *and vice versa*. Thus when $V$ is a Lyapunov function with respect to the set $q_j$, it is simultaneously a Lyapunov function with respect to the set $v_k$.

We now discuss the exceptional ("nongeneric") case in which $q_j$ approaches a saddle point. According to Sect. 5.3, this occurs if there is an initial degeneracy

$$|(v_k^+ q_j)| = |(v_{k'}^+ q_j)| \tag{10.152}$$

for a specific index $j$ and $k \neq k'$. According to Sect. 5.3, no saddle point is reached if there is some $k$ such that

$$|(v_k^+ q_j)| > |(v_{k'}^+ q_j)| \tag{10.153}$$

for $j$ fixed and all other $k' \neq k$. In this case $q_j(t)$ approaches this specific $v_k$ so that $(v_k^+ q_j) \to 1$ for $t \to \infty$.

While $V_1$ is a decreasing function of the $q_j$'s, and thus of the $v_k^+(t)$'s via (10.145), this alone does not guarantee that the $q_j(t)$'s $j = 1, \ldots, N$ approach the *full* set of the $q_j$'s$\equiv v_k$ in (10.145) since two initially different $q_j(t_i)$'s may converge to the same $q_j(t_f)$ if they started in the same basin of attraction. To resolve this problem, we again refer to Sect. 5.3. According to that section, different basins of attraction are reached, if, for each $j$, the relation (10.153) is fulfilled for a specific $k$ that we denote by $k_j$ and that is different from all other $k$'s. By a relabeling of the $k$'s, putting $k_j = j$, we can formulate a necessary and sufficient condition for $V_1$ to be a Lyapunov function for the $q_j(t)$'s and thus for the $v_k^+(t)$'s. This inequality condition reads

$$|(v_j^+ q_j)| > |(v_{k'}^+ q_j)| \quad \text{for all } k' \neq j \quad \text{and all } j = 1, \ldots, M \ ,$$

and

$$|(v_j^+ q_j)| \neq |(v_{j'}^+ q_{j'})| \ , \quad \text{for all pairs } j \neq j' \ . \tag{10.154}$$

In this case, the set $v_k^+(t_\mathrm{i})$ converges to the full set $v_k^+(t_\mathrm{f})$. The inequality condition can be met in a variety of ways. For instance, for a given set of $q_j$, the initial values of the $v_k^+$'s can be constructed consecutively so that the inequality condition is met. An elegant solution consists in making a random choice of the $v_k^+(t_\mathrm{i})$'s. This guarantees their linear independence and the fulfillment of the inequality condition with an overwhelming probability.

### 10.6.2 Projection onto the $q_j$-Space

In the above argument we have used the constraints that $v_k$ and $v_k^+$ lie in the space spanned by $q_k$. For computational reasons it is more advantageous to introduce a potential function $V_2$ which is minimal if this requirement is met. In order to construct such a potential function we argue as follows: The fact that $\boldsymbol{v}^+$ and $\boldsymbol{v}$ are in the same space spanned by $\boldsymbol{q}_j$ can be expressed by the relation (5.11), which, when written in components, reads

$$v_{kj}^{+} = \sum_{k'} a_{kk'} v_{k'j} \ . \tag{10.155}$$

Now let us consider the projection operator $P$ which has matrix elements given by

$$P_{ij} = \sum_{k} v_{ki} v_{kj}^{+} \ . \tag{10.156}$$

Because of (10.155), expression (10.156) can be cast in the form

$$P_{ij} = \sum_{kk'} v_{ki} a_{kk'} v_{k'j} \ . \tag{10.157}$$

We use the symmetry of the coefficients $a$, i.e.

$$a_{kk'} = a_{k'k} \tag{10.158}$$

and exchange the summation variables $k$ and $k'$ in (10.157). We may thus rearrange (10.157) in the form

$$P_{ij} = \sum_{k} \Big(\sum_{k'} a_{kk'} v_{k'i}\Big) v_{kj} \ , \tag{10.159}$$

which, because of (10.155), can finally be written

$$P_{ij} = \sum_{k} v_{kj}^{+} v_{ki} \ . \tag{10.160}$$

We now define the projection operator $P_1$ by

$$P_1 = \sum_{k} \boldsymbol{v}_k^{+}(t) \cdot \boldsymbol{v}_k(t) \tag{10.161}$$

and a second projection operator $P_2$ by

$$P_2 = \sum_{k} \bar{\boldsymbol{v}}_k(t) \cdot \bar{\boldsymbol{v}}_k^{+}(t) \ . \tag{10.162}$$

We allow the vectors $\boldsymbol{v}_k^{+}$ in (10.161, 162) to be time-dependent because they then are subjected to a dynamics. $\bar{\boldsymbol{v}}_k$ and $\boldsymbol{v}_k^{+}$ are the transposed vectors of $\boldsymbol{v}_k$ and $\boldsymbol{v}_k^{+}$, respectively. We introduce the potential function $V_2$ by

$$V_2 = \frac{\gamma_1}{2} \left[ |(1-P_1)\boldsymbol{q}|^2 + |(1-P_2)\boldsymbol{q}|^2 \right] \ . \tag{10.163}$$

The quantity $\gamma_1$ is a decay constant which will be chosen appropriately later. In order to derive a dynamics for $\boldsymbol{v}_k$ and $\boldsymbol{v}_k^+$ we still have to average $V_2$ over the distribution function of the patterns $\boldsymbol{q}$. If a specific set of patterns must be learnt, we may make the replacement

$$\langle V_2 \rangle = \frac{\gamma_1}{2} \sum_j \mu_j [|(1-P_1)\boldsymbol{q}_j|^2 + |(1-P_2)\boldsymbol{q}_j|^2] \tag{10.164}$$

where $\mu_j$ are weight factors which represent the relative frequencies of the offered patterns $q_j$. As a lengthy but elementary algebraic calculation shows, the minimum of (10.163), $V_2 = 0$, is acquired for all $\boldsymbol{q}_j$ if the relations (10.133, 155) are fulfilled and, in particular, if $\boldsymbol{v}_k^+$ and $\boldsymbol{v}_k$ are vectors of the space spanned by $\boldsymbol{q}_j$. We are now in a position to formulate the dynamics which fixes the set of $\boldsymbol{v}_{k'}, \boldsymbol{v}_k^+$.

We require that

$$V_{\text{tot}} = V_1 + V_2 = \min! \tag{10.165}$$

and apply the gradient dynamics with respect to the variables

$$v_{ki} \quad \text{and} \quad v_{ki}^+ \; . \tag{10.166}$$

We arrive at this dynamics by forming

$$\dot{v}_{ki}^+ = -\frac{\partial V_{\text{tot}}}{\partial v_{ki}^+} \tag{10.167}$$

and

$$\dot{v}_{ki} = -\frac{\partial V_{\text{tot}}}{\partial v_{ki}} \; . \tag{10.168}$$

In order to simplify these equations somewhat, we have dropped the argument $t$ everywhere, i.e. $\boldsymbol{v}_k$ and $\boldsymbol{v}_k^+$ are to be understood as time-dependent functions

$$\boldsymbol{v}_k = \boldsymbol{v}_k(t) \tag{10.169}$$

and

$$\boldsymbol{v}_k^+ = \boldsymbol{v}_k^+(t) \; . \tag{10.170}$$

Equations (10.167, 168) read explicitly

$$\begin{aligned} \dot{\boldsymbol{v}}_k^+ = \; & \lambda \langle (\boldsymbol{v}_k^+ \boldsymbol{q})\boldsymbol{q}\rangle - B \sum_{k \neq k'} \langle (\boldsymbol{v}_k^+ \boldsymbol{q})(\boldsymbol{v}_{k'}^+ \boldsymbol{q})^2 \boldsymbol{q}\rangle \\ & - C \sum_{kk'} \langle (\boldsymbol{v}_k^+ \boldsymbol{q})(\boldsymbol{v}_{k'}^+ \boldsymbol{q})^2 \boldsymbol{q}\rangle \\ & + \gamma_1 [2\langle (\boldsymbol{v}_k \boldsymbol{q})\boldsymbol{q}\rangle - \sum_{k'} (\bar{\boldsymbol{v}}_k \boldsymbol{v}_{k'}) \langle (\boldsymbol{v}_{k'}^+ \boldsymbol{q})\boldsymbol{q}\rangle \\ & - \sum_{k'} \langle (\bar{\boldsymbol{v}}_k \boldsymbol{q})(\bar{\boldsymbol{v}}_{k'} \boldsymbol{q})\rangle \boldsymbol{v}_{k'}^+ ] \end{aligned} \tag{10.171}$$

and

$$\dot{v}_k = \gamma_1 [2\langle(v_k^+ q)q\rangle - \sum_{k'} \langle(v_{k'}^+ q)(v_k^+ q)v_{k'}\rangle - \sum_{k'} (v_k^+ \bar{v}_{k'}^+)\langle(\bar{v}_{k'} q)q\rangle] \ . \tag{10.172}$$

The calculations can now be performed in various ways; for instance, we may first form the averages or we may offer the patterns to be learned subsequently in a random fashion. The actual computation can be performed most simply by using the trick introduced in Sect. 10.5, namely by replacing the averages by time-dependent functions

$$\langle q_i q_j\rangle \equiv \langle q_i q_f\rangle_f \rightarrow q_i(t) q_j(t) \tag{10.173}$$

where $q_i(t)$ denotes patterns which are offered time and again to the equations (10.171) and (10.172) which were solved during the time in which these patterns are offered. In other words, (10.173) and similar terms act as some kind of a random force. This is particularly convenient if the $\boldsymbol{q}_j$ that is repeatedly offered is a noisy pattern. On the other hand, from the purely theoretical point of view, our approach is equivalent to one in which the sums over $j$ are replaced by the average values

$$\sum_j q_{ji} q_{jl} \rightarrow \langle q_i q_l\rangle \tag{10.174}$$

and correspondingly

$$\langle q_i q_j q_l q_m\rangle \ . \tag{10.175}$$

In this way we may claim that our algorithm allows us to recover the prototype vectors $\boldsymbol{v}_k$ and their adjoints, provided the second- and fourth-order moments of the patterns are given.

Figure 10.13a–c shows how the system learns three patterns offered to it. The pattern vectors $\boldsymbol{v}_k$ and their adjoints $\boldsymbol{v}_k^+$ are represented here as two-dimensional arrays, enabling us to simultaneously visualize the working of the algorithm. As is seen here, the whole formalism works very well with vectors having $60 \times 60$ pixels. This is clearly no longer a toy problem. The whole procedure can be applied to far more than three patterns of this size. Let us study how the computer can learn prototype patterns from a series of noisy patterns. We shall use the same basic set as in Fig. 10.13a, onto which Gaussian noise is now superimposed. Figure 10.14a shows a section of a time series of patterns offered to the computer during the learning procedure. Figures 10.14b, c show the time-evolution of $\boldsymbol{v}_k$ and $\boldsymbol{v}_{k'}^+$, respectively. The robustness of our procedure is demonstrated still more clearly when a time-series of faces is offered, each being partially hidden by a square whose position is chosen randomly. Figure 10.15a shows a part of the time-series of patterns offered and Fig. 10.15b the learning of the prototype patterns $\boldsymbol{v}_k$. Quite clearly, our approach can be applied not only to the *learning* of patterns but also to their *reconstruction* in the presence of noise.

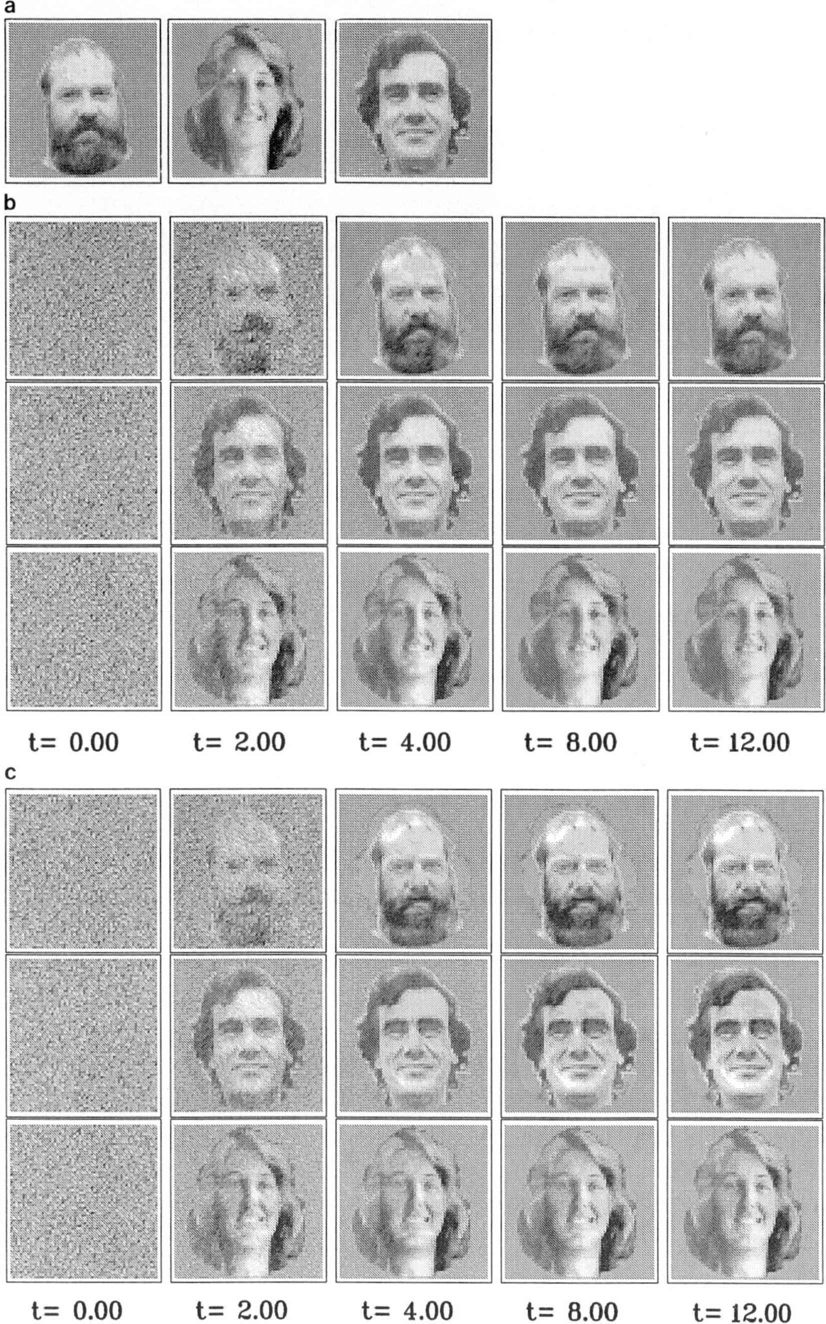


**Fig. 10.13.** (**a**) Three patterns to be learnt simultaneously. (**b**) Temporal evolution of the vectors, $\boldsymbol{v}_k$. The initial state was chosen randomly. (**c**) Temporal evolution of the adjoint vectors, $\boldsymbol{v}_k^+$. The initial state was chosen as $\boldsymbol{v}_k^+ = \boldsymbol{v}_k^{\mathrm{T}}$. From Haken et al. (1989)

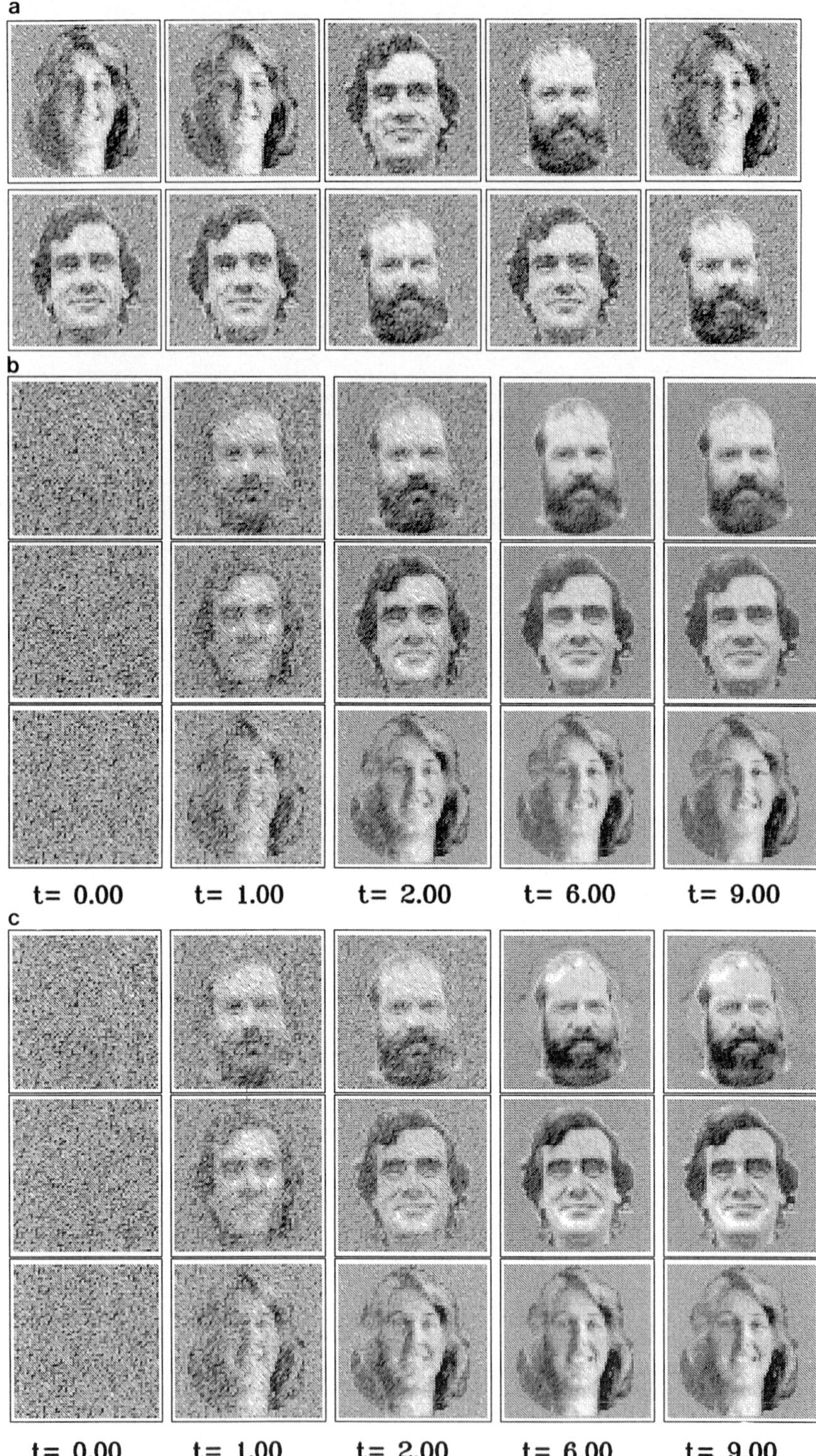


**Fig. 10.14.** Caption see opposite page

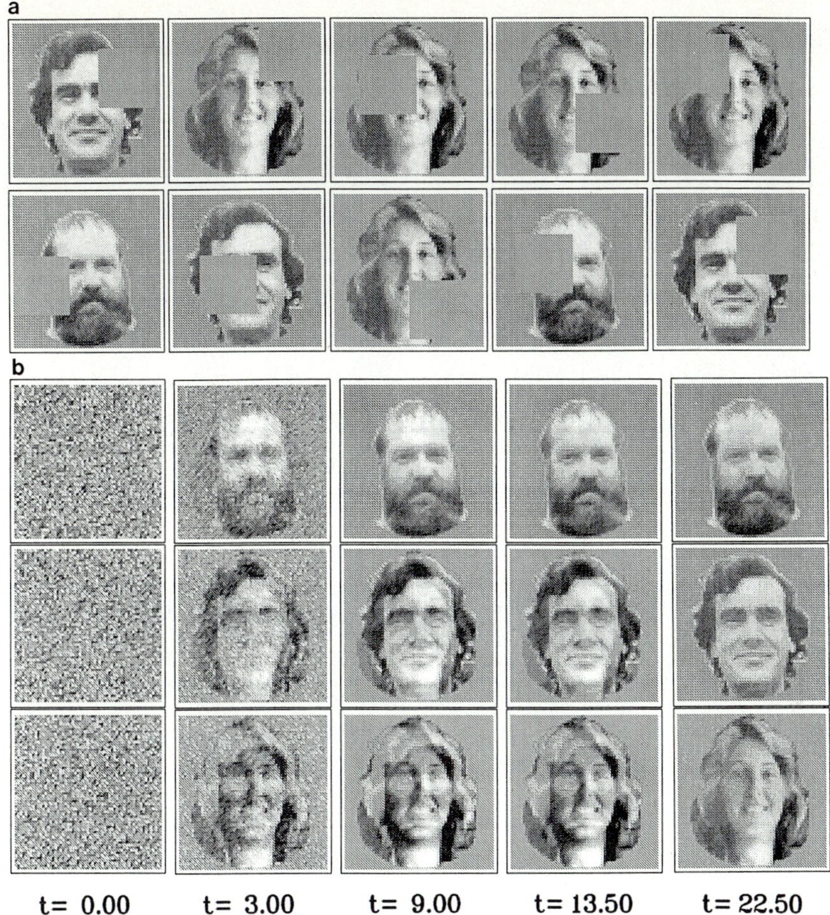


**Fig. 10.15.** (**a**) Section of a time series of randomly offered patterns, where the original faces of Fig. 10.13a were partially hidden by squares of equal size but with random positions. (**b**) Temporal evolution of the $v_k$ corresponding to the pattern sequence of part (**a**). Note that the time scales differ by a factor of 50. From Haas (1989)

As just mentioned, the algorithm allowed us to determine the prototype vectors simultaneously. The formalism can also be applied to sequential learning. Here for instance first a series comprising a single noisy pattern is given and only one $\boldsymbol{v}$ is used. Then in the next step we may offer the computer the same $\boldsymbol{v}$ again and a new set of noisy patterns which are assumed to belong to a new class such that an additional vector $\boldsymbol{v}_2$ is determined. In this way we may proceed stepwise.

◀

**Fig. 10.14.** (**a**) Section of a time series of randomly offered patterns, where Gaussian noise was superimposed on the original faces of Fig. 10.13a. (**b**) Temporal evolution of the $\boldsymbol{v}_k$ corresponding to the pattern sequence of part (**a**). Note that the time scales differ by a factor of 100. The initial state was chosen randomly. (**c**) As in (**b**), but for $\boldsymbol{v}_k^+$. The initial state was chosen as $\boldsymbol{v}_k^+ = \boldsymbol{v}_k^{\mathrm{T}}$. From Haas (1989)

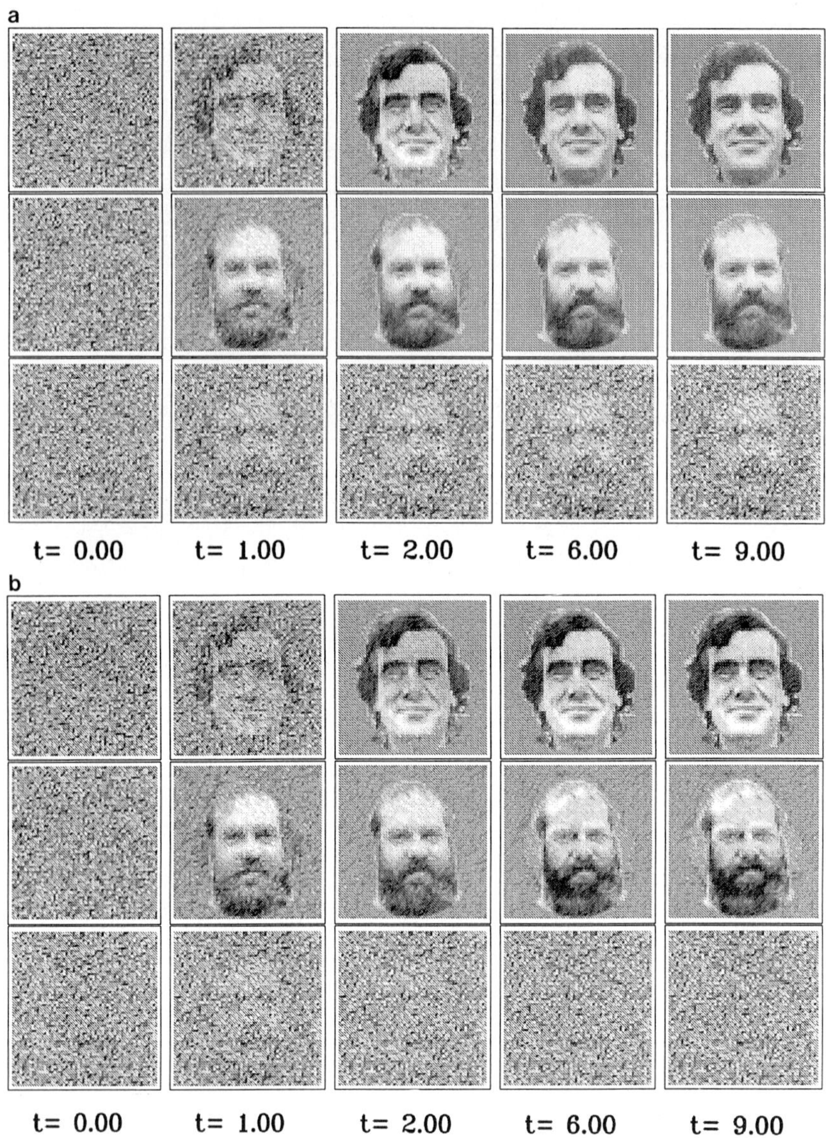


**Fig. 10.16.** **(a)** Temporal evolution of $v_1, v_2, v_3$ when only two of the patterns of Fig. 10.13a are offered. **(b)** As in part **(a)** but for $v_1^+, v_2^+, v_3^+$. From Haas (1989)

Our approach can be generalized in various ways, e.g. we may require a minimum angle between the prototype vectors or we could prescribe a limited number of $v$'s in order to perform a classification.

To study classification, let us consider a few examples. We first treat the case in which *two* patterns (the two male faces of Fig. 10.13a) are to be learnt, but *three* $v_k$'s admitted. The results for $v_k$ and $v_k^+$ are shown in Fig. 10.16a, respec-

**Fig. 10.17.** (**a**) Four faces offered to the computer for classification. (**b**) If only one $v$ is permitted, a single prototype is formed whose temporal evolution is shown here. From Haas (1989)

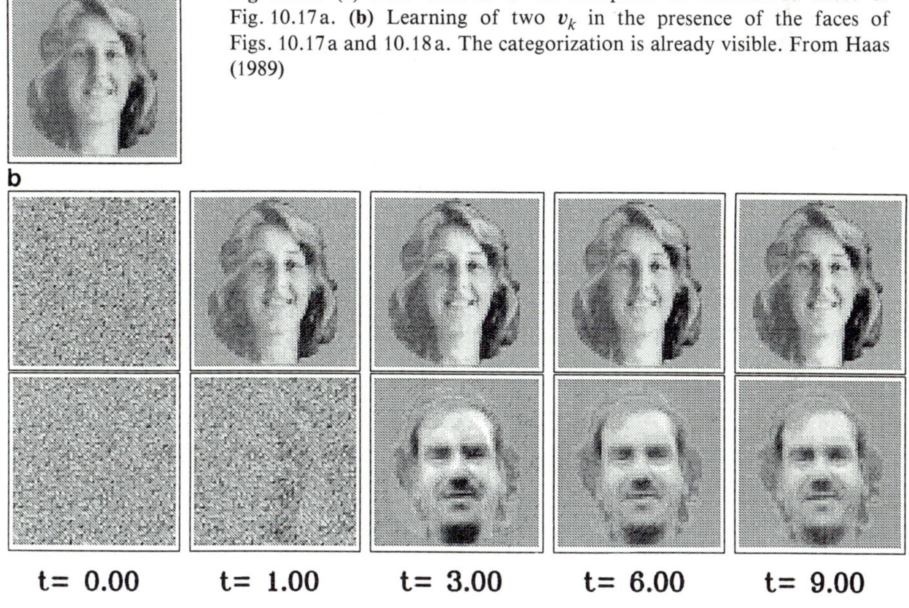


**Fig. 10.18.** (**a**) Face offered to the computer in addition to those of Fig. 10.17a. (**b**) Learning of two $v_k$ in the presence of the faces of Figs. 10.17a and 10.18a. The categorization is already visible. From Haas (1989)

tively. The next examples refer to the process of classification itself. The patterns to be classified are shown in Fig. 10.17a. But now, only a single $v$ is admitted. Figure 10.17b shows the time evolution of $v_k$. Then the female face of Fig. 10.13a was offered in addition to the faces of Fig. 10.17a, and now *two* prototype patterns were allowed. The result of the learning procedure is shown in

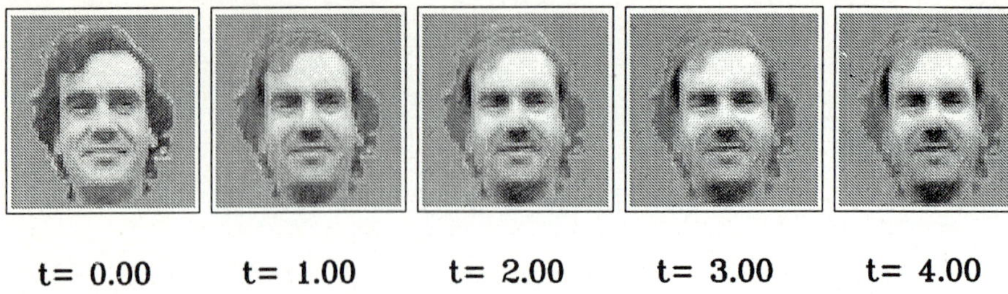


**Fig. 10.19.** A test of the effect of categorization. A face out of those of Fig. 10.17a is put into the category established in Fig. 10.17b. From Haas (1989)

**Fig. 10.20.** The two categories corresponding to Figs. 10.17a and 10.18a. From Haas (1989)

Fig. 10.18b. We then tested how the system recognizes a face out of Figs. 10.17a, 18a in the sense of classification with respect to the prototype patterns of Fig. 10.18b. The results are presented in Fig. 10.19. We thus find two classes of sequential learning. Class 1 is represented by the upper part of Fig. 10.20, class 2 by its lower part.

A warning should be added. Our results might suggest that the algorithm leads to a straightforward classification of male and female faces. In this way our specific results may be fortuitous and more criteria for distinction may be needed. After all, discrimination and classification are done by means of certain scalar products only. On the other hand, we expect that it is possible to steer the categorization, at least to some extent, by sequential learning. Here, for instance, female faces are offered first and only one prototype vector is allowed; then the whole set of male and female faces is offered and two prototype vectors are admitted whose initial states $\boldsymbol{v}_k, \boldsymbol{v}_k^+$ are taken as follows: $\boldsymbol{v}_1, \boldsymbol{v}_1^+$ are chosen as the vectors determined in the first run, whereas $\boldsymbol{v}_2, \boldsymbol{v}_2^+$ are chosen randomly.

## 10.7 Summary

Because of the length of this chapter, it is useful to summarize what we have ourselves learnt about the learning process. In Sect. 10.2 we assumed that the system has already learnt a number of patterns which were then encoded in the synaptic strengths $v_{kl}^{+}$ which connect the cell $l$ of the input layer with the cell $k$ of the order parameter layer in the sense of Fig. 7.2. A new pattern labeled by $n+1$ was then offered to the system. The algorithm presented in Sect. 10.2 tells us how the synaptic strengths which were already present need to be changed, and what new synaptic strengths must be established to the new order parameter cell $n+1$. We then demonstrated how the network can make these changes using channels which are already present, or which are to be newly established between the input layer and the new cell $n+1$ of the order parameter layer. In this approach no approximation was used. Thus in summary we may say that this approach is rigorous but clumsy.

In Sect. 10.4 and particularly Sect. 10.5 we dealt with the learning of patterns which may be noisy and which obey some distribution function that is unknown to the network. We showed (Sect. 10.4) how the network may make unbiased guesses about the distribution function which then lead to a wiring of the network, i.e. to a definition of its synaptic strengths. As we saw, the patterns to be learnt are characterized by the maxima of their frequency of occurrence. The network learns to reproduce the most probable patterns it had previously been offered. By means of its wiring it can reconstruct these patterns once a set of initial data is given that uniquely determines the basin of attraction to which a specific test pattern belongs. Quite obviously there is no semantics whatsoever. Thus the whole procedure is quite in accordance with traditional information theory where any meaning is exorcised.

Here we clearly see a drawback of the procedure, which is present not only in our synergetic computer, but also in any other neural computer. Namely, whilst learning, the network does not make contact with any other stored data so that there can be no associations with already known facts. In other words, the network does evaluate the patterns on criteria no other than their frequency of the occurrence. The network does not ask whether the patterns to be learnt are of any use to itself or to the system of which the network is a part. Or, in still another interpretation, the computer does not understand what it is learning. In particular, the network cannot handle unexpected (improbable) new data which would be classified as important by humans or animals. Indeed, in the course of evolution certain patterns have turned out to be important for survival, and humans and animals have learnt how to evaluate them. It is evident that humans and animals have developed a variety of strategies which include making "large scale estimates" of situations and generalizing. With respect to computers, we can still hope to build in semantics in some sense or another if adequate linkages to other relevant stored facts can be made by the computer.

Since some of the patterns may be offered to the computer with a broad distribution function because of noise, the corresponding basins of attraction may be shallower than those of other patterns with sharper distributions. Therefore, in Chap. 5 we devised a synergetic computer in which all the valleys are of equal depth so that the prototype patterns are all sharply defined. In order to allow for a process in which the valleys can be defined by $\boldsymbol{v}_k$ and $\boldsymbol{v}_k^+$ and therefore sharply with equal depth, we devised the gradient dynamics of Sect. 10.6. In contrast to other approaches used in neural computers, the patterns offered need not be orthogonal to each other, and the system can learn non-orthogonal patterns precisely. This is important when patterns, which are classified as being different, differ only in one or a few features. The approach of Sect. 10.6 is capable of performing classification.

In conclusion we may state that learning by computers is still a largely unexplored field, and many questions may be asked with respect to the synergetic computer: What is the role of attention parameters in learning? How are the features to be selected? Here they were just fixed, but can the computer deal with features and patterns in what one might call a self-consistent way? For instance in language, words and sentences with their meaning condition each other (letters and words are "enslaved" by the meaning which is the order parameter!).

# 11. Learning of Processes and Associative Action

## 11.1 Derivation of the Fokker-Planck Equation

While in the preceding chapter we did not prescribe the path (trajectory) along which the system reaches the final attractor states corresponding to the originally offered patterns (prototype patterns), we now wish to show that the system can even learn to reproduce specific paths (trajectories). Or, in other words, the system may learn to perform specific motions in its space of dynamic variables. While in Sects. 11.1 and 11.2 it will be assumed that all motions are taught, in Sect. 11.3 we shall study the case in which only examples are provided such that the system has to interpolate. It will turn out that we may proceed in analogy to Sect. 10.4, i.e., we first derive a Fokker-Planck equation by means of some generalization of the maximum information principle. We then establish an analogy to the Langevin equation which may be interpreted as a network (Sect. 11.2). The whole chapter is rather mathematical and its results will not be needed later in this book, but this approach has important potential for applications.

Throughout this chapter we make the assumption that the processes which the system has to learn are Markovian. To illustrate what this means we first ignore fluctuations and consider the overdamped motion of a system described by the state vector $\boldsymbol{q}(t)$. The corresponding equation is given by

$$\dot{\boldsymbol{q}}(t) = \boldsymbol{K}(\boldsymbol{q}) \ . \tag{11.1}$$

This differential equation can be considered as the limit $\tau \rightarrow 0$ of the difference equation

$$\boldsymbol{q}(t+\tau) = \boldsymbol{q}(t) + \tau \boldsymbol{K}[\boldsymbol{q}(t)] \ . \tag{11.2}$$

Evidently the value $\boldsymbol{q}(t+\tau)$ is uniquely given by its value at time $t$ and no memory of previous states at $t' < t$ is preserved. This, in essence, is the property of a Markov process. On the other hand, when we consider the equation of motion of a particle with mass $m$

$$m\ddot{\boldsymbol{q}} = \boldsymbol{K}(\boldsymbol{q}) \tag{11.3}$$

the determination of $\boldsymbol{q}(t+\tau)$ requires not only the value of $\boldsymbol{q}$ at the previous time $t$ but also at a still earlier time, say $t-\tau$. Thus $\boldsymbol{q}$ does not obey a Markov process.

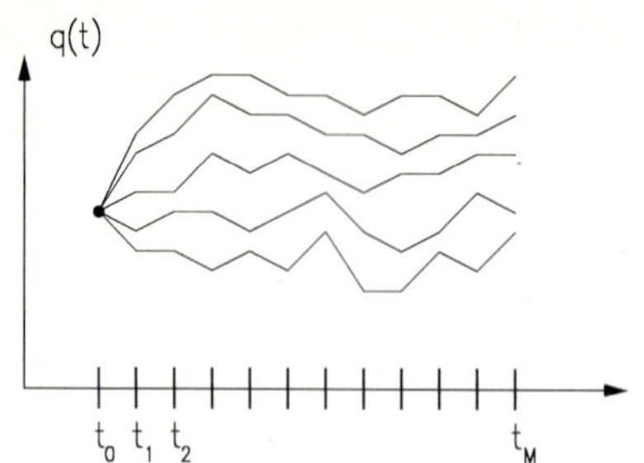


**Fig. 11.1.** Several paths $q(t)$ starting from the same initial state $q(t_0)$

However, by introducing an auxiliary variable $\boldsymbol{p}$, which in mechanics can be identified as momentum,

$$m\dot{q} = \mathbf{p} \ , \tag{11.4}$$

we may replace (11.3) by (11.4) together with

$$\dot{p} = K(q) \tag{11.5}$$

where the extended state vector $(\boldsymbol{q},\boldsymbol{p})$ now obeys a Markovian process. Indeed, each value of this state vector at time $t+\tau$ is uniquely determined by its value at the earlier time $t$. The concept of a Markovian process also extends to stochastic processes where for example (11.1) is replaced by an equation in which fluctuating forces have been added.

In order to express the definition of a Markov process in a rigorous mathematical form, we choose a time sequence $t_0, t_1, \dots t_M$. We may attribute a probability distribution to the path taken by the state vectors at the corresponding times (Fig. 11.1). The joint probability distribution for this path (trajectory) is given by

$$P(\boldsymbol{q}_M, t_M; \boldsymbol{q}_{M-1}, t_{M-1}; \dots; \boldsymbol{q}_0, t_0) \ . \tag{11.6}$$

If the process is Markovian, the $P$ of (11.6) can be split into a product

$$\prod_{i=0}^{M-1} P(\boldsymbol{q}_{i+1}, t_{i+1} | \boldsymbol{q}_i, t_i) P(\boldsymbol{q}_0, t_0) \tag{11.7}$$

where $P(\boldsymbol{q}_0, t_0)$ is the initially given probability distribution, whereas $P(\boldsymbol{q}_{i+1}, t_{i+1} | \boldsymbol{q}_i, t_i)$ is the conditional probability of finding the state vector $\boldsymbol{q}$ at the position $\boldsymbol{q}_{i+1}$ at time $t_{i+1}$ given that the system was in the state $\boldsymbol{q}_i$ at time $t_i$.

In the following we shall allow the time $t$ to change continuously so that we replace the index $i+1$ by $i+\tau$ or, occasionally, by $t+\tau$, where $t$ corresponds to $i$. Furthermore it will be necessary to exhibit the individual components of the state vector $\boldsymbol{q}$. For these reasons we shall adopt the following notation: We replace the *index* $i+1$ of the state vector by the *argument* $i+\tau$ and we reserve the index to denote the individual components. Thus we make the following replacement:

$$q_{i+1} \to \boldsymbol{q}(i+\tau) \equiv [q_1(i+\tau), q_2(i+\tau), \ldots, q_N(i+\tau)] \ . \tag{11.8}$$

Since the argument of $\boldsymbol{q}$ clearly indicates the time at which the variables of the conditional probability are to be taken, and since we shall treat stationary processes, the arguments $t_{i+1}$ and $t_i$ in (11.7) will be dropped altogether. Thus the conditional probability will be represented in the abbreviated form

$$P[\boldsymbol{q}(i+\tau)|\boldsymbol{q}(i)] \ . \tag{11.9}$$

Since it is known from the theory of Markov processes that the Fokker-Planck equation describing a continuous and stationary Markov process is determined by the first and second moments, we shall introduce the following constraints:

$$f_{1,l} = \langle q_l(i+\tau)\rangle_{\boldsymbol{q}(i)} = \int q_l(i+\tau) P[\boldsymbol{q}(i+\tau)|\boldsymbol{q}(i)]\, d^N q(i+\tau) \tag{11.10}$$

and

$$f_{2,l,k} = \langle q_l(i+\tau) q_k(i+\tau)\rangle_{\boldsymbol{q}(i)} \tag{11.11}$$

where (11.11) is defined in complete analogy to (11.10). The subscript $\boldsymbol{q}(i)$ in (11.10, 11) means that the average values are taken under the assumption that the state vector is precisely known at time $t = i$. This is also exhibited explicitly by the right-hand side of (11.10) where the conditional probability $P$ depends on $\boldsymbol{q}(i)$. We now consider $\boldsymbol{q}(i)$ as a fixed parameter, whereas the $q_l(i+\tau)$ represent a set of variables. We may then apply the maximum information principle [cf. Sect. (10.3)] where $P$ replaces $p_j$ and the vector $\boldsymbol{q}(i+\tau)$ replaces the index $j$. The application of this principle is then straightforward and we obtain the result

$$P[\boldsymbol{q}(i+\tau)|\boldsymbol{q}(i)] = \exp\Big[-\lambda - \sum_l \lambda_l q_l(i+\tau) - \sum_{kl} \lambda_{kl} q_k(i+\tau) q_l(i+\tau)\Big] \ . \tag{11.12}$$

We note that the Lagrange multipliers $\lambda$, $\lambda_l$, and $\lambda_{kl}$ are still functions of the initial value of the state vector $\boldsymbol{q}_i$:

$$\lambda(\boldsymbol{q}_i), \lambda_l(\boldsymbol{q}_i), \lambda_{kl}(\boldsymbol{q}_i) \ . \tag{11.13}$$

Our final goal will it be to derive a Fokker-Planck equation for the conditional probability (11.12). To this end we make a few transformations and introduce the vector of the Lagrange parameters $\lambda_l$ by means of

$$\boldsymbol{\lambda} = \begin{pmatrix} \lambda_1 \\ \lambda_2 \\ \vdots \\ \lambda_N \end{pmatrix} \ . \tag{11.14}$$

and the matrix

$$\Lambda = (\lambda_{kl}) \ . \tag{11.15}$$

In the following we shall assume that the determinant of $\Delta$ does not vanish

$$\det \Delta \neq 0 \ . \tag{11.16}$$

We then define a new vector $\boldsymbol{h}$ by means of

$$\boldsymbol{h} = \tfrac{1}{2} \Delta^{-1} \boldsymbol{\lambda} \ . \tag{11.17}$$

Using this newly defined vector $\boldsymbol{h}$ we may write $P$ (11.12) in the form

$$P = \exp\{-\tilde{\lambda} - \sum_{kl} [q_k(i+\tau) - h_k] \lambda_{kl} [q_l(i+\tau) - h_l]\} \tag{11.18}$$

where we have used the abbreviation

$$\tilde{\lambda} = \lambda - \sum_{kl} h_k \lambda_{kl} h_l \ . \tag{11.19}$$

In the limit $\tau \to 0$, the state vector $\boldsymbol{q}(i+\tau)$ must approach $\boldsymbol{q}(i)$, i.e. $P$ must meet the requirement

$$\tau \to 0: \quad P \overset{!}{\to} \delta[\boldsymbol{q}(i+\tau) - \boldsymbol{q}(i)] \ . \tag{11.20}$$

Thus $P$ becomes a singular function, namely the $\delta$ function. As is well-known, the $\delta$ function can be approximated by a Gaussian (compare Fig. 11.2). This leads us to the idea that the matrix $\lambda_{kl}$ becomes singular as $\tau \to 0$. We thus put

$$\lambda_{kl} = \frac{1}{\tau} G_{kl}[\boldsymbol{q}(i)] \ . \tag{11.21}$$

Furthermore we may read off from (11.20) that $h_k$, which depends on $\boldsymbol{q}(i)$, approaches $q_k(i)$ for $\tau \to 0$. To satisfy this requirement, we make the hypothesis

$$h_k = q_k(i) + \tau K_k[\boldsymbol{q}(i)] \ . \tag{11.22}$$

Under the assumptions (11.21, 22) the conditional probability $P$ is transformed into

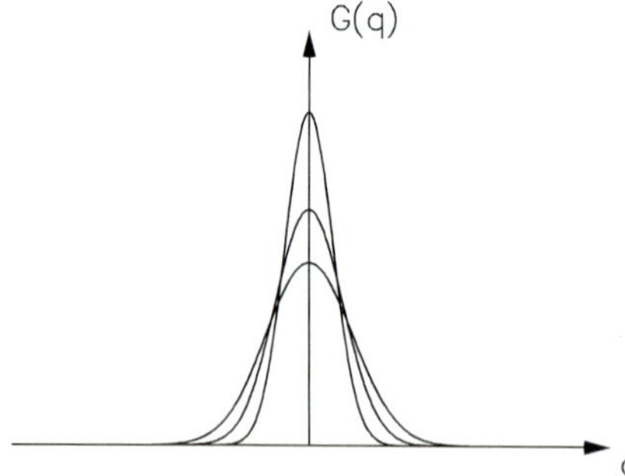


**Fig. 11.2.** Construction of the delta function $\delta(q)$ by means of Gaussian functions $G(q)$ of decreasing width

$$P(q_{i+\tau}|q_i) = \exp[-\tilde{\lambda}(q_i)] \exp\left\{-\frac{1}{\tau}\sum_{kl}[q_k(i+\tau)-q_k(i)-\tau K_k]G_{kl}\right.$$
$$\left.\times[q_l(i+\tau)-q_l(i)-\tau K_l]\right\} . \quad (11.23)$$

It will be now our goal to derive a Fokker-Planck equation for the distribution function belonging to (11.23). To this end we start from an equation defining the probability distribution function $P$ which depends on $q(i+\tau)$ alone. It obeys the Chapman-Kolmogorov equation

$$P(q_{i+\tau}) = \int P(q_{i+\tau}|q_i)P(q_i)d^Nq_i , \quad (11.24)$$

where the conditional probability is given by (11.23). We wish to derive a differential equation for $P(q_{i+\tau})$. To this end we multiply (11.24) by an arbitrary function $g(q_{i+\tau})$ and integrate over $d^Nq_{i+\tau}$ to obtain

$$I \equiv \int g(q_{i+\tau})P(q_{i+\tau})d^Nq_{i+\tau}$$
$$= \int d^Nq_iP(q_i)\underbrace{\int d^Nq_{i+\tau}g(q_{i+\tau})P(q_{i+\tau}|q_i)}_{F(q_i)} . \quad (11.25)$$

To evaluate $F(q_i)$ we introduce a new variable vector

$$q_{i+\tau}-q_i-\tau K(q_i) = \xi , \quad (11.26)$$

which yields

$$F = \int d^N\xi N(q_i)\exp\left(-\xi\frac{G}{\tau}\xi\right)g(q_i+\tau K(q_i)+\xi) \quad (11.27)$$

where $N(q_i) = \exp[-\tilde{\lambda}(q_i)]$, and $G$ is the matrix $(G_{kl})$.

In order to evaluate the integral up to terms linear in $\tau$, we expand $g$ in (11.27) into a power series in $\xi$ up to second order and into a power series in $\tau$ up to first order. Using the normalization

$$\int N(q_i)\exp\left(-\xi\frac{G}{\tau}\xi\right)d^N\xi = 1 , \quad (11.28)$$

the properties of Gaussian integrals,

$$\int N(q_i)\exp\left(-\xi\frac{G}{\tau}\xi\right)\xi_k\xi_l d^N\xi = \frac{\tau}{2}(G^{-1})_{kl} , \quad (11.29)$$

and knowing that integrals over odd powers of $\xi$ vanish, we readily obtain

$$F(q_i) = g(q_i)+\tau K(q_i)\nabla_{q_i}g(q_i)$$
$$+\tau\tfrac{1}{4}\sum_{kl}(G^{-1})_{kl}\partial^2g/\partial q_{ik}\partial q_{il} \quad (11.30)$$

where $\nabla$ is the nabla (or gradient) operator.

Inserting (11.30) into (11.25) and performing a partial integration we obtain in place of (11.25) the relation

$$I=\int d^N q_i g(q_i)\left[1-\tau\nabla_{q_i}K(q_i)+\frac{\tau}{4}\sum_{kl}\left(\frac{\partial^2}{\partial q_{ik}\partial q_{il}}\right)[G^{-1}(q_i)]_{kl}\right]P(q_i)\ . \tag{11.31}$$

We now introduce the notation

$$P(q_{i+\tau})\rightarrow f(q;t+\tau)\ , \tag{11.32}$$

$$P(q_i)\rightarrow f(q;t)\ . \tag{11.33}$$

Because $g$, which occurs in the middle part of (11.25) and on the r.h.s. of (11.25, 31) is an arbitrary function, the corresponding expressions must be equal even without integration. This leads us to the relation

$$f(q;t+\tau)=f(q;t)+\tau Lf(q;t) \tag{11.34}$$

where $L$ is the Fokker-Planck operator

$$Lf=-\nabla_q[K(q)f]+\frac{1}{4}\sum_{kl}\left(\frac{\partial^2}{\partial q_k\partial q_l}\right)\{[G^{-1}(q)]_{kl}f\} \tag{11.35}$$

which occurs in the Îto calculus. Bringing $f(q_i;t)$ in (11.34) to the l.h.s., dividing both sides of the resulting equation by $\tau$ and letting $\tau\rightarrow 0$, we obtain the Fokker-Planck equation

$$\frac{\partial f}{\partial t}=Lf\ . \tag{11.36}$$

## 11.2 Derivation of the Îto-Langevin Equation

We now derive the Îto-Langevin equation corresponding to the Fokker-Planck equation (11.36). (A brief introduction to the formalism of the Îto-Langevin equation can be found in H. Haken, Advanced Synergetics, Chap. 4). We write the Îto-Langevin equation in the form

$$dq_l(t)=K_l[q(t)]\,dt+\sum_m g_{lm}[q(t)]\,dw_m(t) \tag{11.37}$$

where the stochastic process is defined by

$$\langle dw_m\rangle=0 \tag{11.38}$$

and

$$\langle dw_m(t)\,dw_l(t)\rangle=\delta_{lm}dt\ . \tag{11.39}$$

The diffusion coefficients $G_{kl}$ are connected with the functions $g_{lm}$ by the formula

$$\tfrac{1}{2} G_{kl} = \sum_m g_{km} g_{lm} \ . \tag{11.40}$$

We introduce the matrices $G$ and $g$ by means of

$$(G_{kl}) = G; \quad (g_{km}) = g \tag{11.41}$$

so that (11.40) can be written in the form

$$\tfrac{1}{2} G = g\bar{g} \tag{11.42}$$

where $\bar{g}$ means the transposed matrix. For the solution of (11.40) it will be sufficient to assume that $g$ is a square matrix and also that $g$ is symmetric as is $G$. Equation (11.42) then acquires the form

$$\tfrac{1}{2} G = g^2 \ . \tag{11.43}$$

The solution matrix $g$ can be easily determined by assuming that $G$, which is positive definite, can be diagonalized by means of the orthogonal matrix $U$. We denote the corresponding diagonal matrix by $D$ and its matrix elements by $D_l$. We thus obtain

$$D = \tfrac{1}{2} U G \tilde{U} = (U g \tilde{U})^2 \tag{11.44}$$

where

$$U\tilde{U} = 1 \ . \tag{11.45}$$

We then find

$$(U g \bar{U})_{kl} = \delta_{kl} D_l^{1/2} \tag{11.46}$$

from which we may calculate $g$. To this end we define the diagonal matrix $D^{1/2}$ by means of

$$(D^{1/2})_{kl} = \delta_{kl} D_l^{1/2} \ . \tag{11.47}$$

This allows us to cast (11.46) into the form

$$g = \tilde{U} D^{1/2} U \tag{11.48}$$

so that $g$ is explicitly determined. Thus both the quantities occurring in (11.37), i.e. $K_l$ and $g_{lm}$, are now determined. Equation (11.37) can be solved on a serial computer which uses a random noise generator to realize the terms $dw_m(t)$. Equation (11.37) can also be interpreted as a parallel network with elements ("neurones") labeled by the index $l$. The element $l$ receives inputs from all other elements and processes these by means of $K_l(q)$ and the sum over $m$ in (11.37), where random noise generators are required.

## 11.3 Taking Care of a Reduced Information

In a number of practical applications the network may not be able to measure

$$\langle q_l(i+\tau)\rangle_{q(i)} \quad \text{and} \quad \langle q_l(i+\tau)q_k(i+\tau)\rangle_{q(i)}$$

for all the values of the state vector $\boldsymbol{q}(i)$ but rather only some moments of $\boldsymbol{q}(i)$ determined by samples of $\boldsymbol{q}(i)$. We assume that the measurements are made under steady-state conditions. In this case we can express the joint probability by a product of the conditional probability and the steady-state probability distribution

$$P(q_{i+\tau}, q_i) = P(q_{i+\tau}|q_i)P_{\mathrm{st}}(q_i) \ . \tag{11.49}$$

In order to define moments or other correlation functions, we shall introduce the functions $U_j(\boldsymbol{q}_i)$ which may be assumed for instance in the form

$$U_j(\boldsymbol{q}_i) \equiv U_{j,i} = q_{1,i}^{\mu_1} q_{2,i}^{\mu_2} \dots q_{N,i}^{\mu_N} \ ; \quad \mu_1+\mu_2+\dots+\mu_N = R \tag{11.50}$$

Note that the index $i$ refers to the time index whereas the other indices 1, 2, ... refer to components of a vector. We then introduce the following constraints

$$\langle U_{j,i}^{(1)} \rangle = \int U_j^{(1)}(\boldsymbol{q}_i) P_{\mathrm{st}}(\boldsymbol{q}_i) d^N q_i \ , \quad j = 1, 2, \dots \tag{11.51}$$

$$\langle q_{k,i+\tau} U_{m,i}^{(2)} \rangle = \int q_{k,i+\tau} U_m^{(2)}(\boldsymbol{q}_i) P(\boldsymbol{q}_{i+\tau}, \boldsymbol{q}_i) d^N q_{i+\tau} d^N q_i \ , \qquad k = 1, \dots N_j, \quad m = 1, 2, \dots \tag{11.52}$$

and

$$\langle q_{k,i+\tau} q_{l,i+\tau} U_{u,i}^{(3)} \rangle \ , \quad \begin{array}{l} k = 1, \dots, N \\ l = 1, \dots, N \\ n = 1, 2, \dots \end{array} \tag{11.53}$$

which is defined in complete analogy to (11.52)

Using our previous results we may immediately determine the steady-state distribution in the form

$$P_{\mathrm{st}}(\boldsymbol{q}_i) = \exp\Big(-\lambda_{\mathrm{st}} - \sum_j \lambda_{j,\mathrm{st}} U_{j,i}^{(1)}\Big) \ . \tag{11.54}$$

We now make use of a generalization of Jaynes' maximum entropy principle to the space-time domain as made by Jaynes himself, i.e. we may now subject a multi-time joint probability to the maximum information (entropy) principle. For our present approach it is sufficient to consider the two-time joint probability, which, by means of the maximum information principle, acquires the form

$$P(q_{i+\tau}, q_i) = \exp\left[-\lambda_0 + A(q_i) + B(q_i)q_{i+\tau} + \bar{q}_{i+\tau}C(q_i)q_{i+\tau}\right] \tag{11.55}$$

where we have used the following abbreviations

$$A(q_i) = -\sum_j \lambda_j^{(1)} U_j^{(1)}(q_i) \tag{11.56}$$

$$B_k(q_i) = -\sum_m \lambda_{km}^{(2)} U_j^{(2)}(q_i) \tag{11.57}$$

$$C_{kl} = -\sum_n \lambda_{kln} U_n^{(3)}(q_i) \tag{11.58}$$

where the $\lambda$'s are the Lagrange multipliers.

Using (11.49, 54, 55) we readily obtain the conditional probability in the form

$$P(q_{i+\tau}|q_i) = \exp\left[-\hat{\lambda} + \hat{A}(q_i) + B(q_i)q_{i+\tau} + \bar{q}_{i+\tau}C(q_i)q_{i+\tau}\right] \tag{11.59}$$

where we have used the abbreviations

$$\hat{\lambda} = \lambda_0 - \lambda_{\mathrm{st}} \tag{11.60}$$

and

$$\hat{A} = A + \sum_j \lambda_{j,\mathrm{st}} U_j^{(1)}(q_i) \ . \tag{11.61}$$

A comparison of the result (11.59) with (11.12) reveals that we may now make the following identifications between the Lagrange parameters which appeared previously and those which appear now:

$$\lambda(q_i) \leftrightarrow \hat{\lambda} - \hat{A}(q_i) \ , \tag{11.62}$$

$$\lambda_l(q_i) \leftrightarrow -B_l(q_i) \ , \tag{11.63}$$

and

$$\lambda_{kl}(q_i) \leftrightarrow -C_{kl}(q_i) \ . \tag{11.64}$$

In this way we may again derive an Îto-Fokker-Planck equation in complete analogy to Sect. 11.2. If we use the constraints in the form of the functions (11.50) we have polynomials in the drift coefficients $\boldsymbol{K}$ and the diffusion coefficients $G_{kl}$. In practical applications one may try to use only polynomials of low order, but this problem must be addressed by further research. Because of the formal analogy between two-time probability distribution functions and the stationary distribution function we may now transcribe the learning procedure of Sect. 10.5 to our present case. Since the formulas become rather lengthy, we shall not treat this problem here.

# Part II

# Cognition and Synergetic Computers

# 12. Comparisons Between Human Perception and Machine "Perception"

## 12.1 Introductory Remarks

In this second part of the book we shall investigate how one can establish relations between the concept and the performance of a synergetic computer and our understanding of cognitive processes in the human brain. Or, to be more modest, we shall ask the question: To what extent can the synergetic computer mimic mental abilities?

We first discuss the aspects for which this comparison will be made, what its limitations are, and what its prospects may be. First of all there are some general indications that the brain behaves as a synergetic system. It is an *open system* that consumes energy. By means of PET (positron emission tomography) one may even make visible the areas in the brain where enhanced energy consumption takes place when specific tasks, e.g. speaking, are performed. As neuroanatomy and neurophysiology tell us, the brain is composed of a large number ($\approx 10^{10} - 10^{11}$) of interacting parts (the neurones). It is self-organizing – for instance our thoughts can be produced without external inputs. Rather unspecific control parameters may change the macroscopic state of the brain. These control parameters may be drugs supplied from the outside, or internal neurotransmitters such as serotonin or dopamin. Within certain limits, their action can in turn be controlled from the outside, for instance by blocking dopamin$_2$-receptors by haloperidol. Even the staunchest behavioralist, who ignores internal states of the brain, will have to admit that upon taking certain drugs a person will change his or her behavioral pattern. In perception we observe a further phenomenon known from synergetics, namely symmetry breaking (vase-face), or more precisely, oscillations (Chap. 13). Critical fluctuations and critical slowing down – two typical effects known from nonequilibrium phase transitions in synergetics – were found in the motor system (Haken et al.; Kelso, Schöner).

In the following we shall attempt to put the idea that the brain is a synergetic system on a still stronger footing. We shall compare the performance of a synergetic computer with that of a brain under specific conditions. In doing so we shall use known experimental facts, and make predictions that can be checked experimentally. Thus our approach is fully operational. We must be aware of at least two problems in this study, however:

1) Our brain undoubtedly is a complex system, and probably the most complex system we know of. Complex systems can be viewed under many aspects, and their behavior is practically inexhaustible. We shall thus be able to study only a limited number of specific features of the brain's performance, maintaining the

hope, however, that in the course of time more and more features can be subsumed under a general concept (conceivably that of synergetics!)

2) In synergetics it has been shown that even the most diverse systems may behave in an analogous fashion. This implies that the same phenomena can be realized in quite different material systems. Synergetics is thus a theory of structural relationships and not a theory of matter per se. This may provide some philosophical basis for our attempt to compare the performance of a brain with a synergetic computer.

On the other hand, from a knowledge of the macroscopic phenomena alone we cannot draw unique conclusions about the structure of a system (e.g. a network) at the microscopic level. A typical and explicit example is provided by the quite different network-realizations of a synergetic computer that were discussed in Chap. 7.

Summarizing, we may state that synergetics can establish profound analogies between different systems at the macroscopic level and it may also give hints as to where to look on the microscopic level; but it definitely cannot replace the detailed experimental work at the macroscopic and microscopic levels. Thus the excitement aroused by experimental work is quite justified and will continue to play an important part in advancing our knowledge. After these general remarks, let us make some attempts at the announced comparison between brain and computer.

Let us begin by discussing whether one might experimentally check the paradigm of synergetic computers as a model of cognitive brain functions. As we have seen in Chaps. 4 and 5, the systems may acquire specific attractor states $q$. If one attractor is occupied, the system cannot simultaneously occupy another one. There are strong suggestions from speech research, which support this approach.

One of the simplest tasks in language is naming objects. Let us review some studies of the path connecting thought to the spoken word. Levelt and coworkers found that there are two well-defined steps on this path. When we wish to name something, first a so-called lemma is activated, i.e. a mental representation of the meaning of the word. Only then, in a second step, is a sound produced. Sometimes we arrive at the lemma but not at the sound of the word.

The experiments are performed as follows. The scientist shows the test person a picture, for instance a sheep, on a screen. The test person has to name the object. Usually after 0.6 seconds the test person says "sheep". During this latency time, first the lemma and then the form of the sound ("Gestalt" of the sound) must be produced in the brain. To study whether meaning and form of sound of the word are present simultaneously, the following experiments were done.

Shortly after the picture of a sheep had been shown, but before the subject could pronounce the word sheep, words of similar meaning *or* similar sound are offered to him or her by a loudspeaker. The results are: In the first half of the latency period words with similar meaning (such as cow or goat) but not those with similar sound are recognized *with delay*. In the second half of that period, the words with similar sound are suppressed.

These findings can be quite simply explained if we assume that lemmas and formation of sound are represented by two kinds of state vectors each belonging to its own network. Look at the first step: When the lemma "sheep" is formed, the network has made a transition into a *specific* attractor state ("sheep"). Being there, the network cannot occupy a *different* attractor state simultaneously. When we think of the representation of the network's state by means of order parameters (corresponding to "sheep", "cow", "goat", etc.) we understand immediately that only *one* can be present because of their "exclusion" principle. In order that the network can form a new state corresponding to a different order parameter (say "cow"), first the network must be cleared, for instance by setting the attention parameter corresponding to "sheep" equal to zero. This is strongly reminiscent of the way our computer functioned when offered a complex scene, e.g. that of Fig. 9.1.

The above statements about the formation of lemmas apply equally well to sound production. In conclusion these experiments support the concept of an "attractor landscape". On the other hand, they do not allow us to decide which kind of material network is the substrate, i.e. we cannot single out one of the networks of Figs. 7.1, 7.2, or 7.3, or possibly still other ones.

## 12.2 Rotational Invariance. Adaptation and Assimilation. Gestalt. Decomposition of Scenes

### 12.2.1 Rotational Invariance

In Sect. 8.1 we saw that the recognition of faces by the synergetic computer can be made invariant with respect to translation, rotation and scaling. It is part of our everyday experience that we recognize objects independently of their position and size, at least to within certain limits, and without necessarily requiring eye movements. What about rotation? Consider Fig. 12.1: The two images do not seem to exhibit any pronounced difference. But now turn them around by 180°! The two faces now show remarkable differences! In contrast, recognition by a

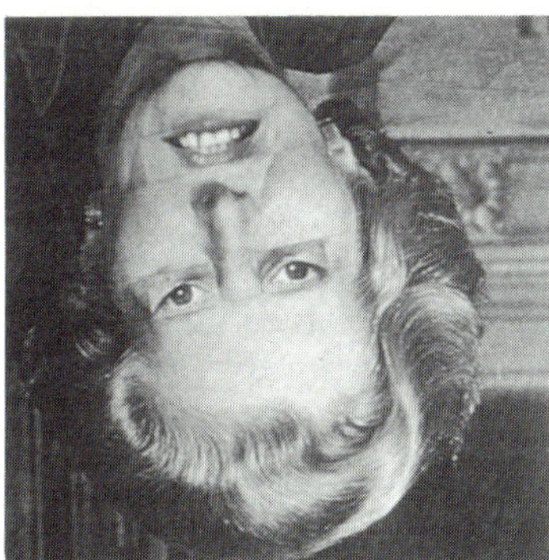
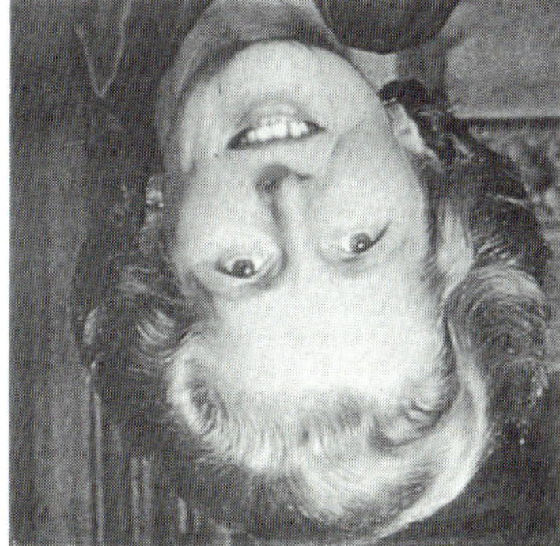

**Fig. 12.1.** How much does the left face differ from the right face?

machine based on the procedure of Sect. 8.1 is fully invariant with respect to rotation. This means that the machine fully perceives the difference between the two faces even if they are upside down. On the other hand, the procedure described in Sect. 8.2 allows pattern recognition only within a certain rotation angle. Thus it is likely that the procedure of Sect. 8.2 is a better model for human perception, but, of course, still other models may exist. Nevertheless, Sect. 8.2 and especially Sect. 8.3 are a good starting point to discuss adaptation, assimilation and Gestalt from the point of view of the synergetic computer.

### 12.2.2 Adaptation and Assimilation. Gestalt

Recall for a moment the essentials of Sect. 8.3. There we studied deformations of patterns by means of the coordinate transformation

$$\boldsymbol{x} \to \boldsymbol{x}' = \boldsymbol{S}(\boldsymbol{x}) \ ,$$

where $\boldsymbol{S}(\boldsymbol{x})$ was to be chosen such that there was a maximal overlap between the test pattern $q(\boldsymbol{x})$ and one of the prototype patterns $v[\boldsymbol{S}(\boldsymbol{x})]$. In this procedure $\boldsymbol{S}(\boldsymbol{x})$ had to obey specific constraints. This procedure may be called *adaptation* of the prototype pattern to the test pattern. As we saw in that section, the deformation of the pattern by means of $\boldsymbol{S}(\boldsymbol{x})$ can be transferred to the test pattern $q$ by means of $\boldsymbol{S}^{-1}(\boldsymbol{x})$, where $\boldsymbol{S}^{-1}$ denotes the inverse of the transformation $\boldsymbol{S}(\boldsymbol{x})$ (as long as $\boldsymbol{S}^{-1}$ exists). In this case, the prototype patterns are fixed whereas $q[\boldsymbol{S}^{-1}(\boldsymbol{x})]$ is *assimilated.* Provided the inverse exists, *adaptation* and *assimilation* are equivalent in the synergetic computer.

We are now able to express the concept of Gestalt in a mathematical form. A gestalt of type $k_0$ is recognized within a test pattern $q$ if, in the decomposition

$$q(\boldsymbol{x}) = \sum_k \xi_k T v_k(\boldsymbol{x}) + \boldsymbol{w} \ ,$$

the transformations $T$ can be chosen, under the given constraints (cost function) such that $|\xi_{k_0}|$ is bigger than any other $|\xi_k|$, $k \neq k_0$. In this way the recognition of a specific gestalt is encoded in the order parameters $\xi_k$ and the recognition is no longer concerned with $v_k$ or $T$. In the spirit of synergetics, $\xi_k$ governs the whole configuration $v_k(\boldsymbol{x})$ including all its permitted transformations, $T$. In Chap. 14 we shall treat the concept of movement gestalts.

### 12.2.3 Decomposition of Scenes

Let us now compare the ability of the synergetic computer to analyze scenes with that of humans. In Chap. 9 we presented examples for the recognition of faces within groups. In most cases the computer gave the correct answer. There were, however, a few exceptional cases in which the computer gave a wrong answer, for instance by "recognizing" another face instead of the faces shown. There are a number of situations in which humans can be similarly deceived. Consider for example Fig. 12.2. At first sight, you will (most probably) recognize the face of Einstein. But when you look at this picture on a finer scale, you will recognize

**Fig. 12.2.** Einstein's face or . . . ? From Del-Prete (1984)

three bathing girls. Thus in pattern recognition some preconception ("Vorverständnis") in the sense of Wittgenstein is required not only by humans but also by computers. One may hypothesize that the saturation of attention parameters might play an important role in the resolution of ambiguous patterns. We shall return to this question in Chap. 13.

## 12.3 Recognition of Low- and High-Pass Filtered Faces

Humans have special abilities to recognize the faces of other people. In order to study these abilities, psychologists have done a number of experiments with human subjects, in which, during the learning phase and the test phase, different pictures of the same faces were offered. Thus it may be hoped that these studies give clues about the roles played by specific features in the recognition of faces. Roughly speaking there are three groups of transformations relating the pictures shown in the learning and in the test phase:

1) Transformations in which the faces were changed in an unusual manner, but without lowering the information content. Examples were studied in which the faces were presented upside-down in the test phase or where they are presented by their photographic negative. The "upside-down" problem was discussed in Sect. 12.2.1. In the case of the "photographic negative", the synergetic computer certainly does better than humans, because its recognition process in invariant with respect to the replacement of the prototype or test pattern vectors by their negatives, i.e. we may replace $\boldsymbol{q}$ and $\boldsymbol{v}_k$ by $-\boldsymbol{q}$ and $-\boldsymbol{v}_k$, respectively. It is an open question how we must change the algorithm of the synergetic computer so that it becomes non-invariant with respect to these transformations.

2) Natural changes of faces; for instance, differential facial expressions or aging of the person by several years.

3) Reduction of the information content; for instance, by employing low- or high-pass filters.

In this section we shall be concerned with the effect of low- and high-pass filtering. Such studies have been performed experimentally by Fiorentini et al. (1983). Their subjects were asked to learn the names of nine photographed faces. When they were able to correctly identify the faces in two subsequent tests in which each face was shown only for about hundred milliseconds, they were given the tasks of recognizing low- or high-pass filtered versions of the faces. These versions were generated by a cut-off of the spatial frequency below or above a limiting frequency. Within a certain frequency range, no significant differences were found in the subjects' ability to recognize the filtered images.

An extension of these studies is provided by the experiments by O'Toole et al. (1988). They divided the subjects into three groups, one of which had to learn the unchanged faces, whereas the other two had to learn high- and low-pass filtered faces, respectively. Then unfiltered, high- and low-pass filtered pictures were all shown to each group, and the number of successes or failures of recogni-

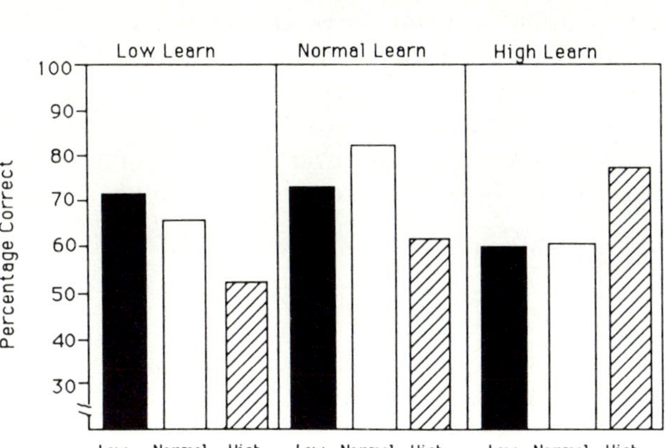


**Fig. 12.3.** Experimental data of O'Toole et al. (1988). For details see text

tion was registered. The limiting (cut-off) frequency was 22 periods within the width of the picture which corresponds to about 11 periods across the faces because these were about half as large as the actual pictures. The results of these experiments are shown in Fig. 12.3. The middle part refers to the case in which unfiltered faces had been learnt. The height of the columns represents the percentage of correctly recognized faces. When unfiltered faces were shown again, they were recognized best (white column). Low-pass filtered faces (black column) were not recognized as well as the unfiltered faces, but still considerably better than the high-pass filtered faces (hatched column). The left-hand side of Fig. 12.3 shows the results for subjects who had learnt low-pass filtered faces. Now the low-pass filtered faces were recognized best (black column), then the unfiltered faces (white column) and then – considerably worse – the high-pass filtered faces (hatched column). Finally, the right box shows the results obtained when high-pass filtered faces had been learnt. The recognition is now best for high-pass filtered faces (hateched column), whereas unfiltered and low-pass filtered faces were recognized with about equal frequency.

These studies were not able to substantiate the result of Fiorentini et al., according to which subjects who had learnt normal faces should recognize low- and high-pass filtered faces almost equally well. These differences are caused by the way in which learning was performed. In the case of Fiorentini et al. the observers had to learn the pictures in such a way that they could identify them in two subsequent tests in which the pictures were shown only for a hundred milliseconds, whereas the subjects of O'Toole et al. were shown the faces only once. In order to study habituation with respect to the faces, O'Toole et al. carried out further experiments in which the subjects were allowed to see the faces two or three times during the learning phase. Then, indeed, it was found that the subjects who had previously learnt the unfiltered faces could recognize the high-pass filtered faces as well as the low-pass filtered ones.

In the next part of this section we will study the ability of the synergetic computer to recognize low- and high-pass filtered faces and investigate the differences that arise when filtered prototype patterns are used. To this end we may start with the results of Sect. 8.1. There we had Fourier analyzed the prototype and test pattern vectors. In order to perform the cut off we first proceed from $x, y$ space to $k_x, k_y$ space, and let the integration over $k_x, k_y$ run only over a specific region. If we use a high-pass filter, the integration runs over

$$k_x^2 + k_y^2 \geq K_s^2 , \tag{12.1}$$

and in the case of a low pass filter over

$$k_x^2 + k_y^2 \leq K_s^2 . \tag{12.2}$$

We then perform the inverse Fourier transform, i.e. we proceed from $k_x, k_y$-space back to $x, y$-space. One may show that, in the case of a low-pass filter, these transformations are equivalent to a convolution of $q(\boldsymbol{x})$ with the function

$$f_{K_s} = \begin{cases} K_s J_1(K_s(x^2+y^2)^{1/2})(x^2+y^2)^{-1/2} & \text{for} \quad x \neq 0 \text{ or } y \neq 0 \\ \frac{1}{2} K_s^2 & \text{for} \quad x = y = 0 \ . \end{cases} \tag{12.3}$$

$J_1$ is the Bessel function of the first kind and of first order. As one may show by a simple calculation, it is immaterial whether one does pattern recognition by using the $q(x, y)$ representation in $x, y$-space or the $c\ (k_x, k_y)$ in Fourier space and in both cases we use the same equations (5.13). Figure 12.4 shows the functions $q(\boldsymbol{x})$ and $|c(\boldsymbol{k})|$. In the following we shall measure the spatial frequency by means of the number of periods per unit length along the edge of the picture. Thus we present $K_s$ as a multiple of $2\pi/L$. Figure 12.5 shows a number of examples of low-pass filtered patterns. Clearly the fine details are lost and sharp edges are smoothed out. On the other hand, high-pass filtered pictures (Fig. 12.6) wipe out information about the brightness of smooth parts whereas jumps in brightness (edges) are enhanced.

We now examine the extent to which the synergetic computer can recognize band-pass filtered faces. We first study the case in which *unfiltered faces* are stored (or had been learnt) by the computer. For this purpose we use the set of prototype patterns of Fig. 6.1a. As the test pattern we choose a pattern out of our basis of Fig. 6.1a and calculate its Fourier transform. After a high- or low-pass filtering has been made and the resulting vectors normalized again, we obtain the pattern to be used as initial value for the equation of motion in Fourier space. Alternatively, we may use the representation in ordinary space as explained above. The patterns obtained in the case of faces $F$ and $D$ are shown in Figs. 12.7 (low pass) and 12.8 (high pass). The time evolution of the order parameters $\xi_j$ is shown in Figs. 12.9 and 12.10 for the example of face "$D$". In order to get a quantitative measure of the recognition process, we proceed as follows: We first have to observe that in all the cases treated, the order parameter $\xi_j$ of the corresponding pattern approaches 1, i.e. the pattern is recognized with

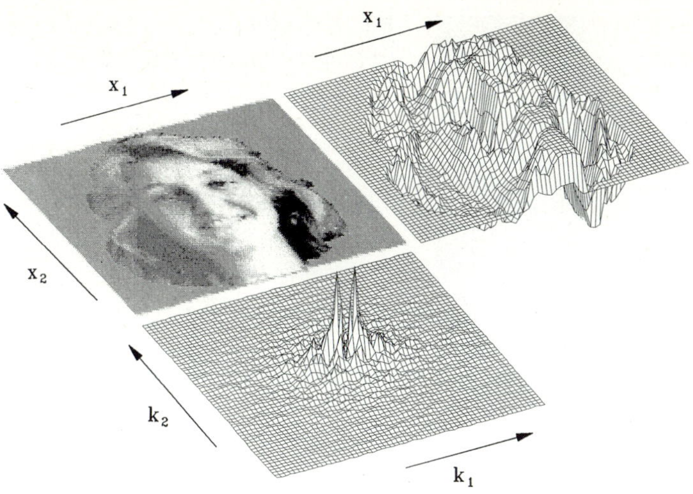


**Fig. 12.4.** The grey values of the face (*upper left corner*) are represented on the plot to the right. The lower left corner shows the absolute values of the Fourier transform. From Hönlinger (1989)

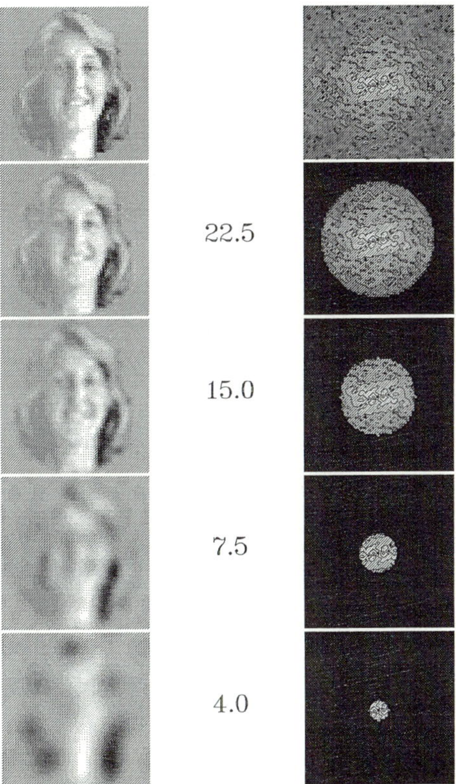


**Fig. 12.5.** Left column: low-band pass-filtered faces. Middle column: values of the radius of cut-off in Fourier space. Right column: regions of equal height of $|(k_x, k_y)|$. From Hönlinger (1989)

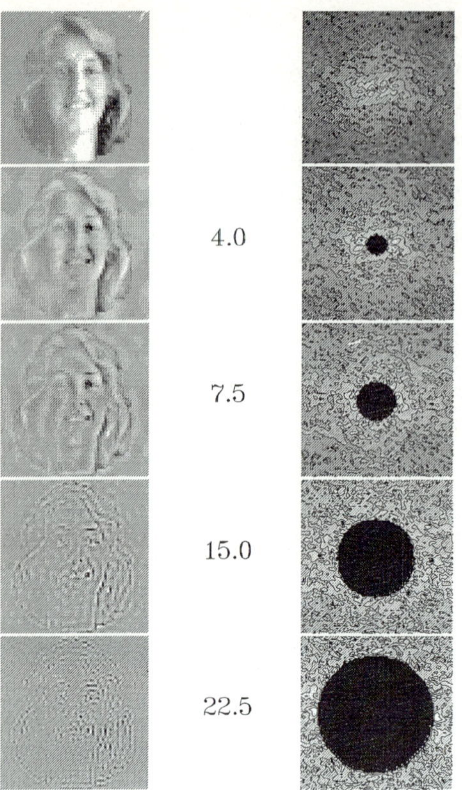


**Fig. 12.6.** As in Fig. 12.5., but for a high pass filter. From Hönlinger (1989)

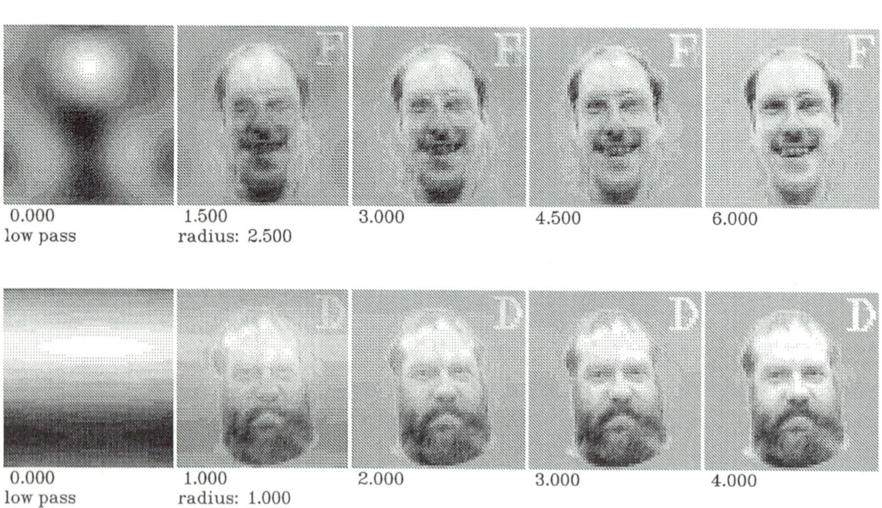


**Fig. 12.7.** Recognition of a low-pass filtered face in the course of time by means of the algorithm of Chap. 5. The lower and upper parts have different cut-off radii as indicated. From Hönlinger (1989)

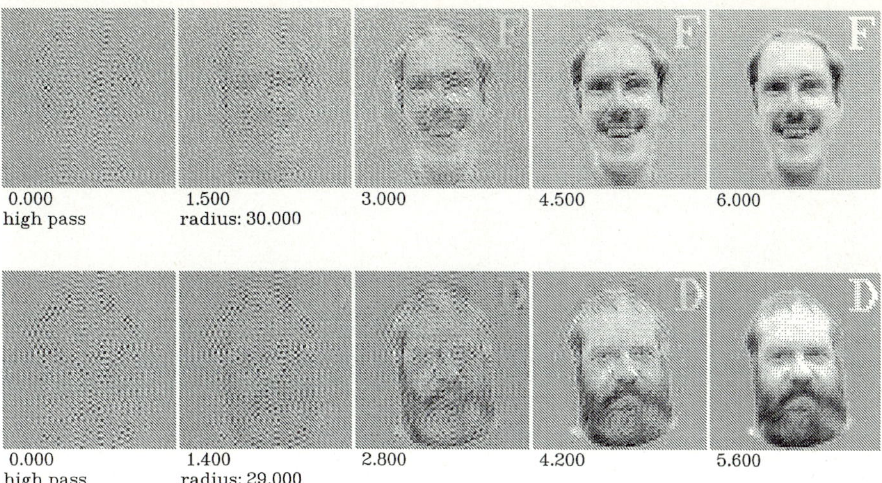


**Fig. 12.8.** As in Fig. 12.7, but for high-pass filtered faces. From Hönlinger (1989)

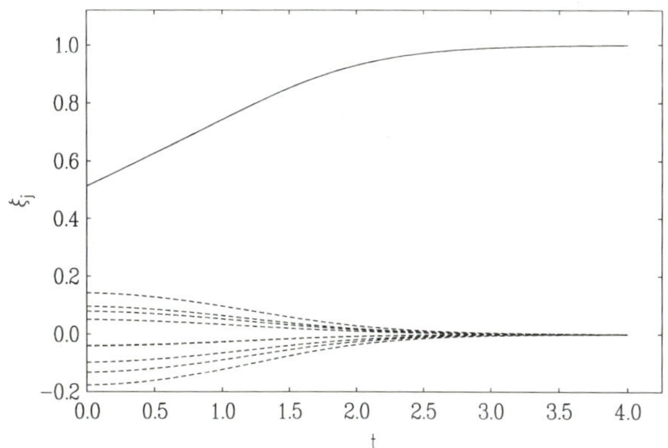


**Fig. 12.9.** Time evolution of the order parameters $\xi_j$ during recognition of face "$D$" after it had been low-pass filtered (with $K_s = 1$). The solid line represents $\xi_4$ (corresponding to face "$D$"). From Hönlinger (1989)

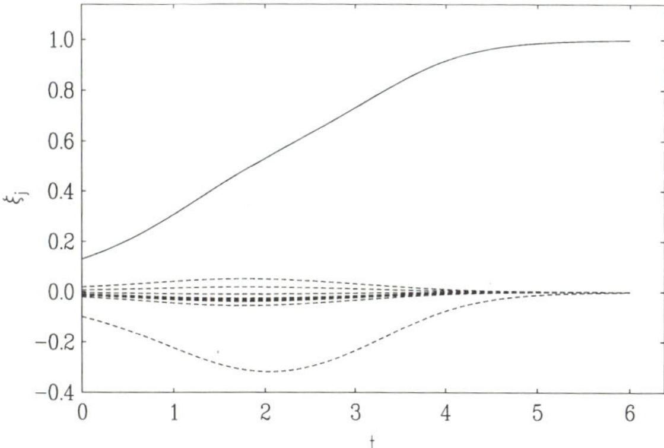


**Fig. 12.10.** As in Fig. 12.9, but after a high-pass filtering with $K_s = 29$. From Hönlinger (1989)

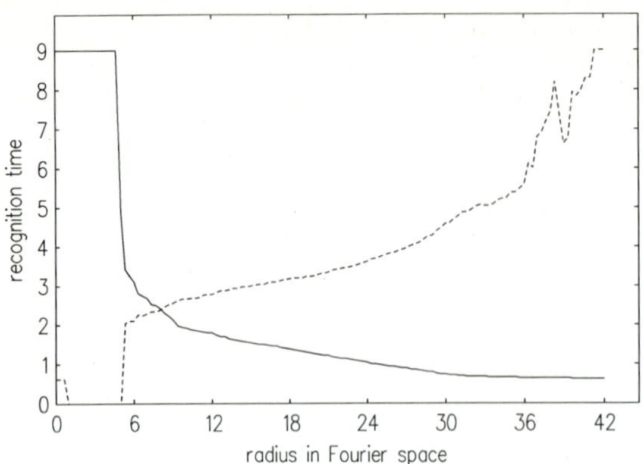


**Fig. 12.11.** Recognition time for pattern *E*. Solid line: low-pass filtered; Dashed line: high-pass filtered. The basis consists of unfiltered prototype patterns. From Hönlinger (1989)

100% certainty. Thus we choose a more sensitive measure. This is provided by the *recognition time* $t_r$, which we define as follows.

$$\xi_j(t_r) = 0.99 \text{ if } \xi_j(0) < 0.99 \quad \text{and} \quad t_r = 0 \text{ if } \xi_j(0) > 0.99 \ .$$

We determine $t_r$ as a function of $K_s$ and plot it in a diagram against $K_s$. Figure 12.11 presents a typical example for a high-pass and low-pass filtered face ($E$). Because of the decrease of available information with increasing $K_s$ in the case of high-pass filtering, $t_r$ increases with $K_s$. Correspondingly, in the case of low-pass filtering, $t_r$ increases as $K_s$ decreases. The area under the two curves is presented for all prototype patterns in Table 12.1. In order to recognize a face in the period $t_r = 2.1 - 2.6$ in the case of low-pass filtering, $0.8 - 6\%$ of the area of the Fourier transformed patterns are sufficient whereas in the case of high-pass filtering at least 93% of the area is needed. Pattern $K$ was not considered. In the cases treated here, low- and high-pass filtered versions of a face do not

**Table 12.1.** Spatial cut-off frequency $K_s$, recognition time $t_r$, and the ratio of the area of the remaining circle in Fourier space to the full area of Fourier space

| Pattern | $K_s$ | $t_r$ | Area | |
|---|---|---|---|---|
| | | | Low pass % | High pass % |
| A | 4.014 | 2.446 | 1.406 | 98.594 |
| B | 6.086 | 2.537 | 3.232 | 96.768 |
| C | 5.320 | 2.124 | 2.470 | 97.530 |
| D | 3.111 | 2.538 | 0.845 | 99.155 |
| E | 8.040 | 2.396 | 5.641 | 94.359 |
| F | 6.057 | 2.249 | 3.202 | 96.798 |
| G | 6.450 | 2.450 | 3.630 | 96.370 |
| H | 8.600 | 2.360 | 6.454 | 93.546 |
| I | 5.083 | 2.247 | 2.255 | 97.745 |
| K | 19.100 | 2.000 | 31.836 | 68.164 |

**Table 12.2.** Recognition times for unfiltered prototype patterns where the test patterns are unfiltered or filtered with low- and high-pass cut-off at $K_s = 22$

| Pattern | Recognition times | | |
|---|---|---|---|
| | Unfiltered | Low pass | High pass |
| A | 0.847 | 0.983 | 4.647 |
| B | 1.044 | 1.289 | 4.177 |
| C | 0.614 | 0.898 | 3.692 |
| D | 0.484 | 0.875 | 4.238 |
| E | 0.621 | 1.149 | 3.449 |
| F | 0.876 | 1.200 | 3.947 |
| G | 0.602 | 1.041 | 3.701 |
| H | 0.970 | 1.396 | 3.222 |
| I | 0.418 | 0.853 | 3.581 |
| K | 0.000 | 1.793 | 2.185 |

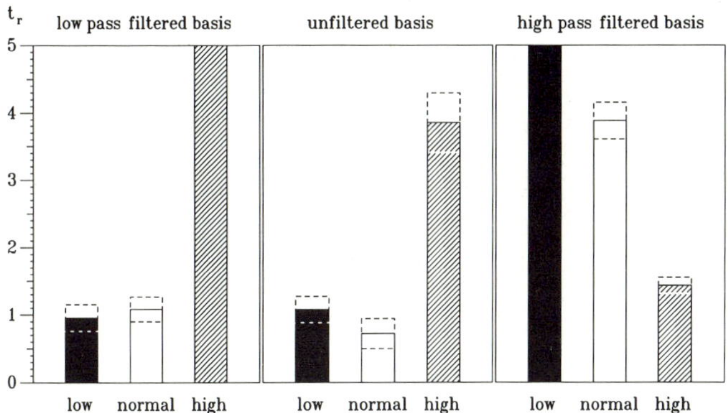


**Fig. 12.12.** Theoretical results for the averaged recognition times, $t_r$, under different conditions. See text for details. From Hönlinger (1989)

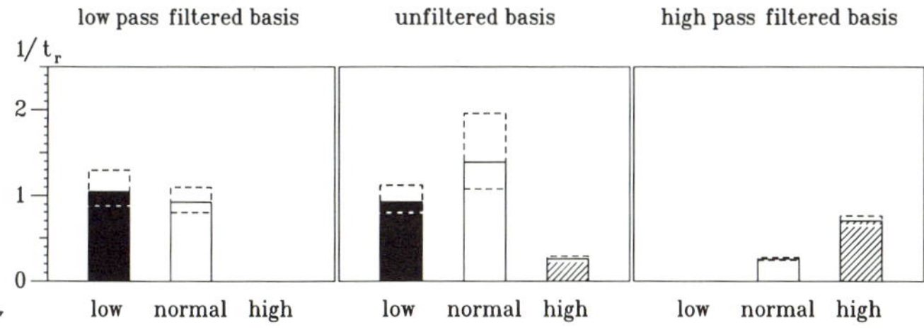


**Fig. 12.13.** Theoretical results for the *inverse* recognition times, $t_r^{-1}$. From Hönlinger (1989)

**Fig. 12.14.** The set of low-pass filtered prototype patterns. From Hönlinger (1989)

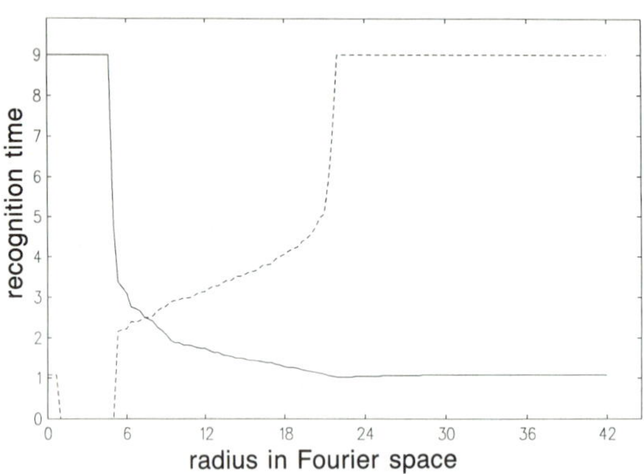


**Fig. 12.15.** Recognition times for low-pass (*solid line*) and high-pass (*dashed line*) filtered face *E*. Low-pass filtered basis. From Hönlinger (1989)

contain any common $k$-vectors because the *same* cut-off fequency $K_s = 22$ is used in order to meet the experimental conditions. Thus the computer has no information on the faces at all, and, not surprisingly, the computer fails to recognize the faces.

Quite surprisingly, the human subjects were able to recognize the faces, at least to some degree (cf. Fig. 12.3). Therefore humans must use other clues. For a comparison with the experiments, the recognition times for unfiltered patterns were also calculated. Because the test pattern is in each ease identical to a prototype pattern without letter, the corresponding value of $\xi_j$ is close to 1 from the very beginning. This is the reason for the short recognition times. Table 12.2 shows the recognition times for low- and high-pass filtered test patterns with $K_s = 22$ and for unfiltered test patterns. By means of the average values and standard deviations of $t_r$ over the patterns $A - I$, the middle panel of Fig. 12.12 was established. Quite evidently, the recognition of low-pass filtered faces by means of a synergetic computer can be achieved considerably faster than the recognition of high-pass filtered faces. In order to allow a more direct comparison with the experimental data, Fig. 12.13 plots the inverse times of Fig. 12.12.

**Table 12.3.** Recognition times for low-pass filtered prototype patterns and test patterns that are unfiltered, low- or high-pass filtered ($K_s = 22$ in all cases)

| Pattern | Recognition times | | |
|---|---|---|---|
| | Unfiltered | Low pass | High pass |
| A | 1.064 | 0.995 | – |
| B | 1.258 | 1.203 | – |
| C | 1.017 | 0.808 | – |
| D | 0.889 | 0.816 | – |
| E | 1.088 | 1.012 | – |
| F | 1.067 | 0.942 | – |
| G | 0.983 | 0.886 | – |
| H | 1.471 | 1.283 | – |
| I | 0.905 | 0.659 | – |
| K | 1.850 | 0.800 | – |

We now turn to the case of *filtered faces as prototype patterns.* In the preceding sections we found that low- and high-pass filtered patterns can be recognized even if they contain only a few spatial frequencies. One might now ask whether this is also true for a basis of filtered patterns. Can a high-pass filtered face be recognized by the computer if a basis of low-pass filtered patterns is used? To answer this question we construct a low-pass filtered basis by cutting off all spatial frequencies which are bigger than $K_s = 22$. After back-transformation and the addition of a letter, the patterns were normalized. The result of this operation is shown in Fig. 12.14. The recognition times of different filtered patterns can now be determined in the same manner as in the preceding section. Figure 12.15 shows the recognition times of pattern $E$ for low- and high-pass filtered faces and a low-pass filtered basis. The results for unfiltered low- and high-pass filtered patterns with $K_s = 22$ for all prototype patterns are collected in Table 12.3.

The average values and standard deviations averaged over the patterns $A-I$ are represented on the left-hand side of Fig. 12.12. A comparison with the case

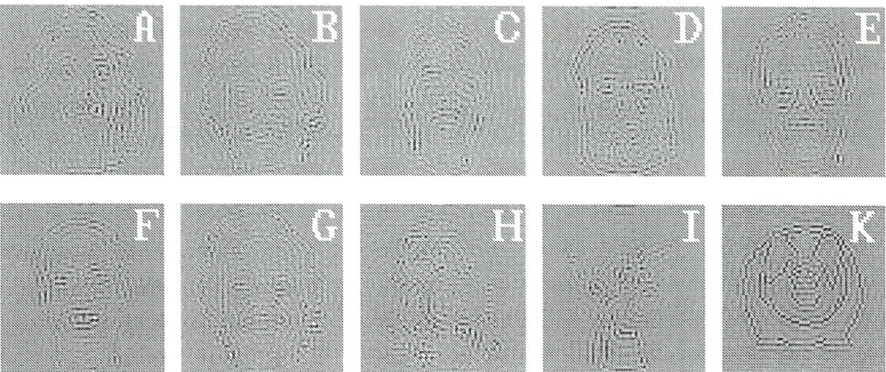


**Fig. 12.16.** The set of high-pass filtered prototype patterns. From Hönlinger (1989)

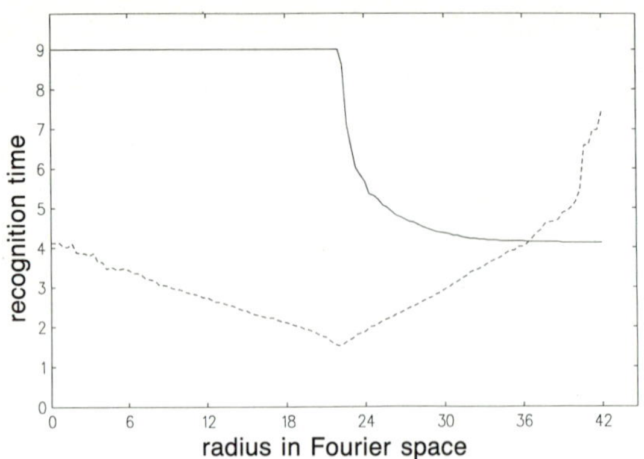


**Fig. 12.17.** Recognition times for low-pass (*solid line*) and high-pass (*dashed line*) filtered faces. High-pass filtered basis. From Hönlinger (1989)

of the unfiltered basis (middle part) shows that a prototype pattern from which only a letter was removed cannot be recognized so quickly when a low-pass filtered basis is used. For a high-pass filtered basis (Fig. 12.16) with $K_s = 22$, which was constructed in complete analogy to the low-pass filtered basis, the recognition times of pattern $E$ are those depicted in Fig. 12.17. Having calculated the recognition times of all patterns, for high- and low-pass filtered and unfiltered prototype patterns, we may compare the results. Because of the great difference between pattern $K$ and all other patterns, we have formed the average values only for the patterns $A-I$.

As Fig. 12.12 (middle part) shows, low-pass filtered patterns can be recognized more quickly than high-pass filtered patterns when an unfiltered basis is used. O'Toole et al. find that their subjects can correctly recognize low-pass filtered patterns more frequently than high-pass filtered patterns. If low-pass filtered faces had been learnt, unfiltered faces could still be recognized comparatively well, but high-pass filtered faces hardly better than 50%. As a detailed comparison between Figs. 12.1 and 12.13 reveals, our results based on the synergetic computer agree qualitatively quite well with the experimental findings. The only pronounced disagreement occurs for basis patterns that are low-pass filtered with high-pass filtered test patterns, or vice versa, when the same cut-off $K_s$ is used.

# 13. Oscillations in the Perception of Ambiguous Patterns

## 13.1 Introduction

The study of ambiguous (or ambivalent) patterns such as Fig. 13.1 has intrigued psychologists for a long time. Such patterns can be traced back as far as Roman times (Lorscheid and Hofmeister 1980) (Fig. 13.2). In 1759 Porterfield and in 1832 Necker reported on such patterns (Fig. 13.3). For more recent studies and reviews see Fisher (1967), Gombrich (1973), Gräser (1977), Pöppel (1982), Kawamoto and Anderson (1985).

There exists a large variety of ambivalent patterns with respect to perspective (Fig. 13.4). Another category consists of figure-ground patterns, which were studied by Rubin (1921) (Fig. 13.5). For further examples see Attneave (1971). Escher's work provides us with many artistic examples (cf. Fig. 2.5).

Semantic ambiguities [young/old woman (Fig. 13.6), duck/rabbit (Fig. 13.7), etc. (Figs. 13.8, 13.9)] are also well known; see for example Jastrow (1900),

**Fig. 13.1.** Vase or faces? From Rubin (1921)

**Fig. 13.2.** Lovers or an old woman? An early ambiguous sculpture. By courtesy of Römisch-Germanisches Museum Köln ►

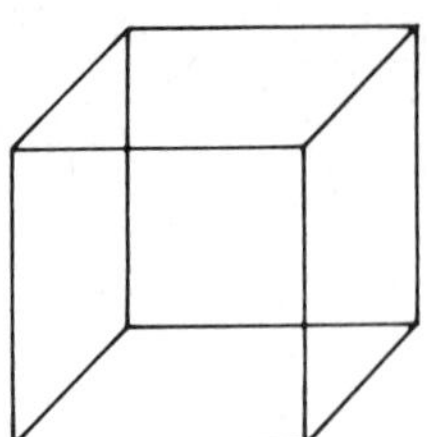

**Fig. 13.3.** Necker cube. After Necker (1832)

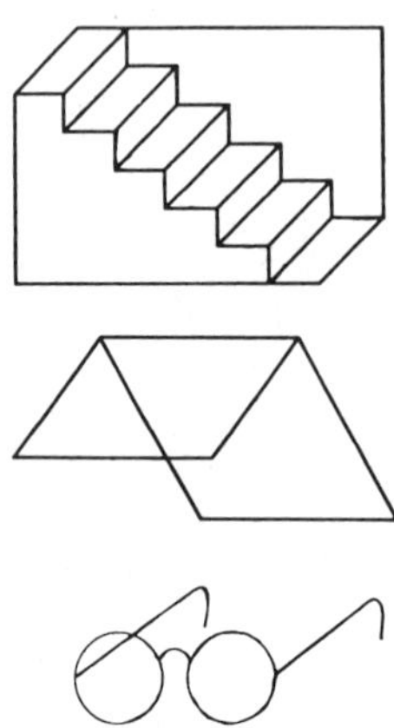

**Fig. 13.5.** Examples of figure-background ambivalence. See Attneave (1971), E. Rubin (1921)

**Fig. 13.4.** Examples of patterns that are ambivalent with respect to perspective. [Schröder's staircase after Schröder (1858)]

**Fig. 13.6.** Young or old woman? From Hill (1915)

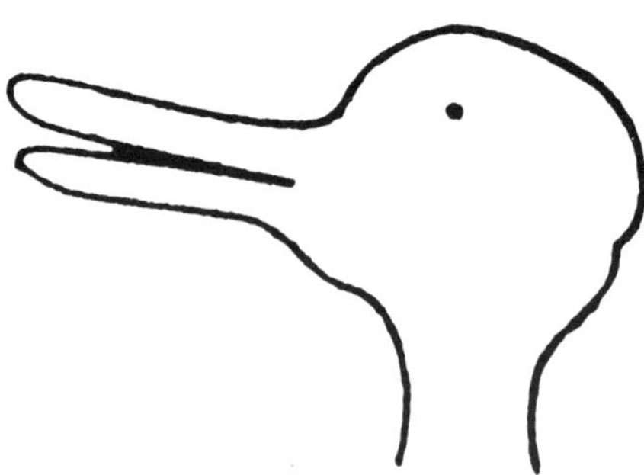

**Fig. 13.7.** Duck or rabbit? After Jastrow (1900)

Wallach and Austin (1954), Botwinick (1961), and Bugelsky and Alampay (1961).

When a person looks at such figures, he or she experiences an oscillation in perception, e.g. the young woman is perceived for some seconds, then the old woman, then the young woman again, etc. These oscillations have been studied

**Fig. 13.8.** Mouse or face? From Bugelski (1961)

**Fig. 13.9.** Slave market by Salvadore Dali (1904). Voltaire's sculpture may or may not be seen

by numerous authors [Marbe (1893), Eichler (1930), Köhler (1940), Orbach et al. (1963), Stadler and Erke (1968), Pöppel (1982), Gräser (1977)].

The best known hypothesis to explain these findings is that of saturation, proposed by Köhler (1940). He assumes that a given pattern, once it has been transmitted from the retina to the visual cortex triggers an electrochemical current which in turn enhances the resistance of the neural medium such that the neurones become saturated. Thus eventually the current has to change its direction. Although (not surprisingly!) not all psychologists accept this model, there seems to be general agreement that the observed oscillations (also called reversions) result from neuronal fatigue, inhibition or saturation. Based on these ideas, a variety of theories have been published [e.g. Kruse (1988), Attneave (1971)].

In this chapter we shall show how these oscillations result from a straightforward extension of the approach presented in Chaps. 5, 6 and 9. It turns out that a specific set of parameters, which we had previously identified as "attention parameters", now become time dependent due to the saturation of synaptic connections.

This chapter is organized as follows: Section 13.2 summarizes the properties of ambivalent patterns, Sect. 13.3 deals with ambivalent patterns without bias and Sects. 13.4 – 6 treat ambivalent patterns with bias, cases with more than two ambiguous patterns, and finally hysteresis. Section 13.7 is concerned with the role played by fluctuations of the attention parameters.

## 13.2 Properties of Ambivalent Patterns

In this section we describe some of the most important experimental findings related to ambivalent patterns. The aim of subsequent sections will be to explain them by means of our approach.

*Property A:* The pattern must possess two or more alternatives of perception.

*Property B:* When a particular alternative has been perceived, it remains stable over some time until suddenly the other alternative is perceived.

*Property C:* The time during which one alternative is perceived is approximately constant for a given person, a given pattern, and under the same circumstances. Significant differences may occur for different persons and patterns, however. This explains why the results of different authors vary considerably. According to Table 13.1 the average reversion time may vary from 1.5 to 5.7 s. Gräser's (1977) value is based on the best statistics, because an average was taken over 133 people each presented with 48 different patterns.

*Property D:* The two alternatives of perception are rarely of exactly equal strength. In most cases one is preferred over the other. Despite this, provided neither alternative has too strong a bias, a reversion will occur, but the reversion times of the individual components will be different. The stronger the bias, the

**Table 13.1.** Average reversion times

| Authors | Average reversion time in seconds |
|---|---|
| Marbe (1893) | 5.7 |
| Eichler (1930) | 1.5 |
| Köhler (1940) | 5 |
| Orbach et al. (1963) | 2 |
| Stadler and Erke (1968) | 4.5 |
| Pöppel (1982) | 2 – 3 |
| Gräser (1977) | 3.65 |

**Fig. 13.10.** Unambiguous patterns. Young woman (*left*) and old woman (*right*)

longer the reversion time. Strictly speaking, every pattern may be considered as an incomplete ambivalent pattern, but one alternative can dominate so strongly over the other(s) that no reversion occurs.

*Property E:* The period, defined as the sum of the reversion times (i.e. the time taken to return to the originally perceived image) becomes longer with increasing bias of one alternative of perception. Thus, if the ambivalent patterns are without bias, the period is the shortest.

*Property F:* Which alternative of perception is realized first depends, on the one hand, on accidental factors, e.g. on the section that is first looked at by the observer. Thus one can only measure a probability distribution corresponding to the likelihood that a certain alternative is perceived first. On the other hand, the result also depends on what the subject has perceived immediately before the test. When a group of subjects are first shown Fig. 13.10a and then Fig. 13.6, all of the persons recognized the young woman first. If, on the other hand, Fig. 13.10b is shown first to another group of test persons and then Fig. 13.6, 94% of them perceive the old woman first. Without previous "preparation" of this kind the ratio is 40% old, and 60% young woman (Leeper 1935).

*Property G:* The reversion time of a particular alternative, expressed as a percentage of the period (Property E), is a function of the probability that this alternative is perceived first.

*Property H:* The temporal evolution of the reversion rates shows a duration of habituation of 1 – 3 min during which the frequency increases (i.e. the reversion times decrease). After that a stable average period is observed. This is shown in Fig. 13.11. In most cases discussed in the literature the transitory phase is not considered but only the stable phase.

*Property I:* The reversion can be influenced by will and by practice but cannot be prevented.

*Property J:* Hysteresis occurs. If one considers in turn the sequence of pictures of Fig. 13.12 from the upper left corner to the lower right corner and then in the opposite direction, one observes that the transition from the face of a man to a girl occurs at different points.

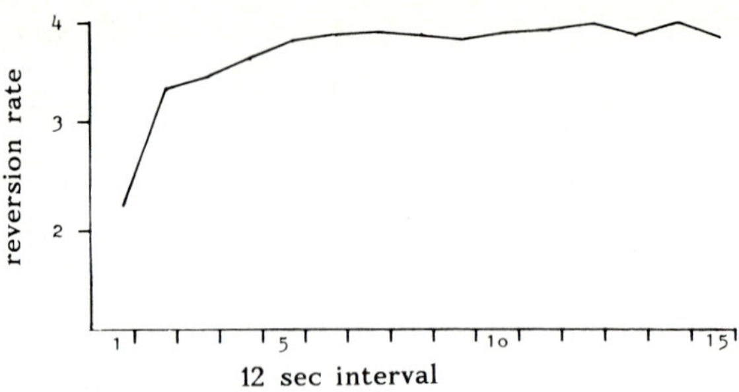


**Fig. 13.11.** Time evolution of the reversion time in seconds. The time scale is in intervals of 12 s. The learning phase lasts about 70 s. After that, stable reversion times are found. After Gräser (1977)

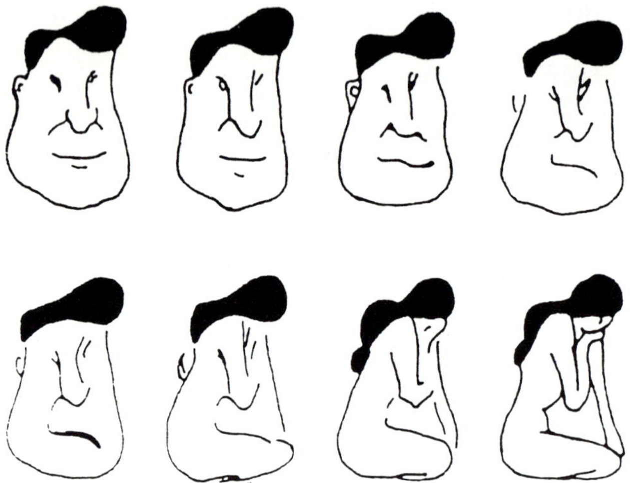

**Fig. 13.12.** Hysteresis effect in the perception of a face or a girl. Note that the switch in perception occurs at a different point depending on whether the faces are viewed from left to right starting at the top left, or in the reverse order. After Fisher (1967)

*Property K:* If one measures not only the average values of the reversion times, but also their probability distribution over time a characteristic curve emerges. It increases rapidly at small time intervals between reversions whereas at high time intervals it decreases much more slowly.

## 13.3 Perception of Ambivalent Patterns Without Bias

In order to illustrate the essence of our approach, we first consider patterns which allow for two different perceptions without bias. In this case the equations (5.32) reduce to

$$\dot{\xi}_1 = \xi_1(\lambda_1 - A\xi_1^2 - B\xi_2^2) \tag{13.1}$$

$$\dot{\xi}_2 = \xi_2(\lambda_2 - B\xi_1^2 - A\xi_2^2) \tag{13.2}$$

where

$$A = 4C_2 \quad \text{and} \quad B = 4(C_1 + C_2) \ . \tag{13.3}$$

But in contrast to our previous approach we now allow saturation of the attention parameters $\lambda_1, \lambda_2$. We shall assume that the attention parameters saturate if their corresponding pattern *increases* in perception amplitude $\xi_1$ or $\xi_2$. Because the equations (13.1, 2) are *invariant* upon replacement of $\xi_1$ and $\xi_2$ by $-\xi_1$ and $-\xi_2$, we wish to retain this property in the equations for $\lambda_1$, $\lambda_2$. These ideas lead us, in a straightforward manner, to the following differential equations for $\lambda_1$ and $\lambda_2$

$$\dot{\lambda}_1 = a - b\lambda_1 - c\xi_1^2 \tag{13.4}$$

$$\dot{\lambda}_2 = a - b\lambda_2 - c\xi_2^2 \ . \tag{13.5}$$

In the following we shall assume that

$$a = b = c = \gamma > 0 \ . \tag{13.6}$$

To study the basic properties of (13.1 – 5) we may apply the standard methods of dynamical systems theory. We first determine the fixed points and their stability as functions of the various parameters occurring in these equations. As this analysis shows, oscillations occur once the condition

$$B - A < 1 \tag{13.7}$$

is fulfilled.

Figure 13.13 shows the oscillatory behavior of the order parameters (perception parameters) $\xi_1$ and $\xi_2$ and of the attention parameters $\lambda_1$ and $\lambda_2$ for $\gamma = 0.1$, $C_1 = 0.2$, $C_2 = 0.25$.

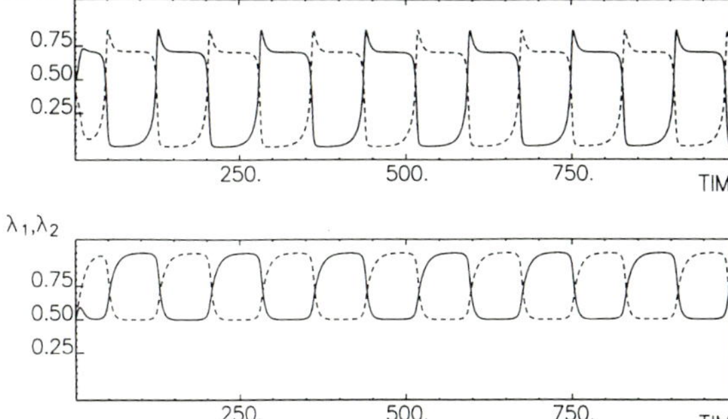


**Fig. 13.13.** The upper trace shows the time evolution of the order parameters $\xi_1$, $\xi_2$ indicating which pattern is perceived at a particular moment. The lower trace shows the time dependence of the attention parameters $\lambda_1$, $\lambda_2$. From Ditzinger and Haken (1989)

## 13.4 Oscillations in Perception in the Presence of a Bias

As we have mentioned before, unprepared persons may initially perceive an ambiguous pattern with differing probabilities for each interpretation – they show a bias. For instance, 60% of them may first see a young woman, 40% an old woman in Fig. 13.6. (For a further example, see Fig. 13.14.) If we label the prototype pattern vector of "old woman" by 1, and that of "young woman" by 2, we may reformulate the above statement by saying that a percentage $p_1 = 40\%$ of the persons identify the test pattern vector, $\boldsymbol{q}$, which corresponds "objectively" to the actually presented pattern with $\boldsymbol{v}_1$ and a percentage $p_2 = 60\%$ with $\boldsymbol{v}_2$. This leads us to the idea of reconstructing the test pattern vector $\boldsymbol{q}$ from these experimental data by putting

$$\boldsymbol{q} = p_1 \boldsymbol{v}_1 + p_2 \boldsymbol{v}_2 \ . \tag{13.8}$$

In order to model this intrinsic bias, we resort to the fundamental mechanism introduced in the original model of Chap. 5. With respect to two dimensions, this model means that the "landscape" of the potential $V$ over the plane spanned by $\xi_1, \xi_2$ is divided by a ridge along the diagonal. In this case there is no intrinsic bias, so that $p_1 = p_2 = 50\%$ and $\boldsymbol{q}$ coincides with the ridge along the diagonal. But with bias the ridge must be displaced so that the line of "neutral force" is given by (13.8). How can we represent this displacement mathematically? The function representing the ridge of the potential $V$ is inherent in the part $V_1$ of the total potential $V$. A simple analysis shows that this can be achieved by simply changing the angle between the diagonal and the $\xi_1$ axis (Fig. 13.15). If the

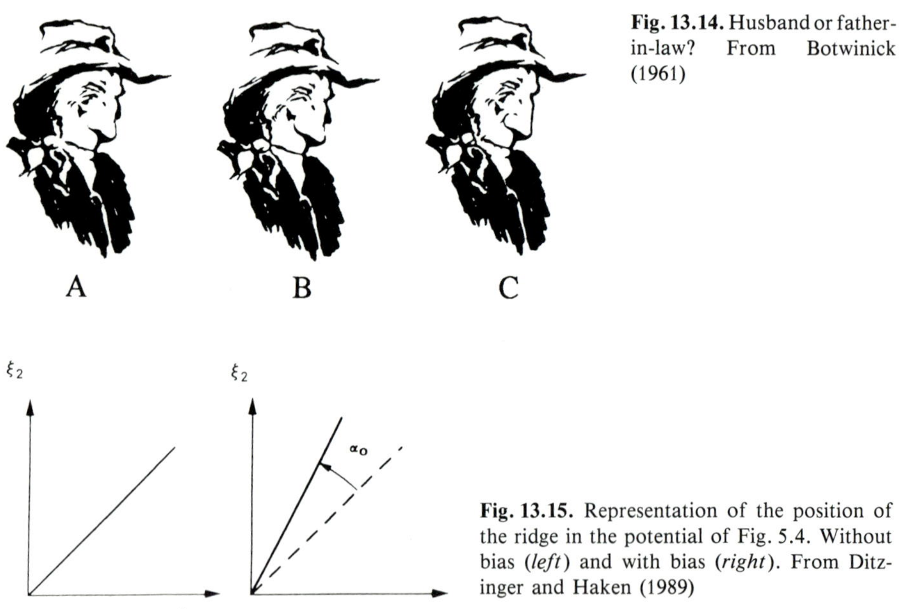


**Fig. 13.14.** Husband or father-in-law? From Botwinick (1961)

**Fig. 13.15.** Representation of the position of the ridge in the potential of Fig. 5.4. Without bias (*left*) and with bias (*right*). From Ditzinger and Haken (1989)

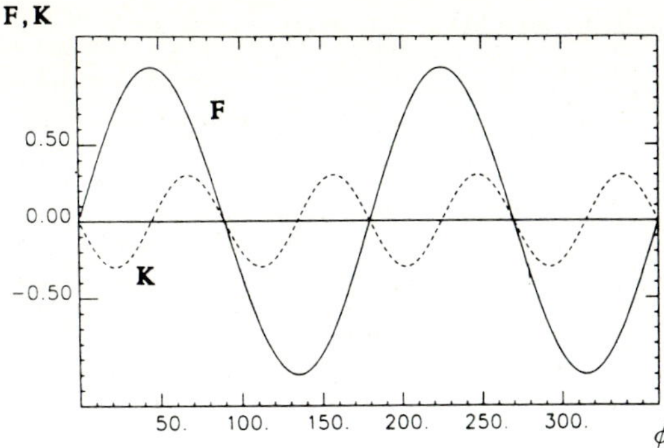


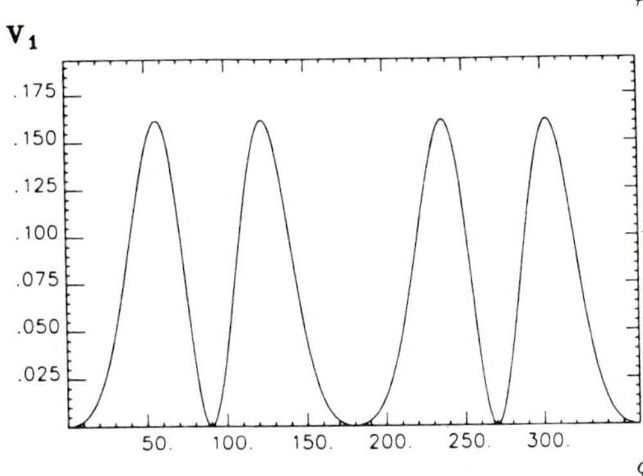


**Fig. 13.16.** The upper plot shows how the potential $V_1$ is altered in the presence of bias. Plotted are the components $F = \sin 2\phi$ and $K = -\alpha_0 \sin 4\phi$ versus $\phi$. Below: the extended expression $V_1$ as a function of $\phi$ according to (13.10). A value $\alpha_0 = 0.3$ was used. From Ditzinger and Haken (1989)

displacement angle is $\alpha_0$, we introduce a new potential $V_1$ in place of the former $V_1$:

$$V_1 = \frac{C_1}{2} |q|^4 (F+K)^2 \tag{13.9}$$

where $F = \sin 2\phi$ and $K = -\alpha_0 \sin 4\phi$. For small enough angles $\alpha_0$ we may retain the term linear in $\alpha_0$ and drop the second-order term. We then arrive at (cf. Fig. 13.16)

$$V_1 = \frac{C_1}{2} |q|^4 \sin^2 2\phi (1 - 4\alpha_0 \cos 2\phi) \ . \tag{13.10}$$

Using some trigonometric relationships we readily realize that $V_1$ can be expressed in terms of $\xi_1$ and $\xi_2$ by means of

$$V_1 = 2C_1 \xi_1^2 \xi_2^2 \left(1 - 4\alpha_0 \frac{\xi_1^2 - \xi_2^2}{\xi_1^2 + \xi_2^2}\right) \ . \tag{13.11}$$

Equations (13.1, 2) must now be replaced by the equations

$$\dot{\xi}_1 = \xi_1 \left[\lambda_1 - A\xi_1^2 - B\xi_2^2 + 4(B-A)\alpha_0 \xi_2^2 \left(1 - \frac{2\xi_2^4}{(\xi_1^2+\xi_2^2)^2}\right)\right] \tag{13.12}$$

$$\dot{\xi}_2 = \xi_2 \left[\lambda_2 - B\xi_1^2 - A\xi_2^2 - 4(B-A)\alpha_0 \xi_1^2 \left(1 - \frac{2\xi_1^4}{(\xi_1^2+\xi_2^2)^2}\right)\right] \tag{13.13}$$

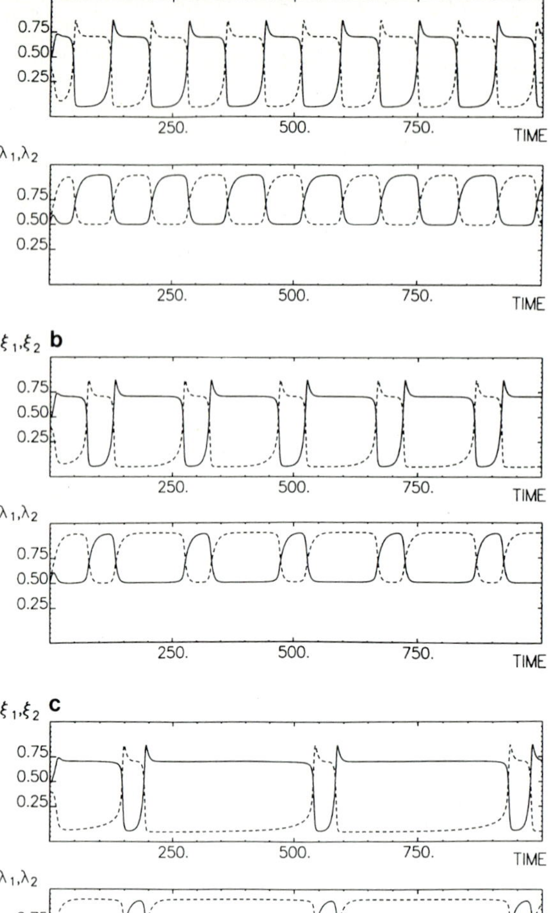


**Fig. 13.17 a – c.** These plots show the time evolution of the order parameters $\xi_1$, $\xi_2$, and of the attention parameters $\lambda_1$, $\lambda_2$. In **(a)** no bias is present ($\alpha_0 = 0.0$). In **(b)** the bias is increased slightly ($\alpha_0 = 0.03$), and in **(c)** the bias is further increased ($\alpha_0 = 0.05$). From Ditzinger and Haken (1989)

while (13.4, 5) remain unchanged. In the following we shall again use (13.6) and put $\gamma = 0.1$. The properties of (13.12, 13) and (13.4, 5) can again be analyzed by dynamic systems theory. If $A = 1$, $B = 2$, and $\alpha_0$ is small enough, oscillations again occur. If, however, $\alpha_0$ exceeds a critical value $\alpha_{0\text{crit}}$, the oscillations stop and the system runs into one or another fixed point. In other words, if the intrinsic bias is too large, only one pattern (or the other, if the observer is adequately prepared) can be observed. Figure 13.17 a – c shows the behavior of $\xi_1, \xi_2$ for increasing values of the bias $\alpha_0$. The reversion times $T_k$ of the individual components $k (k = 1, 2)$ become different and the length $T$ of a period becomes longer in good agreement with properties $D$ and $E$ (Sect. 13.2). Clearly the following relations are valid:

$$T_1 = T_2 \quad \alpha_0 = 0$$
$$T_1 > T_2 \quad \alpha_0 < 0 \qquad (13.14)$$
$$T_2 < T_1 \quad \alpha_0 > 0$$

The simplest hypothesis relating $\alpha_0$ to $T_1$ and $T_2$ that fulfills (13.14) is given by

$$\alpha_0 = c\,\frac{T_2 - T_1}{T}\ , \quad \text{where} \quad T = T_1 + T_2\ . \qquad (13.15)$$

The accuracy of this hypothesis can be checked by a numerical calculation of $T_1$ and $T_2$ as a function of $\alpha_0$. In Table 13.2 we present $T_1/T$ and $T_2/T$ and their difference $(T_2 - T_1)/T$ for varying $\alpha_0$. In the last column $\alpha_0$ is divided by this difference. Quite evidently an almost constant value results, as was postulated by (13.15). Thus the hypothesis (13.15) is fulfilled to an excellent degree. As it turns out, this constant coincides with $\alpha_{0\text{crit}}$ which was determined independently by our analysis of the situation where oscillations stop and fixed-point behavior occurs. This value was determined to be

$$c = \alpha_{0\text{crit}} = \frac{1}{4}\left(\frac{1}{B-A} - 1\right)\ . \qquad (13.16)$$

As our numerical calculations show, the relation (13.15) with $c$ given by (13.16) remains approximately valid also for values of the parameters $A$ and $B$ other than those used in Table 13.2. In our model it has been possible to relate the reversion times $T_1$ and $T_2$ to the bias $\alpha_0$. In this way we obtain a link between the bias and the observed data.

On the other hand, as we have seen above, the bias $\alpha_0$ can also be related to the vector $q$ of (13.8). Some simple rules of geometry and trigonometry lead us to a relation between $\alpha_0$ and $p_2 - p_1$, namely,

$$\alpha_0 = \arctan(p_2 - p_1)\ , \qquad (13.17)$$

**Table 13.2.** Recognition times as a function of $\alpha_0$. The parameters used are $\lambda = 0.1$, $C_1 = 0.24$, $C_2 = 0.25$

| $\alpha_0$ | $T_1/T$ | $T_2/T$ | $(T_2 - T_1)/T$ | $c$ |
|---|---|---|---|---|
| 0.001 | 0.4536572 | 0.5463428 | 0.0926856 | 0.0107891 |
| 0.002 | 0.4071759 | 0.5928242 | 0.1856483 | 0.0107730 |
| 0.003 | 0.3606642 | 0.6393358 | 0.2786715 | 0.0107653 |
| 0.004 | 0.3139986 | 0.6860015 | 0.3720029 | 0.0107526 |
| 0.005 | 0.2670623 | 0.7329377 | 0.4658754 | 0.0107324 |
| 0.006 | 0.2196693 | 0.7803307 | 0.5606614 | 0.0107016 |
| 0.007 | 0.1718999 | 0.8281001 | 0.6562002 | 0.0106674 |
| 0.008 | 0.1235106 | 0.8764895 | 0.7529789 | 0.0106244 |
| 0.009 | 0.0742883 | 0.9257116 | 0.8514233 | 0.0105705 |
| 0.010 | 0.0233689 | 0.9766310 | 0.9532620 | 0.0104902 |

critical $\alpha_0$: 0.010416687

where we have used

$$p_1+p_2=1 \ . \tag{13.18}$$

As a comparison between (13.15) and (13.17) reveals, we obtain

$$p_k=\frac{1}{2}\{1+\tan[c(2T_k/T-1)]\}\equiv f\left(\frac{T_k}{T}\right) \ . \tag{13.19}$$

In this way it has been shown that $p_k$ is a function, $f$, of $T_k/T$ and thus property $G$ of Sect. 13.2 has been derived.

In conclusion we mention an interesting extension, of or alternative to, our model of the effect of bias: Instead of introducing the displacement angle $\alpha_0$, we may leave the ridge unshifted, but introduce different strengths of saturation of the attention parameters, i.e. we put

$$\dot{\lambda}_1=a-b\lambda_1-c_1\xi_1^2 \ , \tag{13.20}$$

$$\dot{\lambda}_2=a-b\lambda_2-c_2\xi_2^2 \ , \tag{13.21}$$

where $a, b, c_1, c_2$ are all positive, and $c_1>c_2$ if pattern 2 is preferred. As one may show, (13.20, 21) can be brought to a form with $c_1=c_2=c$ by means of the transformation

$$\xi_1\rightarrow\sqrt{\frac{c}{c_1}}\xi_1 \ , \qquad \xi_2\rightarrow\sqrt{\frac{c}{c_2}}\xi_2 \ . \tag{13.22}$$

This transformation shifts the neutral line of the "force field" in (13.1, 2) in practically the same way as the ridge was shifted by the angle $\alpha_0$. The model (13.20, 21) with unshifted ridge can be more easily interpreted as far as the resulting duration of the reversion times $T_1$ and $T_2$ is concerned. For instance $c_1>c_2$ clearly implies a quicker saturation of $\lambda_1$ than of $\lambda_2$ and thus $T_1<T_2$.

## 13.5 Ambiguous Patterns with More Than Two Alternatives

Our results can be generalized in a straightforward manner to the case in which there are several alternatives (e.g. the four possibilities of Fig. 13.18). Labelling

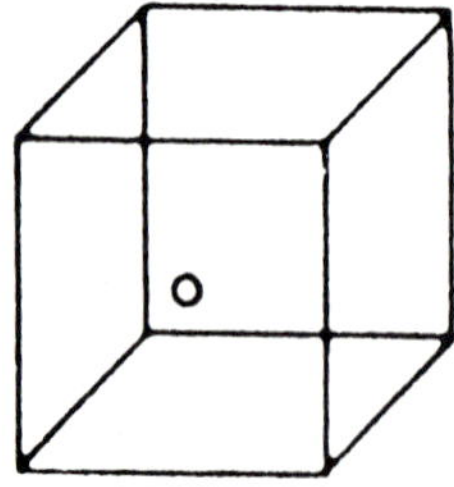

**Fig. 13.18.** A Necker cube with a spot. The spot may be perceived as being on the front face or on the rear face of the cube. Thus a total of four interpretations become possible

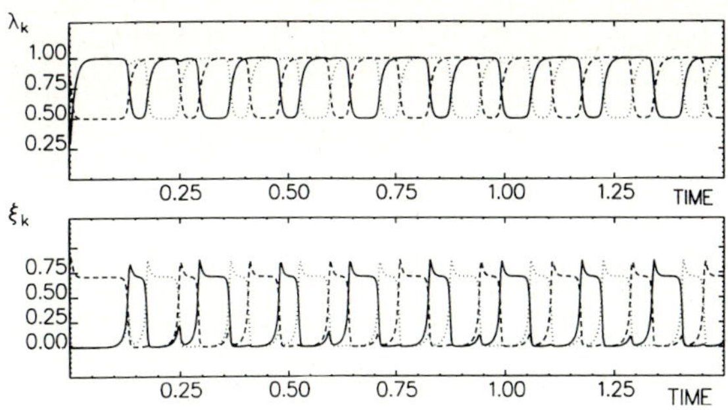


**Fig. 13.19.** Time dependence of the order parameters $\xi_k$ and the attention parameters $\lambda_k$ for the case of an ambiguous pattern with three possible interpretations. The different interpretations are distinguished by the solid, the dashed, and the dotted curves. From Ditzinger and Haken (1989)

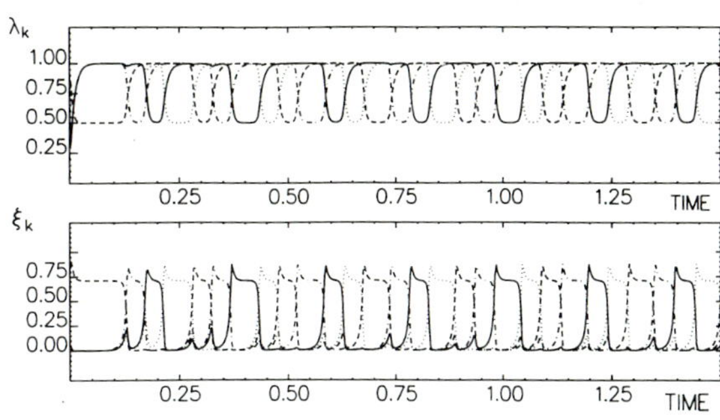


**Fig. 13.20.** As in Fig. 13.19, but now with four possible interpretations. From Ditzinger and Haken (1989)

the corresponding order parameters $\xi_k$ and attention parameters $\lambda_k$ by $k = 1, \ldots M$, we may formulate the corresponding equations as

$$\dot{\xi}_k(t) = \lambda_k(t)\xi_k(t) - 4C_1\xi_k(t) \sum_{k' \neq k}^{M} \xi_{k'}^2(t) - 4C_2\xi_k(t) \sum_{k'}^{M} \xi_{k'}^2(t) \tag{13.23}$$

$$\dot{\lambda}_k(t) = -\gamma[\lambda_k(t) + \xi_k^2(t) - 1] \qquad k = 1, \ldots, M \; .$$

We have solved these equations on a computer for the examples of $M = 3$ (Fig. 13.19) and $M = 4$ (Fig. 13.20). The sequence of the occurrence of the individual order parameters $\xi_k$ is determined by the initial conditions $\xi_k(0)$ and $\lambda_k(0)$ and is maintained during the course of time. As is evident from Figs. 13.19 and 13.20, the system needs a long transient time until it reaches stable oscillations.

So far we have considered the case in which there is no bias. When there is a bias, we may generalize our model in the following way: The angle $\alpha_0$ which described the bias in the case $M = 2$ must now be replaced by a matrix $\underset{\sim}{\alpha}_0$ which represents the shift of the ridge of the potential $V_1$ within all $M$ dimensions. Using a generalization of Fig. 13.15 we obtain

$$\tan\left(\alpha_{0kk'} + \frac{\pi}{4}\right) = \frac{\xi_{k'}}{\xi_k} \tag{13.24}$$

and thus for $\alpha_{0kk'}$

$$\alpha_{0kk'} = \arctan\left(\frac{\xi_{k'}}{\xi_k}\right) - \frac{\pi}{4} \ . \tag{13.25}$$

We thereby obtain a relation between $\alpha_{0kk'}$ and $\alpha_{0k'k}$:

$$\alpha_{0k'k} = \operatorname{arccot}\left(\frac{\xi_{k'}}{\xi_k}\right) - \frac{\pi}{4} = \frac{\pi}{2} - \arctan\left(\frac{\xi_{k'}}{\xi_k}\right) - \frac{\pi}{4} \ ,$$

whence

$$\alpha_{0k'k} = -\alpha_{0kk'} \ . \tag{13.26}$$

This allows us to generalize the potential $V_1$ in the following way:

$$V_1 = C_1 \sum_{k \neq k'}^{M} \xi_k^2 \xi_{k'}^2 \left(1 - 4\alpha_{0kk'} \frac{\xi_k^2 - \xi_{k'}^2}{\xi_k^2 + \xi_{k'}^2}\right) \ . \tag{13.27}$$

Inserting (13.27) into the order parameter equations for $\xi_k$, we obtain our basic system of equations

$$\begin{aligned}
\dot{\xi}_k(t) = {} & \lambda_k(t)\xi_k(t) - 4C_1\xi_k(t) \sum_{k' \neq k}^{M} \xi_{k'}^2(t) \\
& \times \left(1 - 4\alpha_{0kk'} \frac{\xi_k^2(t) - \xi_{k'}^2(t)}{\xi_k^2(t) + \xi_{k'}^2(t)}\right) \\
& + 32C_1\xi_k^3(t) \sum_{k' \neq k}^{M} \alpha_{0kk'} \frac{\xi_{k'}^4(t)}{[\xi_k^2(t) + \xi_{k'}^2(t)]^2} - 4C_2\xi_k(t) \sum_{k'}^{M} \xi_{k'}^2(t) \\
\dot{\lambda}_k(t) = {} & -\gamma[\lambda_k(t) + \xi_k^2(t) - 1] \\
k = {} & 1, \ldots, M \ .
\end{aligned} \tag{13.28}$$

In order to determine the matrix $\alpha_0$ uniquely, we have to know $M-1$ matrix elements. Let us assume that the elements $\alpha_{01k'}$ with $k' = 1, \ldots, M$ are known, where $\alpha_{011} = 0$. The other elements $\alpha_{0kk'}$ where $k \neq 1$, can be calculated as follows: We insert (13.24) for $k = 1$, i.e.

$$\xi_x = \xi_1 \tan\left(\alpha_{01x} + \frac{\pi}{4}\right) \ , \quad x = k, k' \tag{13.29}$$

into (13.25) and obtain

$$\alpha_{0kk'} = \arctan\left(\frac{\tan[\alpha_{01k'} + (\pi/4)]}{\tan[\alpha_{01k} + (\pi/4)]}\right) - \frac{\pi}{4} \ . \tag{13.30}$$

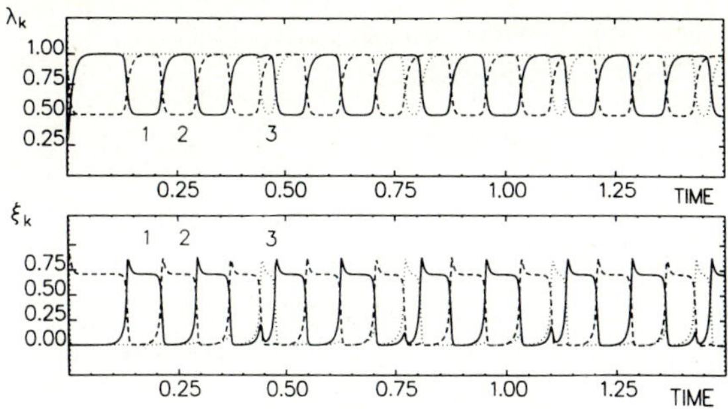


**Fig. 13.21.** Oscillations of the attention and order parameters for the case of three differently biased alternatives. From Ditzinger and Haken (1989)

In this way we obtain the remaining matrix elements from the known $\alpha_{01k'}, k' = 1, \ldots, M$. In analogy to Sect. 13.4 we may find the $\alpha_{01k'}$ by means of one of the interpretations of the angles $\alpha_{01k'}$ (13.15, 16) or (13.17). In Fig. 13.21 the oscillations of the perception (order parameters) are represented for three differently biased alternatives. We have chosen $\alpha_{012} = 0, \alpha_{013} = -0.022$. In this way we attempted to simulate the states of a Necker cube (Fig. 13.3). The unbiased alternatives $k = 1$, 2 are the two spatial interpretations, whereas $k = 3$ corresponds to the perception of a plane which is somewhat less favored. As we see in Fig. 13.21, the alternative $k = 3$ appears, after the transient period, only every fifth time whereas the other two possibilities materialize every second or third time.

## 13.6 Hysteresis

A well-known example of hysteresis effects was shown in Fig. 13.12. When we look at the individual patterns in turn, starting from the upper left corner and finishing at the lower right corner, the transition from a man's face to a girl will occur only after the second pattern on the lower row. In contrast, when we proceed in the opposite direction the switch from the perception of a girl to the face of a man occurs only in the top row. We have called this effect hysteresis (H. Haken, *Synergetics. An Introduction*) in analogy to the switching processes in physical systems. In order to treat this effect within the framework of the present approach, we begin with the following consideration: If we have not seen a pattern before, or at least not for a long time, we will attach a bias parameter (angle $\alpha_0$) after a certain duration of habituation (cf. property H of Sect. 13.2). When looking at a somewhat different picture, the original bias will fade away and will relax towards the bias attached to this new picture. However, this adaptation will take some while so that we now let the bias parameter $\alpha_0$ in (13.12, 13) become a time-dependent function which obeys an equation of the form

$$\dot{\alpha}(t) = -\mu[\alpha(t) - \alpha_{0j}] \ . \qquad (13.31)$$

Here $\mu$ is the damping parameter, whereas $\alpha_{0j}$ represents the "objective" bias of the pattern with label $j$. (The "objective" bias can be measured by means of the reversion times, though this is not our concern at present). The solution of (13.31) for $t \geq t_j$, where $t_j$ is the initial time, is given by

$$\alpha(t) = \alpha_{0j} + [\alpha(t_j) - \alpha_{0j}]\,\mathrm{e}^{-\mu(t-t_j)} \ . \tag{13.32}$$

We now proceed as follows: We assume that at time $t = t_1$ the observer starts to regard pattern 1 for some time, say $\tau$. The index $j$ is put equal to 1 and thus $\alpha_{0j} = \alpha_{01}$. The initial value $\alpha(t_1)$ is subjective and may be chosen arbitrarily in our simulation. After time $\tau$, i.e. at time $t = t_1 + \tau \equiv t_2$, the observer begins to

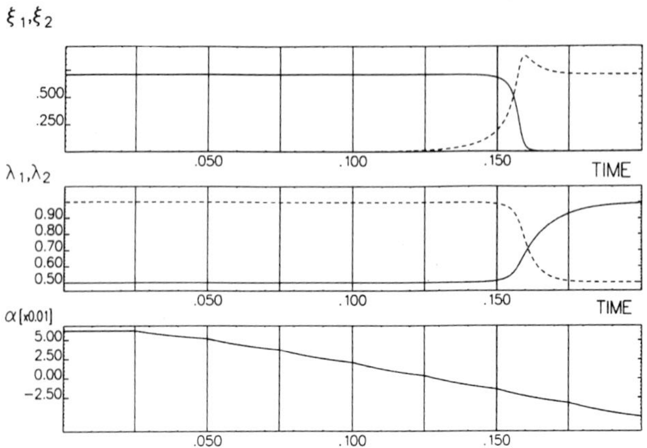


**Fig. 13.22.** The hysteresis effect (see also Fig. 13.23). The solid line refers to the percept "face", the dashed line to the percept "girl". The upper part of this figure shows the time evolution of the order parameters $\xi_1$, $\xi_2$. The sudden switch between the two percepts is clearly visible. The middle panel represents the time evolution of the attention parameters, where the saturation effects are quite pronounced. The bottom part shows the time evolution of the bias $\alpha$. From Ditzinger and Haken (1989)

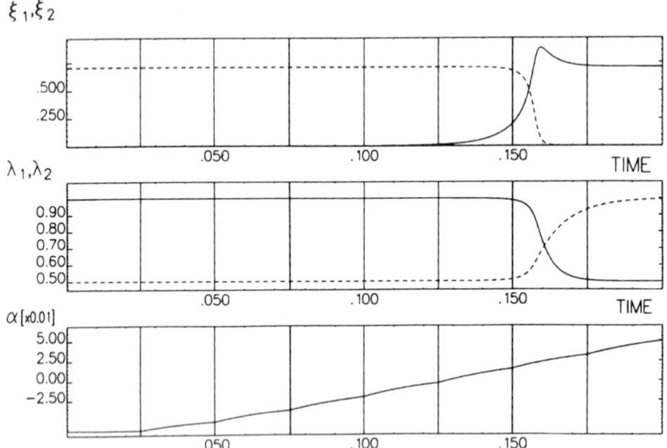


**Fig. 13.23.** As in Fig. 13.22, but for the case in which the pictures of Fig. 13.12 are considered in the reverse order. From Ditzinger and Haken (1989)

look at a second picture, $j=2$. $\alpha_{0j}$ is chosen equal to $\alpha_{02}$, whereas the initial value of $\alpha$, $\alpha(t_2)$, is chosen by means of the solution of (13.32) at its final time, i.e. $t_2=t_1+\tau$. We may continue this procedure in a piecewise fashion, where each time the final value of $\alpha$ in one interval serves as the initial value in the next interval. In this way we obtain a curve such as that shown in the lower part of Fig. 13.22. Simultaneously we solve the equations for $\xi_k$ and $\lambda_k$ where the time evolution of $\alpha(t)$ is taken into account. The time evolution of $\xi_1, \xi_2$ and $\lambda_1, \lambda_2$ is shown in the two upper parts of Fig. 13.22. When we perform the same calculation, now going backwards in time (Fig. 13.23), we immediately find that the crossing over between the two order parameters $\xi_1$ and $\xi_2$ occurs at a different pattern. This then is the hysteresis effect. In fact, the properties $F$ and $H$ can also be realized by (13.31).

## 13.7 The Role of Fluctuations of Attention Parameters

In this section we wish to show how our previous results can be refined when fluctuations of the attention parameters are taken into account. In this way excellent qualitative agreement with psychophysical results obtained by Price (1967) and Borsellino (1982) are obtained. The agreement can even be made quantitative if the fluctuation parameters and the other parameters of the model system are chosen appropriately. We first briefly remind the reader of the basic experiments of Price and of Borsellino et al. Both experiments are based on the fact that human perception of ambiguous patterns oscillates between the two interpretations of the same pattern. Price studied the following effect (Fig. 13.24): When an ambiguous pattern is shown to test persons, the time for which they recognize one or the other pattern itself changes in time, especially during the

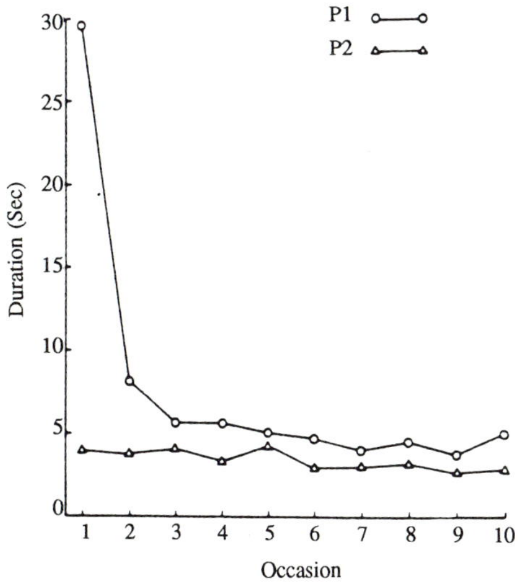


**Fig. 13.24.** Duration of perceived pattern versus occasion of its appearance. From Price (1967)

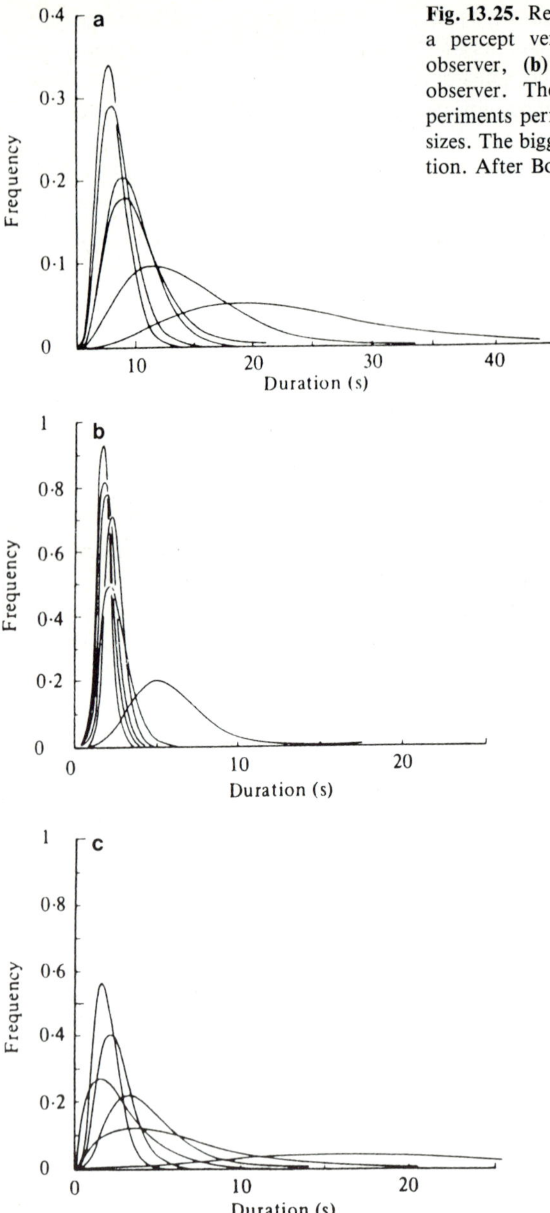


**Fig. 13.25.** Relative frequency of the occurrence of a percept versus its duration for **(a)** a typical observer, **(b)** a fast observer, and **(c)** a slow observer. The different curves result from experiments performed with Necker cubes of various sizes. The bigger the cube, the broader the distribution. After Borsellino et al. (1982)

first few oscillation periods. The duration of recognition of the preferred pattern is initially much longer than that of the less preferred pattern, whereas later on the two times become closer to one another. Borsellino et al. carefully studied the distribution of the oscillation periods, which are not strictly fixed and fluctuate to some extent (Fig. 13.25). By varying the magnification of the objects, e.g. the Necker cubes, shown to the subjects he varied the visual angle (angle subtended by the pattern at the eye) and studied its impact on the fluctuations in the length of the recognition times. On plotting the frequency (number of specific outcomes) versus duration they find a distribution function whose shape and center of gravity depend on the visual angle. While for small angles the distribution function has a narrow width and is located at comparatively short duration times, for increasing angles the width increases and the position of the maximum shifts to longer durations. For different observers the same type of behavior results. Borsellino et al. were able to distinguish between fast, slow and typical observers. In these cases the maxima of the frequency distribution were shifted to shorter times (fast observer) or to longer times (slow observer).

We shall also study the case of three-fold ambiguous patterns. We shall show that the recurrence of perception of a particular interpretation with respect to the other two is no longer unique, i.e. that the sequence in which the interpretation of a specific pattern reoccurs is to some extent random.

### 13.7.1 The Model

To describe the time development of the order parameters we adopt (13.12, 13), or, in the absence of bias, (13.1, 2). The time-dependent attention parameters $\lambda_1$ and $\lambda_2$ are now assumed to obey the equations

$$\dot{\lambda}_1 = a - b\lambda_1 - c\xi_1^2 + F_1(t) \tag{13.33}$$

$$\dot{\lambda}_2 = a - b\lambda_2 - c\xi_2^2 + F_2(t) \ . \tag{13.34}$$

As in the previous section we shall assume that $a = b = c = \gamma$, $\gamma > 0$. However, $\lambda_1$ and $\lambda_2$ are now subjected to fluctuating forces $F_1$ and $F_2$ as indicated in (13.33, 34) above. We shall assume as everywhere in this book that

$$\langle F_j(t) \rangle = 0 \tag{13.35}$$

$$\langle F_j(t) F_k(t') \rangle = \delta_{jk} Q \delta(t - t') \ , \quad j, k = 1, 2 \ . \tag{13.36}$$

In our simulations we shall allow the size of the fluctuations to be varied.

### 13.7.2 Results

The equations (13.12, 13, 33, 34) were solved by means of an Euler forward procedure on a VAX 8300. The impact of the fluctuating forces was mimicked by a random number generator. To simulate the experimental results obtained by Price we made 33 test runs where the initial values $\xi_1(0), \xi_2(0)$ were chosen randomly, taking care of the bias prescribed by $\alpha$. In this way $\xi_j(t)$ curves resulted for each test run. A typical example is shown in Fig. 13.26. The reversion times resulting for each individual percept were then determined as a function of the number of periods after which that time was measured. Eventually these measured values of the durations were averaged and plotted versus the number of oscillations after which this period occurred. The results are plotted in Fig. 13.27 and are in excellent agreement with the result of Price (Fig. 13.24). To obtain this

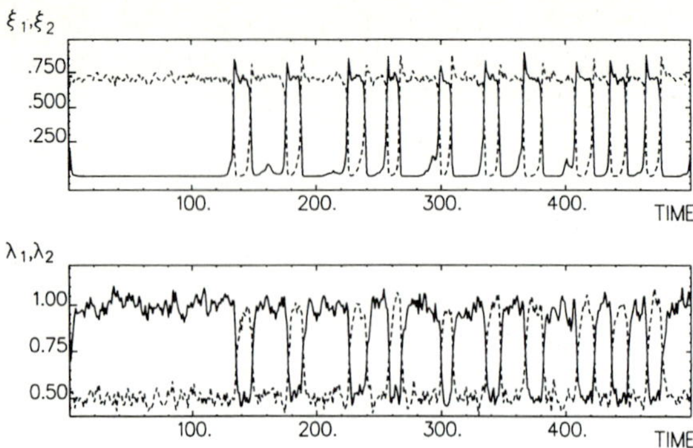


**Fig. 13.26.** Time evolution of the order parameters $\xi_1$, $\xi_2$ and of the attention parameters $\lambda_1$, $\lambda_2$. The statistical variation of the duration of the individual percepts is clearly visible. The results were obtained by integrating equations (13.11, 12, 31, 33, 34). From Ditzinger and Haken (1990)

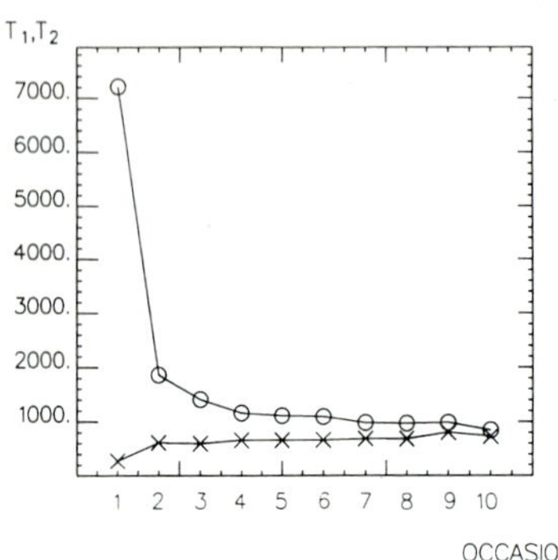


**Fig. 13.27.** Duration versus occasion of percept. Theoretical results. From Ditzinger and Haken (1990)

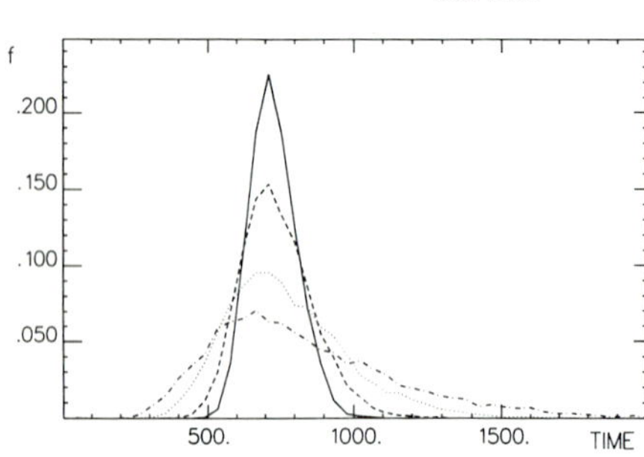


**Fig. 13.28.** Relative frequency versus duration. Theoretical results. The parameters of the fluctuating forces are: $Q = 0.08$ (*solid line*); $Q = 0.12$ (*dashed line*); $Q = 0.2$ (*dotted line*); $Q = 0.3$ (*dash-dotted line*). The other parameters were chosen as $C_1 = 0.2$; $C_2 = 0.25$; $\gamma = 0.11$; $\alpha(t) = 0$; iteration length $5 \cdot 10^6$. From Ditzinger and Haken (1990)

agreement the size of the fluctuating forces had to be fixed. Thus the comparison of our calculation with results of Price allows us to determine that parameter.

In order to simulate the experimental results obtained by Borsellino et al. we proceed in a similar manner. The initial values of $\xi_1, \xi_2$ were chosen at random in the range $0-1$ and the test run was continued long enough to enable us to define a statistics of the frequency of duration, i.e. we could determine a distribution function of frequencies versus duration.

In subsequent test runs the size of the fluctuating forces was changed and each time the distribution function was determined. The resulting curves are

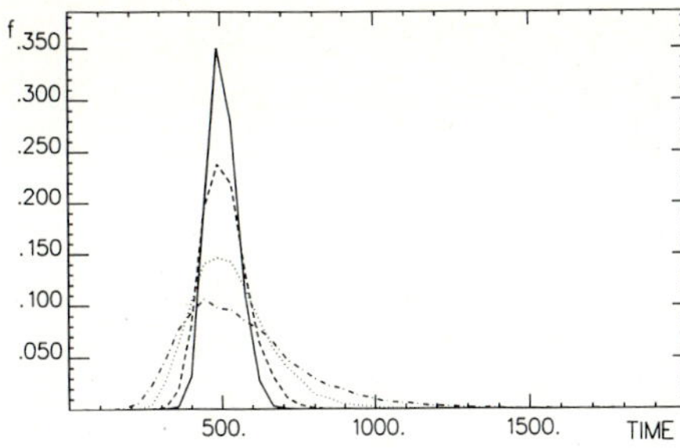


**Fig. 13.29.** Same as Fig. 13.28 but for a fast observer (with $\gamma = 0.15$). From Ditzinger and Haken (1990)

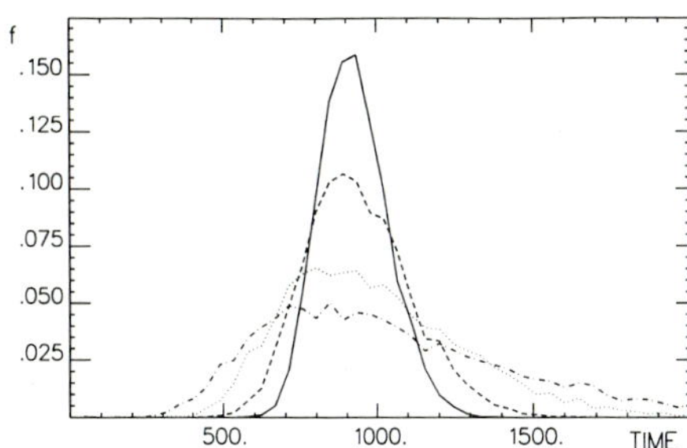


**Fig. 13.30.** Same as Fig. 13.28 but for a slow observer (with $\gamma = 0.09$). From Ditzinger and Haken (1990)

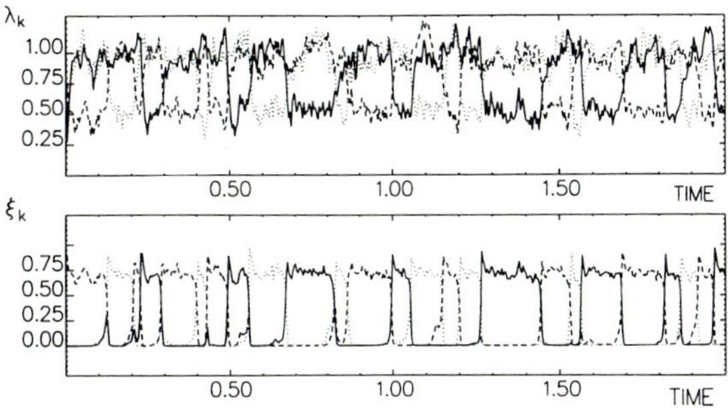


**Fig. 13.31.** Time evolution of the attention parameters $\lambda_k$ and the corresponding order parameters $\xi_k$ for the case of three interpretations within one ambivalent figure. Shown are theoretical results obtained by integrating the corresponding order parameter equations and the equations for the attention parameters under the impact of noise. From Ditzinger and Haken (1990)

shown in Fig. 13.28. They agree qualitatively quite well with the results obtained by Borsellino et al.

In order to compare our results with his results for fast and slow observers we changed the relaxation constant $\gamma$ of the attention parameters. The results are shown in Figs. 13.29 and 13.30. Again quite a good qualitative agreement is found which can be made, to some extent, quantitative when the parameters are chosen appropriately.

Finally we studied the impact of fluctuations on the reoccurrence of pattern interpretation when 3 interpretations are possible. The results are shown in Fig. 13.31. As is evident, the patterns are recognized in a random sequence.

### 13.7.3 Discussion

One might ask whether fluctuations act only on the attention parameters or also on the order parameters describing recognition. Our numerical results, which took into account both kinds of fluctuations, showed that meaningful results can be obtained only when we allow for the impact of fluctuations on the *attention parameters* but not on the order parameters. These results need not necessarily exclude the possibility that fluctuations acting directly on the order parameters play some role. But as a general conclusion we may definitely state that the impact of the fluctuations on the attention parameters is by far the more important.

The good agreement between our results and the experimental results of Borsellino et al. is surely quite significant. It supports the idea that the change in shape and position of the distribution function found in Borsellino's experiments can be explained by a change in the size of the fluctuations. As mentioned before, the experimentally determined distribution function changed as a function of the vision angle. This function became broader with increasing vision angle (magnification). In our interpretation this means that the attention parameters had to fluctuate more intensely with a bigger vision angle which is certainly a plausible assumption.

# 14. Dynamic Pattern Recognition of Coordinated Biological Motion

## 14.1 Introduction. Perception of Structure in Biological Motion

So far in this book we have been concerned with static patterns. As humans, we may also recognize patterns of movement such as walking and trotting of horses. This leads us to ask whether movement patterns can also be recognized by the synergetic computer.

Let us first consider some classical experiments on human perception. Classical demonstrations by Johansson (1973) attest to the fact that the visual system can extract rather abstract information from optics. Using only lights mounted on the joints of a human, Johansson showed that perceivers could easily determine whether the (otherwise invisible) person was walking, climbing, performing press-ups, and so forth. Cutting and colleagues, in an extensive set of studies, using "point light walker displays" have shown that even the gender of a walking person can be accurately determined, merely from the relational structure among the lights, with all other clues removed [see Cutting and Proffitt (1981) for a review]. Similarly, observers can recognize themselves and others from these time-varying displays, which evidently carry somehow an individual's signature. Hoenkamp (1978) and Todd (1983) in studies of computer-animated stick figures have provided evidence that the perception of human gait (walk, run, limp) is influenced by certain variables, such as the movements of the lower leg and ankle joint. With these exceptions, however, [see also Bingham (1987)], the nature of the perceptual information extracted from biological motion remains a mystery. The only certainty is that the visual system can extract whatever this information is and use it to make decisions remarkably quickly (e.g. $<400$ ms in Johansson's studies).

On the computational side, Hoffman and Flinchbaugh (1982) have used hypothesized anatomical constraints – that each limb tends to move approximately in a single plane for extended periods of time – to develop structure-from-planar-motion algorithms. In our approach, we use functional, spatio-temporal constraints that have been found in studies of coordinated behavioral patterns and their dynamics (Sect. 14.4).

Our approach to the recognition of dynamic patterns of biological motion is continuous with the methods described previously, but it uses order parameters that have been identified in studies of coordinated behavioral patterns as the relevant macroscopic observables (Haken et al. 1985) upon which to base the encoding of prototypes. In this sense, the dynamics of the synergetic computer for the recognition process is specific to the order parameters that characterize the formation of those patterns.

## 14.2 The Pattern Generation and Pattern Recognition Experiments

We do not know a priori, of course, what the order parameters for coordinated patterns of biological motion are. In fact, in a structurally complex system (for a human ≈ 100 joints, 792 muscles) it is nontrivial to determine and measure such patterns. As was shown in Chap. 4, in synergetics we use nonequilibrium phase transitions, i.e. qualitative changes in a system's behavior as a means of identifying order parameters for patterns and their nonlinear dynamics (stability, loss of stability, etc.). In fact, in a number of cases, features predicted for nonequilibrium phase transitions have been observed in coordinated movements, and the mechanisms underlying these transitions have been identified [e.g. loss of stability as seen in fluctuation enhancement; critical slowing down of the order parameter; hysteresis, etc., see e.g. Haken (1988, Chap. 11) and Kelso et al. (1987) for recent reviews].

The work was originally done on an experimental model system involving bimanual coordination by Kelso (1981, 1984), and Kelso and Scholz (1985) but has since been generalized to a wide variety of different contexts, including multicomponent (quadrupedal) gait patterns [Schöner et al. (1986)]. Both bimanual (Haken et al. 1985) and gait (Haken and Lorenz 1987) patterns – specified by the relative phases of the components, which act as order parameters – can be derived from the model of coupled nonlinear oscillators.

Here we use recently discovered phase transition in single, multijoint limb movements (Kelso et al. 1989) as an example of changes between movement patterns. There is little doubt, however, that the method we shall develop in this chapter may be used to recognize other patterns of biological motion such as those described in Sect. 14.2. A graphical display of two of the basic patterns produced by a human subject in shown in Fig. 14.1. The multiple vectors connecting infrared light emitting diodes placed on the subject's shoulder, elbow, wrist and hand nicely illustrate observed patterns. Briefly, different initial conditions were studied:

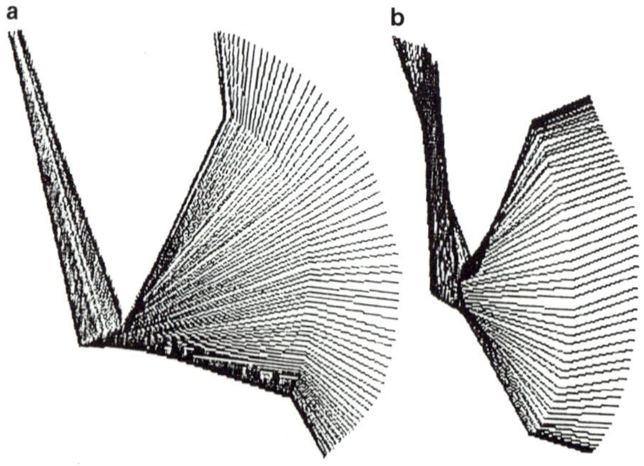


**Fig. 14.1a, b.** Graphic representation of the two basic patterns of multijoint arm motion observed in the experiments of Kelso et al. (1989). Infrared light emitting diodes (IRLEDs) are placed on the shoulder, elbow, wrist and hand. The vectors are created by joining the IRLEDs together. One half cycle is shown for each pattern. From Haken et al. (1990)

1) Flex (extend) the elbow and flex (extend) the wrist together in a cyclical fashion (in-phase) (Fig. 14.1 a);
2) Flex the elbow while extending the wrist, and vice versa (anti-phase) (Fig. 14.1 b).

These two tasks were performed with the forearm pronated or supinated. Subjects were instructed to synchronize peak elbow flexion to an auditory metronome whose frequency increased from 1.0 Hz in steps of 0.25 Hz with 10 cycles of motion per frequency value. The subjects were told that, should they feel the pattern of movement begin to change, they should not resist the change (analogous to the "do not intervene" instruction used in many limb perturbation studies). The subject's task was always to maintain a one-to-one frequency relationship with the metronome. As in earlier work on phase transitions in hand movements, when the forearm was in the supine posture, condition 2 (the antiphase mode of coordination) switched to the in-phase pattern (condition 1) at a certain critical frequency, but not vice versa.

The relative phase dynamics identified earlier by Haken et al. (1985) for the switching dynamics between the hands may easily be applied to this work on single, multicomponent limb movements, thereby, allowing a detailed characterization of the individual patterns and their dynamics. Specifically:

1) Two stable patterns, corresponding to attractors of the relative phase dynamics, exist in rhythmical multijoint limb movements. Which one is observed depends on the initial preparation of the system;
2) A transition from one attractor to the other occurs at a critical control parameter value;
3) Beyond the transition, only one pattern is observed, i.e. the system shifts from a bistable to monostable regime:
4) When the control parameter, frequency, is decreased, the system remains in the same basin of attraction, i.e., together with the phase transition (2), it exhibits hysteresis;
5) Predicted features of nonequilibrium phase transitions, such as critical fluctuations in the order parameter, i.e. the relative phase, are also observed in the experiments (Kelso et al. 1989).

We can now use these results to create synthetic displays with a computer in order to determine whether subjects can identify and categorize these patterns based on the order parameter, relative phase. Forms of motion are captured by modeling articulated limbs as a collection of rigid, connected segments (Fig. 14.2), although point light displays can also be easily created (Kelso and Pandya 1989).

It is possible to synthesize displays that differ only in the phase relationship among different moving components, thereby creating a physical continuum of values from which one can test the ability of persons or the computer to categorize. Stimuli consist of three connected line segments, whose orientations and relative positions may be varied in a cyclic fashion as a function of time. The line segments represent a human arm that performs a motion with different phase relationships between the upper arm, forearm and hand (Figs. 14.1 and 14.2).

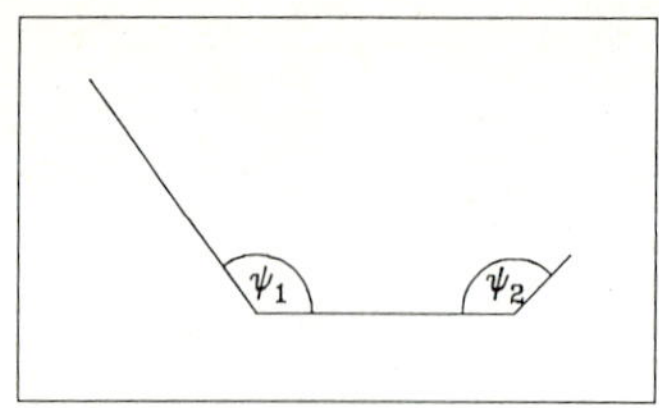


**Fig. 14.2.** Definition of the angles involved in Fig. 14.1. From Haken et al. (1990)

Thirteen displays were constructed with the phase angle between elbow and wrist changing in 30° intervals from 0° to 360°. A sequence of 130 displays was created using each of the 13 displays ten times, and then randomizing them. The observers were seated in front of the video monitor and first presented with the two basic patterns, called $A$ (Fig. 14.1a) and $B$ (Fig. 14.1b). The actual arm motions corresponding to these two dynamic patterns were also demonstrated to subjects. Subjects then carefully examined each subsequent display and indicated on an answer sheet whether the pattern belonged to class $A$ or class $B$. Each display consisted of two complete cycles of arm motion with a fixed relative phase. There was a five second interval between the displays for the observer to respond. The results of the identification or labeling test were unambiguous: Labeling probabilities changed abruptly along the continuum for all ten subjects tested. Around a phase difference of 90°, the identification function possessed a rather steep slope, indicating a category boundary. Mean variability of response was negligible within each category but was quite large at the boundary, defining the point at which responses in both categories were equiprobable. Again around 270°, large variability accompanied by a steep slope revealed a second boundary between the two categories. Note that due to the $2\pi$ periodicity of relative phase, the phase angles of 0° and 360° correspond to the same anchor point (Fig. 14.1a), while 180° corresponds to the second anchor (Fig. 14.1b).

Although much more experimental work can be done here, the pattern recognition experiment reveals that human observers can readily categorize dynamic visual patterns into one "gait" or another. Notwithstanding the availability of many other sources of visual input, subjects appear to classify the patterns according to the identified order parameter, relative phase. Meaningful information, in the present case, may be said to lie in attractors of the relevant phase dynamics (Kelso 1989). Thus, relative phase may be introduced into our pattern recognition algorithm as a relevant (low-dimensional) macroscopic feature capable of distinguishing different dynamic patterns.

## 14.3 The Behavioral Pattern Recognition Algorithm

In this section we develop an algorithm that enables the recognition of biological patterns. Such patterns may be different kinds of hand movements, for instance those of a parallel or antiparallel kind, human walking or running, or the different gaits of quadrupeds, such as horses. We characterize the movement by a set of angles $\psi_k(t)$ which are attached to each joint. These angles are, of course, time dependent and in the case that we analyse in detail (Sect. 14.4) are given by the angles $\psi_1$ and $\psi_2$ in Fig. 14.2 ($k = 1, 2$). Focussing our attention on rhythmic movements, we may represent $\psi_k(t)$ as a Fourier series in the form

$$\psi_k(t) = a_{k0} + \sum_{l=1}^{\infty} [a_{kl} \cos(\omega l t) + b_{kl} \sin(\omega l t)] \tag{14.1}$$

or

$$\psi_k(t) = a_{k0} + \sum_{l=1}^{\infty} A_{kl} \cos(\omega l t + \phi_{kl}) \ . \tag{14.2}$$

It will be sufficient to take only a few terms into account, although the exact number of terms, $N_k$, may depend on the joint $k$. The $\psi_k(t)$ is then characterized by the set

$$\{a_{k0}, a_{kl}, b_{kl}\} \tag{14.3}$$

or

$$\{a_{k0}, A_{kl}, \phi_{kl}\} \tag{14.4}$$

where these alternative descriptions are related by

$$A_{kl}^2 = a_{kl}^2 + b_{kl}^2 \ , \quad \phi_{kl} = \arctan \frac{b_{kl}}{a_{kl}} \ . \tag{14.5}$$

In order to ensure that the recognition process is invariant with respect to time shifts, we introduce the relative phase; for instance, we may fix the angle $\phi_{1l}$, or any other phase angle, as a suitable reference.

A pattern of movement is therefore characterized by the magnitudes $A_{kl}$ and the relative phases $(\phi_{kl} - l\phi_{1l})$ which we lump together in a vector $\boldsymbol{v}$.

Furthermore we wish to distinguish between different patterns so that we supplement the quantities occurring in (14.4) by an upper index u, and, in analogy to our previous treatments of the recognition of static patterns, we label the pattern u by a number $c_{\mathrm{u}}$ that identifies the pattern uniquely.

We then introduce the total pattern vector by means of

$$\boldsymbol{v}_{\mathrm{u}} = (a_{k0}^{(\mathrm{u})}, A_{kl}^{(\mathrm{u})}, \phi_{kl}^{(\mathrm{u})} - l\phi_{1l}^{(\mathrm{u})}, c_{\mathrm{u}}) \ . \tag{14.6}$$

The further steps in our approach are in complete analogy to the pattern recognition procedure presented in Chap. 5. For the $M$ prototype patterns $\boldsymbol{v}_{\mathrm{u}}$ we introduce the adjoint vectors $\boldsymbol{v}_{\mathrm{u}}^{+}$ and require

$$(\boldsymbol{v}_{\mathrm{u}}^{+} \boldsymbol{v}_{\mathrm{u}'}) = \delta_{\mathrm{uu}'} \ , \quad \boldsymbol{v}_{\mathrm{u}}^{+} = \sum_{\mathrm{u}'=1}^{M} g_{\mathrm{uu}'} \bar{\boldsymbol{v}}_{\mathrm{u}'} \ . \tag{14.7}$$

A newly offered test pattern will be described by the vector $\boldsymbol{q}$ which is constructed in complete analogy to (14.6), but without the component $c_{\mathrm{u}}$.

We then introduce the order parameters $\xi_u$ via the scalar product

$$\xi_u = (v_u^+ q) \quad . \tag{14.8}$$

The order parameters are subjected to the dynamics presented in Sect. 5.3

$$\dot{\xi}_u = \xi_u(\lambda - 2D + \xi_u^2) \ , \quad D = \sum_{u'=1}^{M} \xi_{u'}^2 \ . \tag{14.9}$$

According to this dynamics, any test pattern vector $q$ will be pulled into one and only one prototype vector $v_u$, namely the one to which it is most similar. As was demonstrated for the case of static patterns, this method allows us to restore the pattern, i.e. if an incomplete set of data is given, the whole pattern will be found. It allows the discrimination of patterns and as a by-product also their identification. As a consequence of (14.9), only one $\xi_{u_0}$ is different from zero when the dynamics has reached its stationary state. The corresponding restored and identified pattern is then given by $v_{u_0}$.

## 14.4 Application and Results

In order to test our pattern recognition algorithm in detail, we use the simulated data corresponding to the pattern generation experiment described in Sect. 14.2 (Kelso et al. 1989). Figure 14.2 defines the angles $\psi_1$ and $\psi_2$. The time series $\psi_k(t)$, $k = 1, 2$ are determined from the simulation of the multijoint trajectory experiment (Sect. 14.4) using the dynamics of Haken et al. (1985) where a transition from antiphase motion to in-phase motion takes place during the course of time. The time series of the angles and of the difference between them are plotted in Fig. 14.3. Our aim now is to apply the formalism described in the previous section to these time series, i.e., to classify the movement patterns. Because we wanted to distinguish between antiphase and in-phase motion, we built two pro-

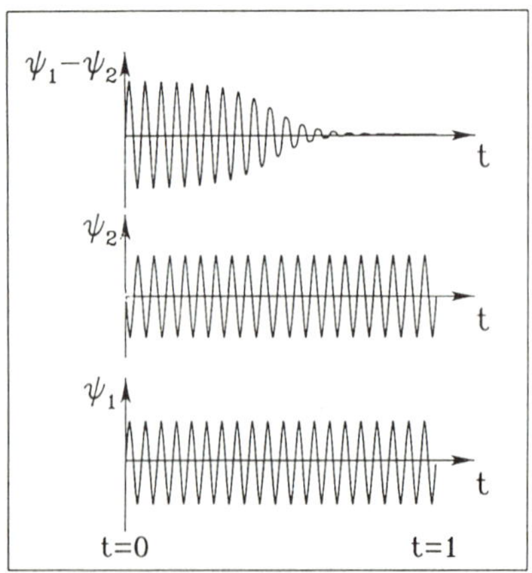


**Fig. 14.3.** Time behavior of the angles $\psi_1$-$\psi_2$, $\psi_2$, $\psi_1$ during the transition from antiphase to inphase motion. From Haken et al. (1990)

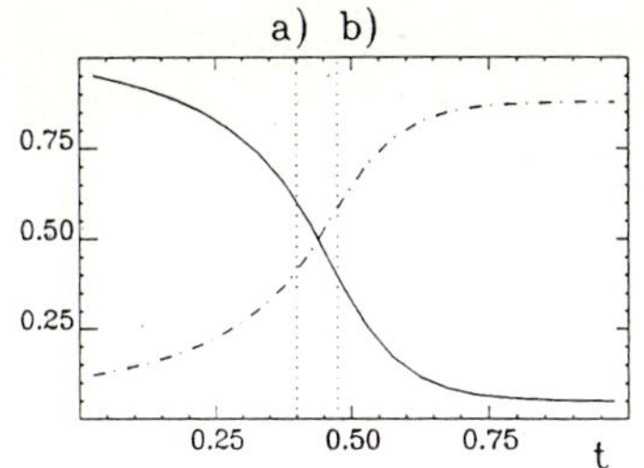


**Fig. 14.4.** Initial values of $\xi_a$ and $\xi_i$ for the different states of the transition. On the left-hand side the antiphase motion is predominant, whereas on the right-hand side the algorithm indicates in-phase motion. From Haken et al. (1990)

totype vectors $\boldsymbol{v}_a$ and $\boldsymbol{v}_i$ as described above, using the magnitudes and relative phases of a Fourier transformation from the first and the last cycle of the time series in Fig. 14.3 at $t = 0$ and $t = 1$. The components $c_a$ and $c_i$, which label the corresponding patterns are set to $-0.5$ and $0.5$, respectively, and the adjoint vectors $\boldsymbol{v}_a^+$ and $\boldsymbol{v}_i^+$ defined by (14.7) were calculated.

Then each cycle of the time series was Fourier transformed, and the vectors $\boldsymbol{q}$, constructed from the resulting Fourier coefficients, served as test patterns for our recognition algorithm. In these cases the components $c_q$ were set to 0. Figure 14.4 shows the time behavior of the order parameters $\xi_a$ and $\xi_i$, given as the scalar product between $\boldsymbol{q}$ and the adjoint vectors, during the transition.

At the cross-over point a switch from the antiphase to the in-phase motion is identified, thereby illustrating that our procedure is capable of classification. Figure 14.5 shows the time evolution of the $\xi_k$ according to the pattern recognition algorithm described in Chap. 5. In Fig. 14.5a the antiphase motion is the predominant one. As we see, the corresponding value of $\xi_a$ increases to a saturation value of 1, whereas the other one, $\xi_i$, referring to the in-phase motion decays to zero. The label $c$ reaches the value $-0.5$ indicating antiphase motion. Figure 14.5b shows the opposite case in which the recognition system indicates in-phase motion. In this section we have shown how behavioral patterns, specifically visually constructed multijoint limb trajectory patterns, can be recognized and categorized. The algorithm can identify both stable patterns and the transition between the patterns. An important feature of the present ap-

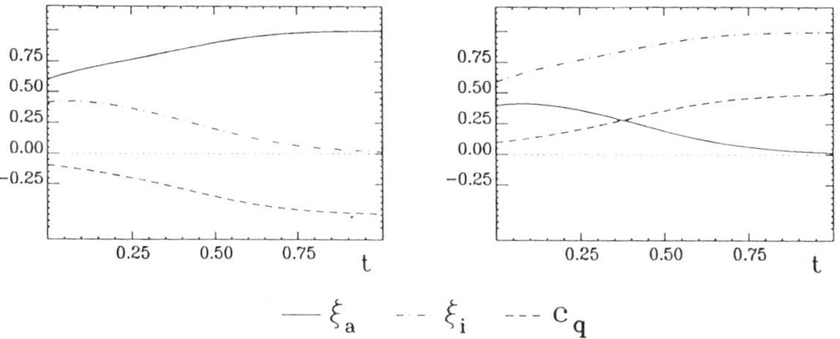


**Fig. 14.5.** Simulations of the dynamics (14.9) for the two cases labeled **(a)** and **(b)** in Fig. 14.4 (see text). From Haken et al. (1990)

proach is its use of the order parameter concept (in this case the relative phases) as a characterization of the behavioral patterns. Order parameters have proved to be an adequate macroscopic observable on which to base the recognition of dynamic patterns. It is clear from our results that the whole approach can be significantly generalized, for instance to more complicated patterns of biological motion, e.g. the point light displays created by walking, running, lifting weights, etc. (Sects. 14.1, 14.2), see e.g. Johansson (1973).

Until now we have assumed that the motion occurs in a plane perpendicular to the direction of observation. We now wish to generalize our approach in at least two ways:

1) As in Johansson's experiments the only information on the subject's motion, such as walking or running, is provided by the motion of lights at the joints.
2) The motion occurs in a plane that may be rotated with respect to the plane of the observer by a time-independent angle $\alpha$.

Finally we shall generalize our analysis to the case of a time-dependent angle, $\alpha$.

## 14.5 Recognition of Patterns of Movement Characterized only be Specific Light Spots

In the preceding section we showed how the algorithm of a synergetic computer can distinguish between movement patterns. In this case the movement pattern was produced by a human arm with its in-phase and antiphase motion characterized by the angles beween upper and lower arm and between lower arm and hand. In this section we want to go one step further. As mentioned above, early ex-

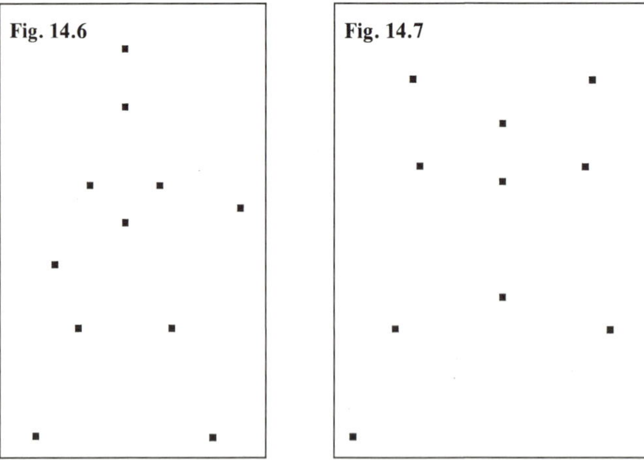


**Fig. 14.6.** Random dots or . . . ? From R. Haas et al. (1990), as are all of the figures in this section

**Fig. 14.7.** Random dots or . . . ?

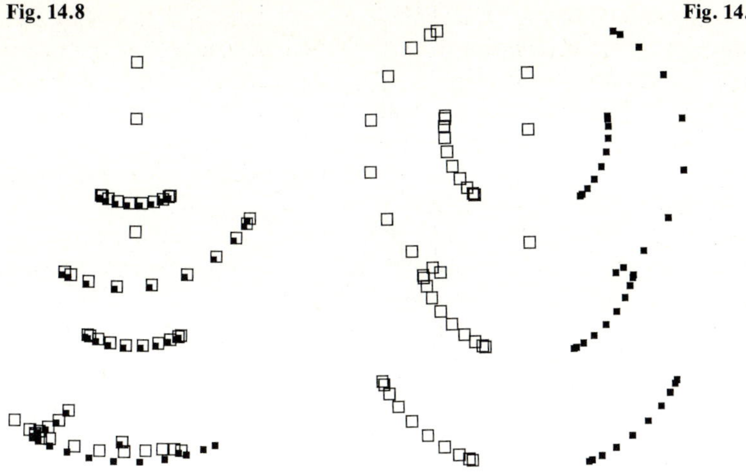


**Fig. 14.8.** Stroboscopic picture of the motion of the dots of Fig. 14.6

**Fig. 14.9.** Stroboscopic picture of the motion of the dots of Fig. 14.7

periments on human recognition of movement patterns have shown that humans can detect these patterns even when the only source of visual information is light emitting diodes fixed at the joints. We now wish to show how this problem can be solved by computers. Typical configurations of light spots are shown in Figs. 14.6, 7. Quite evidently it is impossible for a human observer (or a computer) to make any sense out of these points. The situation changes immediately for the human observer when the individual dots move, as was shown by Johansson. Figures 14.8, 9 show stroboscopic pictures of the movement of these dots. To analyze these patterns we proceed in the following steps. We first let the computer find out which moving dots belong to the same limb section, e.g. lower arm. This is achieved by requiring that the distance between the corre-

**Table 14.1.** Integer numbers label the dots and the other entries specify the separations in cases where these are constant. Dashes imply non-constant, i.e. time-dependent separations

| | 1 | 2 | 3 | 4 | 5 | 6 | 7 | 8 | 9 | 10 | 11 |
|---|---|---|---|---|---|---|---|---|---|---|---|
| 1 | – | 2.60 | – | – | – | – | – | – | – | 2.60 | – |
| 2 | 2.60 | – | – | – | – | – | – | – | – | – | – |
| 3 | – | – | – | 2.60 | – | – | – | – | – | 2.60 | – |
| 4 | – | – | 2.60 | – | – | – | – | – | – | – | – |
| 5 | – | – | – | – | – | 3.46 | – | – | 3.46 | – | – |
| 6 | – | – | – | – | 3.46 | – | – | – | – | – | – |
| 7 | – | – | – | – | – | – | – | 3.46 | 3.46 | – | – |
| 8 | – | – | – | – | – | – | 3.46 | – | – | – | – |
| 9 | – | – | – | – | 3.46 | – | 3.46 | – | – | 3.46 | 5.20 |
| 10 | 2.60 | – | 2.60 | – | – | – | – | – | 3.46 | – | 1.73 |
| 11 | – | – | – | – | – | – | – | – | 5.20 | 1.73 | – |

**Fig. 14.10** **Fig. 14.11**

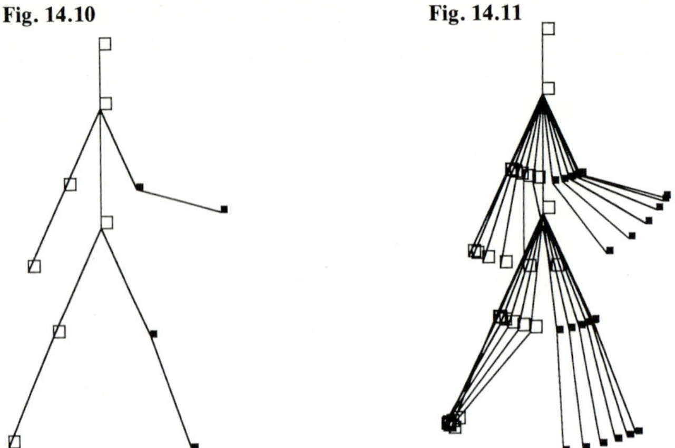

**Fig. 14.10.** Reconstruction of stick figure belonging to Fig. 14.6

**Fig. 14.11.** Stroboscopic reconstruction the stick figure belonging to Fig. 14.8

**Fig. 14.12** **Fig. 14.13**

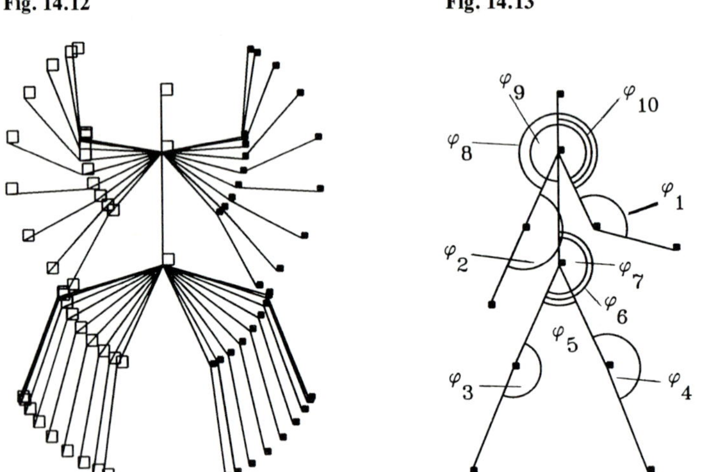


**Fig. 14.12.** Stroboscopic reconstruction of the stick figure belonging to Fig. 14.9

**Fig. 14.13.** Definition of the angles $\phi_k$

sponding pair of dots remains constant in time. Denoting the coordinates of dot $j$ by $\boldsymbol{x}_j(t) = [x_j(t), y_j(t)]$, the computer has to sort out those pairs $j, k$ for which

$$|(\boldsymbol{x}_j - \boldsymbol{x}_k)(\dot{\boldsymbol{x}}_j - \dot{\boldsymbol{x}}_k)| < \varepsilon \ .$$

The result of this calculation is shown in Table 14.1.

The resulting reconstruction of the underlying figures is shown in Fig. 14.10 and, when movement is taken into account, in Fig. 14.11. Figure 14.12 shows the corresponding results for the second kind of movement treated (Fig. 14.9). In order to classify the different kinds of movement patterns, we then let the computer determine the angles according to Fig. 14.13. This is a simple trigonometric task, because the vectors $\boldsymbol{x}_j - \boldsymbol{x}_k, \boldsymbol{x}_k - \boldsymbol{x}_l$ at the joint $k$ are known. In the next step the computer has to plot the time dependence of the phase angles as shown in Figs. 14.14 and 14.15. Now we are in the same position as we were in the preceding section when we took the time dependence of the angles at the joints as the starting point of our analysis. In complete analogy to that treatment, we now Fourier analyze the angles $\phi_k(t)$. The left-hand side of Fig. 14.16 shows the absolute value of the amplitudes, the right-hand side the corresponding phases. The abscissa denotes the index of the Fourier component $n = 0$, 1, 2, etc. Figure 14.17 represents the same results but for the second movement pattern. The two types of movement pattern are next encoded by means of the following vectors

$$v_{\mathrm{u}} = (a_{k0}^{(\mathrm{u})}, A_{kn}^{(\mathrm{u})}, \phi_{kn}^{(\mathrm{u})} - n\phi_{1n}^{(\mathrm{u})}, c^{(\mathrm{u})}) \ .$$

In order to distinguish the two prototype patterns from one another, we added the label $c^{(\mathrm{u})}$. In our practical calculations we chose $k = 1, \ldots, 11$ and $a_{k0}^{(\mathrm{u})}, A_{kn}^{(\mathrm{u})}, \phi_{kn}^{(\mathrm{u})}$ for $n = 1, \ldots 4, c^{(1)} = 0.5$ and $c^{(2)} = -0.5$ for motions 1 and 2, respectively. The formalism is then the same as in the preceding section; typical results are shown in Figs. 14.18 and 14.19.

## 14.6 Recognition of Movement Patterns in a Plane Other than that Perpendicular to the Observer

We study the following problem: As in Sect. 14.5 the movement of a person or animal is characterized by the movement of points at the individual joints. But we shall now allow the person or animal to move in a plane that makes an angle $\alpha$ to the plane of the screen onto which the points are projected; this angle $\alpha$ is not known to the observer. Later on we shall allow the plane of movement to rotate, so that $\alpha$ becomes a time-dependent function, again unknown to the observer. The coordinates of the screen of the observer are called $x$ and $y$, those of the moving object in its plane of movement $x', y'$. We assume that the plane of movement is rotated around the vertical axis. The relations between $x, y$ and $x', y'$ are given by

$$x = x' \cos \alpha \tag{14.10}$$

$$y = y' \ . \tag{14.11}$$

Our first task will it be to identify those (moving) points which are rigidly connected by limbs. We label the corresponding pairs of points by $i$ and $j$. Because the lengths of the limbs do not change during motion, we have to search for combinations $i, j$ which satisfy

$$|\mathbf{r}_i'(t) - \mathbf{r}_j'(t)|^2 = \text{const} \tag{14.12}$$

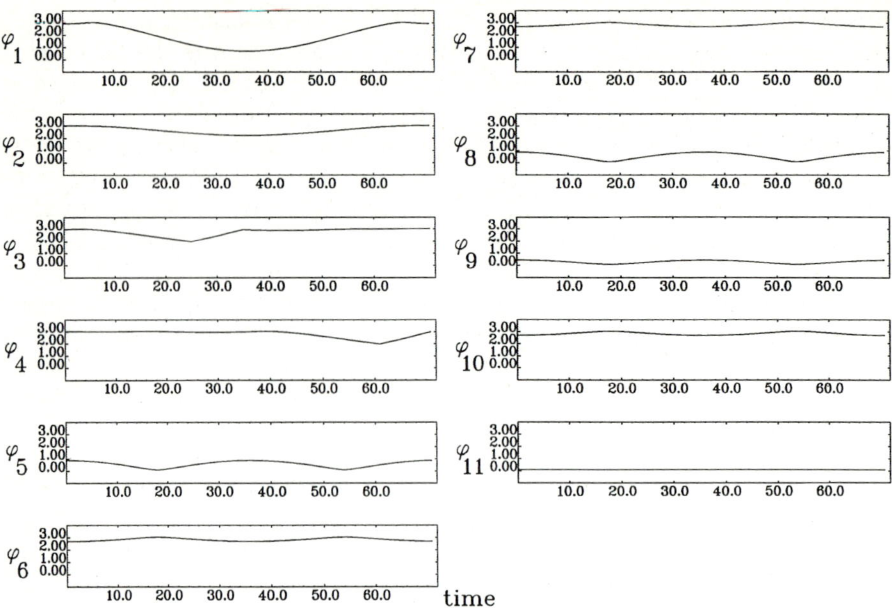


**Fig. 14.14.** Time dependence of the angles $\phi_k(k)$ corresponding to Fig. 14.11

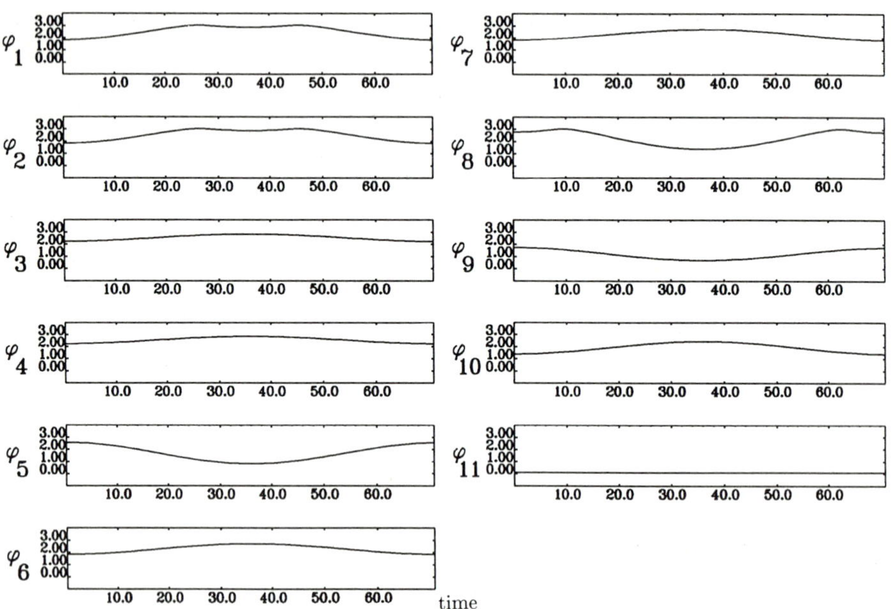


**Fig. 14.15.** Time dependence of angles $\phi_k(t)$ corresponding to Fig. 14.12

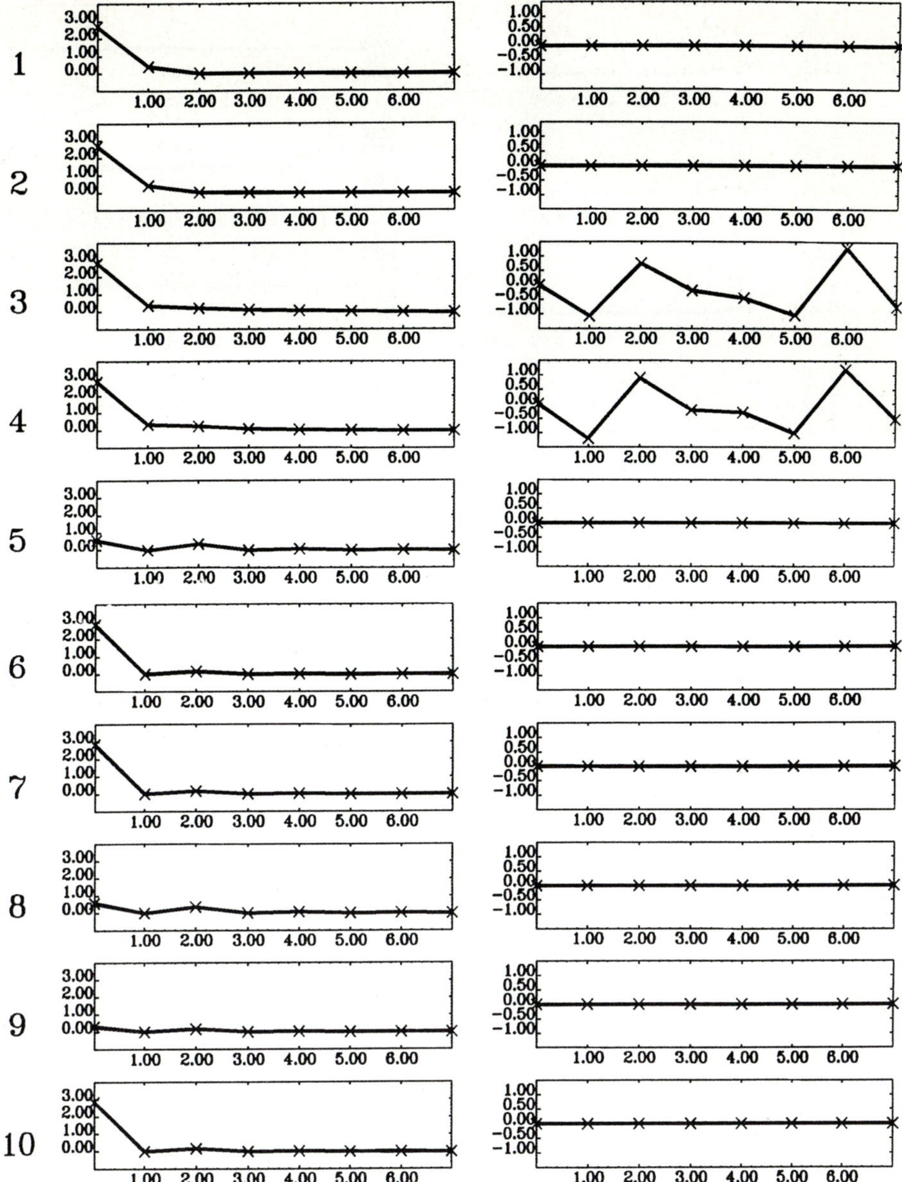


**Fig. 14.16.** Fourier amplitudes (*left*) and phases of $\phi_k(t)$ (*right*) for Fig. 14.14

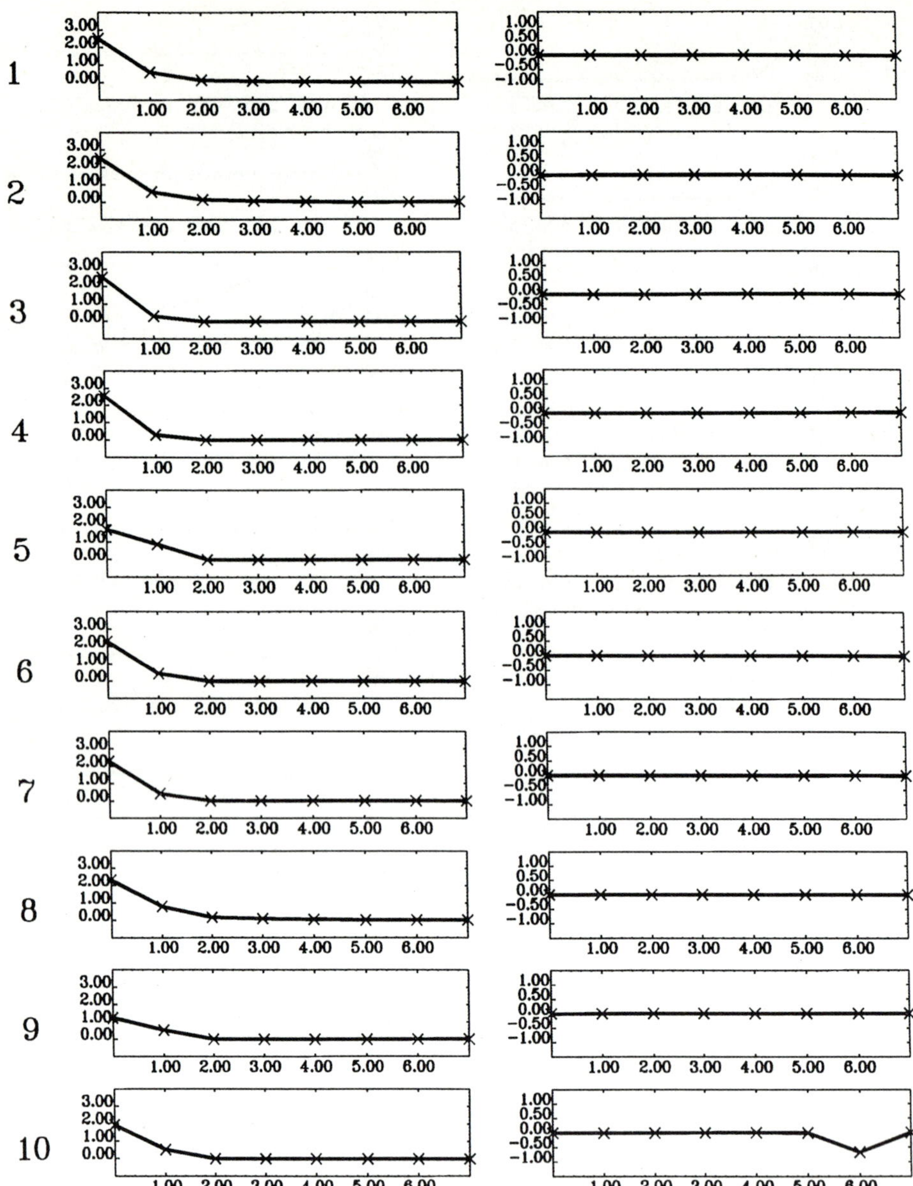


**Fig. 14.17.** Fourier amplitudes (*left*) and phases of $\phi_k(t)$ (*right*) for Fig. 14.15

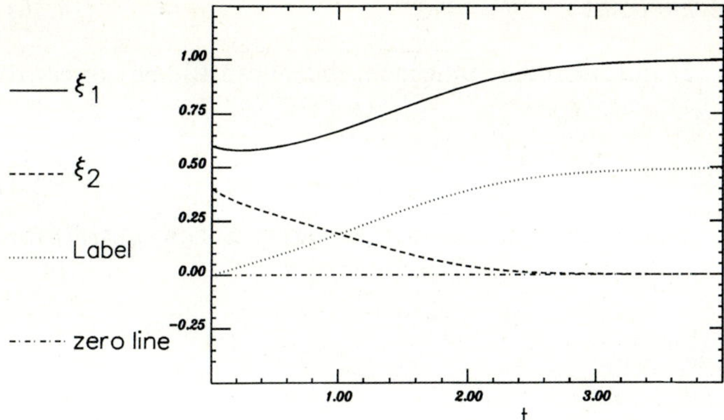


**Fig. 14.18.** Time evolution of the order parameters $\xi_u = (\boldsymbol{v}_u^+ \boldsymbol{q})$, u = 1,2 for a pattern $\boldsymbol{q}$ which is more similar to $\boldsymbol{v}_1$. The dotted curve is the time evolution of "label" $c_u$

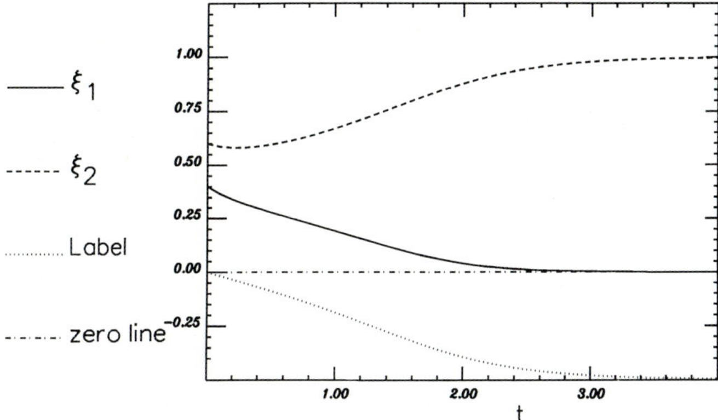


**Fig. 14.19.** Same as Fig. 14.18 but for a different pattern $\boldsymbol{q}$

where the constant is of course time independent. Writing out (14.12) in components, we obtain

$$[x_i'(t)-x_j'(t)]^2+[y_i'(t)-y_j'(t)]^2 = \text{const} \ . \tag{14.13}$$

We introduce the abbreviation

$$\Delta x_{ij} = x_i - x_j \tag{14.14}$$

and use the relation (14.10) to obtain

$$\frac{1}{\cos^2\alpha}(\Delta x_{ij})+(\Delta y_{ij})^2 = \text{const} \ . \tag{14.15}$$

We assume that $\alpha$ is time independent and may thus multiply (14.15) by $\cos^2\alpha$ to yield

$$(\Delta x_{ij})^2 + \cos^2\alpha\,(\Delta y_{ij})^2 = \text{const} \ . \tag{14.16}$$

The condition that (14.12) and (14.16) are time independent can also be expressed in the form

$$\Delta x_{ij}\,\Delta \dot{x}_{ij} + \cos^2\alpha\,\Delta y_{ij}\,\Delta \dot{y}_{ij} = 0 \tag{14.17}$$

where the dots above $x_{ij}$ and $y_{ij}$ indicate the time derivative. Solving (14.17) for $\cos^2\alpha$, we obtain

$$\frac{\Delta x_{ij}\,\Delta \dot{x}_{ij}}{\Delta y_{ij}\,\Delta \dot{y}_{ij}} = -\cos^2\alpha_{ij} \equiv A_{ij} \ . \tag{14.18}$$

We now have to insert the time sequences of the observed data on the left-hand side in order to check whether $\cos\alpha_{ij}(t)$ is time independent, or equivalently whether

$$\frac{dA_{ij}}{dt} = 0 \ . \tag{14.19}$$

The relationship (14.19) can be checked by computer calculations. The computer then has to sort out those combinations of $i$ and $j$ for which (14.19) is fulfilled. In order to verify that the individually identified pairs $ij, kl, \ldots$ describe motion in the same plane, we have to check that

$$A_{ij} = A_{kl} \ , \quad ij \neq kl \ . \tag{14.20}$$

In a generalization of our approach we assume that there is a finite distance $l$ between the plane in which the center of the person or animal moves and the plane in which the limb movement occurs. The relation (14.10) then generalizes to

$$x = l\sin\alpha + x'\cos\alpha \ , \tag{14.21}$$

or when we solve for $x'$, to

$$x' = \frac{1}{\cos\alpha}(x - l\sin\alpha) \ . \tag{14.22}$$

Again we have to study the time dependence or time independence of (14.13). Generalizing the previous steps, this amounts to verifying the time independence of

$$(\Delta x_{ij} - 2l\sin\alpha)^2 + \Delta y_{ij}^2\cos^2\alpha \tag{14.23}$$

or equivalently to checking whether the equation

$$(\Delta x_{ij} - 2l\sin\alpha)\,\Delta \dot{x}_{ij} + \Delta y_{ij}\,\Delta \dot{y}_{ij}\cos^2\alpha = 0 \tag{14.24}$$

holds. In this equation $l$ and $\alpha$ are still unknowns. By inserting the values of

$$\Delta x_{ij}, \Delta \dot{x}_{ij}, \Delta y_{ij}, \Delta \dot{y}_{ij} \tag{14.25}$$

at different times, we may establish a system of equations for $l$ and $\sin\alpha$ which may be solved to yield definite values of $l$ and $\alpha$. Inserting further values for the quantities (14.25) at still different times, one may check the consistency of the solution for $l$ and $\alpha$. If a solution can be found, then the pair $ij$ is coupled by the relationship (14.12), otherwise the points $i$ and $j$ are not rigidly connected by a limb bone.

We now consider a second generalization, namely the case in which $\alpha$ is time dependent. Then we have to check whether the relation

$$\frac{(\Delta x_{ij})^2}{\cos^2\alpha} + (\Delta y_{ij})^2 = \text{const} \tag{14.26}$$

holds where the right-hand side is still time independent. Differentiation of (14.26) with respect to time yields

$$\frac{\Delta x_{ij}\,\Delta \dot{x}_{ij}}{\cos^2\alpha} + 2\,\frac{(\Delta x_{ij})^2}{\cos^3\alpha}\,\sin\alpha\,\dot{\alpha} + \Delta y_{ij}\,\Delta \dot{y}_{ij} = 0\ , \tag{14.27}$$

or when we multiply (14.27) by $\cos^2\alpha$ and introduce suitable abbreviations

$$K(t) + L(t)\,\frac{\sin\alpha}{\cos\alpha}\,\dot{\alpha} + \cos^2\alpha\,M(t) = 0\ . \tag{14.28}$$

We consider (14.28) as a differential equation for $\alpha$. We make the substitution

$$\eta = -\ln|\cos\alpha| \tag{14.29}$$

which allows us to cast (14.28) into the form

$$\dot{\eta} + \mathrm{e}^{-2\eta}\tilde{M}_{ij}(t) = \tilde{K}_{ij}(t) \tag{14.30}$$

where we have used the abbreviations

$$\tilde{K} = -\frac{K}{L} \tag{14.31}$$

and

$$\tilde{M} = \frac{M}{L}\ . \tag{14.32}$$

We consider in addition a different pair $kl$ which is assumed to move in the same plane as the pair $ij$, again with a fixed distance between the points $k$ and $l$. We then obtain

$$\dot{\eta} + \mathrm{e}^{-2\eta}\tilde{M}_{kl} = \tilde{K}_{kl}(t)\ . \tag{14.33}$$

In order to get rid of the time derivative $\dot{\eta}$, we take the difference between (14.30) and (14.33) and obtain

$$e^{-2\eta}[\tilde{M}_{ij}(t)-\tilde{M}_{kl}(t)] = \tilde{K}_{ij}-\tilde{K}_{kl} \; . \tag{14.34}$$

We may solve (14.34) with respect to $e^{-2\eta}$:

$$e^{-2\eta} = \frac{\Delta\tilde{K}}{\Delta\tilde{M}} \, , \tag{14.35}$$

and thus

$$-2\eta = \ln \frac{\Delta\tilde{K}}{\Delta\tilde{M}} \; . \tag{14.36}$$

The right-hand side of (14.36) must obey equations (14.30) and (14.33). A different self-consistency check is obtained by establishing (14.35) for a further pair $i'j'$ so that

$$e^{-2\eta} = \frac{\Delta\tilde{K}'}{\Delta\tilde{M}'} \tag{14.37}$$

holds. Dividing (14.35) by (14.37) we find the relation

$$\frac{\Delta\tilde{K}'}{\Delta\tilde{M}'} = \frac{\Delta\tilde{K}}{\Delta\tilde{M}} \; . \tag{14.38}$$

Making these self-consistency checks for the different pairs, we may identify those pairs for which the relation (14.12) holds. We now know the motion of the limbs.

In the next step of our analysis we introduce the angles of the individual limbs at each joint. We then proceed as in Sects. 14.3, 4. We may now calculate the time dependence of the angles, Fourier analyze them and use the leading Fourier coefficients as features describing the pattern of movement. In the last step of the analysis, the test pattern vector $\boldsymbol{q}$ is made up of the features just mentioned, while the prototype pattern vectors are supplemented with a component explicitly identifying (labeling) the different movement patterns.

# Part III

# Logical Operations and Outlook

# 15. Realization of the Logical Operation XOR by a Synergetic Computer

## 15.1 Introduction

In this section I wish to show how the XOR operation (the exclusive "or") can be performed by a dynamical system which has a close formal resemblance to a liquid forming hexagons in a nonequilibrium state. This will allow us to construct a synergetic computer for this operation. Historically, the XOR operation has played an important role in the discussion of parallel computers, or in other words, connectionist machines or neurocomputers. Following up the basic concepts of McCulloch and Pitts, Rosenblatt (1958) had developed his perceptron. The continuation of this work was "killed" (to use Sejmour Papert's words) by the influential book by Minsky and Papert (1961), "Perceptrons". In that book they showed that Rosenblatt's perceptron cannot perform the XOR operation. Nowadays, the XOR operation can be performed by neurocomputers with several layers and a sigmoid activation curve (instead of the original steep threshold curve of McCulloch and Pitts).

In the previous chapters we have seen that there exists another construction principle that is totally different from that of McCulloch and Pitts and different also from all the neurocomputers proposed so far. We shall now study the applicability of our construction principle.

## 15.2 Solution of the XOR Problem

The truth table of the XOR (exclusive "or") operation reads

|   | 0 | 1 |
|---|---|---|
| 0 | 0 | 1 |
| 1 | 1 | 0 |

Table I

In it, the uppermost row and the left column represent the possible inputs, the middle square the corresponding outputs. For our purposes we encode 0 by $-1$, so that the truth table then reads

|   | $-1$ | $1$ |
|---|---|---|
| $-1$ | $-1$ | $1$ |
| $1$ | $1$ | $-1$ |

Table II

We wish to realize Table II by a dynamical system with the variables $x(t)$, $y(t)$, $z(t)$, that has its fixed point attractors at

$$\begin{array}{lll}(-1, & -1, & -1)\ , \\ (\ 1, & 1, & -1)\ , \\ (-1, & 1, & 1)\ , \\ (\ 1, & -1, & 1)\ .\end{array}$$

and

Its basins of attraction will be constructed in the following way: for instance when $x$ is close to $-1$ and $y$ is close to $-1$, the system will be attracted to

$$x=-1, \quad y=-1, \quad z=-1 \ .$$

By reading off the final value of $z$, the XOR operation is accomplished. This system can be represented by the potential function

$$V=3xyz+\tfrac{1}{2}(x^2+y^2+z^2)^2 \ , \tag{15.1}$$

and the equations of motion:

$$\dot{x}=-\frac{\partial V}{\partial x}=-3yz-(x^2+y^2+z^2)x \ , \tag{15.2}$$

$$\dot{y}=-\frac{\partial V}{\partial y}=-3xz-(x^2+y^2+z^2)y \ , \tag{15.3}$$

$$\dot{z}=-\frac{\partial V}{\partial z}=-3xy-(x^2+y^2+z^2)z \ . \tag{15.4}$$

To discuss (and substantiate) the properties of this system, we use cylindrical coordinates, in which $V$ is given by

$$V=\tfrac{3}{2}r^2 z\sin 2\phi+\tfrac{1}{4}(r^2+z^2)^2 \ . \tag{15.5}$$

The fixed points are then defined by

$$\frac{\partial V}{\partial \phi}=3r^2 z\cos 2\phi=0 \ , \tag{15.6}$$

$$\frac{\partial V}{\partial r}=3rz\sin 2\phi+(r^2+z^2)r=0 \ , \tag{15.7}$$

$$\frac{\partial V}{\partial z}=\frac{3}{2}r^2\sin 2\phi+(r^2+z^2)z=0 \ . \tag{15.8}$$

We (15.6) we obtain

$$r=0\ , \quad \text{or } z=0\ , \quad \text{or } \cos 2\phi=0, \quad \text{i.e. } \sin 2\phi=\pm 1 \ . \tag{15.9}$$

Multiplying (15.7) by $r$ and (15.8) by $-2z$ and taking the sum, we obtain

$$(r^2+z^2)(r^2-2z^2)=0 \ . \tag{15.10}$$

The first factor $r^2+z^2=0$ leads us back to

$$r=0 \quad \text{and} \quad z=0 \tag{15.11}$$

whereas the second factor leads to

$$r^2=2z^2 \ . \tag{15.12}$$

Thus we may identify the following fixed point

$$x=y=z=0 \ . \tag{15.13}$$

Inserting (15.12) and (15.9) into (15.7), we obtain

$$3rz(\pm 1+z)=0 \ . \tag{15.14}$$

Disregarding the already known fixed point $r=z=0$, we find

$$z=1 \tag{15.15}$$

where the upper sign corresponds to $x\cdot y>0$ and the lower to $x\cdot y<0$. Then from (15.12, 15, 9) it follows that

$$\left.\begin{array}{llllll} z=-1 & \text{if} & x=1, & y=\phantom{-}1 & \text{or} & x=-1, \quad y=-1 \\ z=\phantom{-}1 & \text{if} & x=1, & y=-1 & \text{or} & x=-1, \quad y=\phantom{-}1 \end{array}\right. \quad \text{Table III}$$

i.e. the truth Table II.

The fixed point (15.13) is a (higher order) saddle point and is of no concern if we exclude it as initial state. In order to let the system operate one has to choose $x$ and $y$ close to the desired values as indicated in Table III (or II) and $z$ close to zero. The system then pulls $z$ into the correct fixed point. The system can be represented as a single layer network with 3 "neurones" whose activities $x, y, z$ are described by the right-hand sides of (15.2 – 4), which also fix the connections between these "neurones". Note that these neurones have entirely different properties to those of the now "conventional" neurocomputers.

## 15.3 Comparison with Fluid Instabilities

The equations (15.2 – 4) are practically identical to the order parameter equations of a fluid heated from below, where, because of surface effects, a term $xyz$ occurs in the (nonequilibrium) potential. The last term of $V$ represents a saturation effect. The term $xyz$ leads to a coupling between fluid rolls that are rotated with respect to one another by 60° and 120°. This coupling, in turn, gives rise to the formation of the hexagons originally identified by Bénard. In our present analogy the control parameter, i.e. the Rayleigh number minus the critical Rayleigh number, was set equal to zero. For a positive control parameter $a$, the additional term $-a(x^2+y^2+z^2)$ occurs in the potential $V$, giving rise to a splitting of the saddle point at $x=y=z=0$ into a repeller at $x=y=z=0$ and four attractors surrounding it, while the other four attractors persist. In such a case the initial values must be chosen outside the basins of the attractors produced by $a>0$, if the fluid is to act as a XOR device.

## 15.4 Learning

In the present context, learning is again an important issue. For our purposes here, we may start with a potential function of the general form

$$V=\sum_{lm}\lambda_{lm}q_l q_m+\sum_{lmn}\lambda_{lmn}q_l q_m q_n+\sum_{lmnk}\lambda_{lmnk}q_l q_m q_n q_k$$

and subject the $\lambda$'s to the learning algorithm described in Sect. 10.5

We may then demand that the information gain (10.93) is minimized by an iteration procedure in which the $\lambda$'s are subjected to a gradient dynamics. In this way, once the moments have been measured experimentally, the logical operation, in our case XOR, may be learned by the network.

# 16. Towards the Neural Level

## 16.1 Neurones Fire and May Mode-Lock

In previous chapters we have developed mathematical models that can reproduce cognitive abilities and can be implemented on serial or certain kinds of parallel computers. In this chapter we will go one step further: we shall investigate the extent to which such models can be linked to the properties of neurones that have been studied experimentally in a number of animals. It is not our task here to present all the physiological details; we merely discuss a few salient features which are decisive for the functioning of neurones within the neural network of a brain.

Let us consider the visual system. Light impinging of the retina is transformed into nerve excitation which is then transmitted to the layered sheets of the visual cortex. In the visual cortex of animals neurones have been identified which react in a specific manner to specific patterns or objects shown to the animal. An example is provided by a particular cell which reacts once a specific area of the retina is illuminated (an area which corresponds to the so-called visual field), and which reacts strongly only if the object is a bar pointing in a specific direction. If the bar is shown at an angle different to the preferred orientation, the signal becomes correspondingly weaker. There are other cells which respond most strongly to a bar that has both a definite orientation and which moves in a particular direction. Thus the nervous system has specific feature detectors. These may be sensitive to lines (bars), others to edges, and some of them are in addition sensitive to motion. What is most important in the present context is the fact that the signals emitted by the neurones consist of pulses. These pulses are emitted at a mean frequency of around 40 Hz and the strength of the signal is encoded by pulse frequency modulation, i.e. the time interval between pulses becomes shorter the stronger the signal.

More recently, an important new feature of such cells was discovered in the brains of cats. When a bar was moved so that it stimulated a visual field corresponding to (at least) two neurones that are sensitive to the motion and orientation of bars, these two neurones fired synchronously. Expressed in more technical terms, *mode locking* or *frequency locking* occurred. If the bars in the visual fields of the two neurones were moved in different directions, no such frequency locking happened. These discoveries by Gray, Singer, Eckhorn, Reitböck and their coworkers followed an earlier discovery by Freeman of similar frequency locking effects in neurones related to the olfactory bulb. It has been suggested, for instance by Singer, that frequency locking is a means of linking together common features, in the present case common motion. A number of authors have modelled such frequency locking effects between two neurones.

In the context of this work we wish to consider such oscillations and frequency locking effects in a much wider frame. Until now our approach has not taken into account any oscillations. Thus the question arises of whether we can devise a mathematical model which, on the one hand, preserves the cognitive capabilities of the model presented in the first part of this book, and which, on the other hand, can also take the oscillatory properties of neurones into account. We will now show that this can indeed be achieved. Our goal is to treat this problem as far as possible analytically, because only in this way may we gain significant insight into the properties of networks with oscillatory elements. To this end we model a neurone by means of a nonlinear oscillator with the following properties: As long as the incoming signal is below a certain threshold, the oscillator does not react, i.e. it remains quiet. If on the other hand the signal exceeds this threshold, the oscillator begins to oscillate with an amplitude proportional to the incoming signal. This means that we replace the pulse code used by neurones by an amplitude modulation code. Because such oscillators can also show frequency locking, we are still capturing the essential features of the properties of neurones that are important for the network. Once the individual oscillators are switched on by the incoming signals, they may communicate with each other and will eventually establish a particular final state of the network.

## 16.2 Summary of the Main Results

Since the mathematics of our approach will be rather cumbersome, we first summarize the main results. For simplicity we shall not consider neurones detecting bars but neurones responding to grey values which may originate from the rods of the retina. We assume that the amplitude of the individual neuronal oscillator is proportional to the grey value. In accordance with the experimental findings we cannot expect all oscillators to oscillate at precisely the same frequency and phase, at least initially. But, as we shall show, once the frequencies are not too far apart, frequencies and phases will be locked by the nonlinear system. By splitting the amplitude into a rapidly oscillating part and a slowly varying part, we shall demonstrate that the slowly varying part obeys equations which are but slight modifications of the equations that were treated in Chap. 5.

Our network is thus capable of acting as an associative memory and of identifying objects. If the original frequencies of the oscillators are too far apart from one another, the corresponding neurones do not interact efficiently and cannot form a coherent excitation over the network. In the sense of the Hebbian learning mechanism, one may expect that such neurones are not coupled with each other. In our model then the network is split into subnetworks, each of which acts as an associative memory and can thus identify objects. If moving objects stimulate a specific set of neurones to fire, while other objects at rest cause another set of neurones to fire, one can immediately arrive at a model in which foreground-background discrimination is achieved on the basis of motion. We now formulate our mathematical approach.

## 16.3 Oscillator Model of a Neurone: Rotating Wave Approximation and Slowly Varying Amplitude Approximation

We denote the real amplitude of the neural oscillator by $z$, where $z$ is a function of time, $z = z(t)$. The frequency of this oscillator is $\omega$. The intensity of the signal impinging on the oscillator minus any internal losses is denoted by $\varepsilon$. We shall assume that the oscillator can entertain self-sustained oscillations, i.e. the oscillations are intrinsic and not imposed on the oscillator by means of an oscillatory external driving force. The parameter $\varepsilon$ simply serves to regulate the output amplitude. If $\varepsilon$ is smaller than zero, the oscillator does not oscillate at all, whereas for positive $\varepsilon$, the oscillator amplitude increases with increasing $\varepsilon$. A realization of such an oscillator can be found in radio-engineering in the form of the so-called van der Pol oscillator, which also plays an important role in laser physics. The van der Pol equation reads

$$\ddot{z} + (z^2 - \varepsilon)\dot{z} + \omega^2 z = 0 \; . \tag{16.1}$$

In order to study the properties of this oscillator as well as that of the total network of which it will be part, we introduce two well-known approximations from nonlinar physics, namely the rotating wave approximation and the slowly varying amplitude approximation. For this purpose we make the hypothesis

$$z = A\,\mathrm{e}^{\mathrm{i}\omega t} + A^*\mathrm{e}^{-\mathrm{i}\omega t} \tag{16.2}$$

where $A$ and $A^*$ may still be time-dependent functions whose time dependence, however, is assumed to be much slower than that of the exponential function $\mathrm{e}^{\mathrm{i}\omega t}$. Inserting the hypothesis (16.2) into (16.1), we readily obtain

$$\begin{aligned}
&\mathrm{e}^{\mathrm{i}\omega t}(-\omega^2 A + 2\mathrm{i}\omega\dot{A} + \ddot{A}) + \text{c.c.} \\
&\quad + (A^2\mathrm{e}^{2\mathrm{i}\omega t} + 2AA^* + A^{*2}\mathrm{e}^{-2\mathrm{i}\omega t})[(i\omega A + \dot{A})\mathrm{e}^{\mathrm{i}\omega t} + \text{c.c.}] \\
&\quad + \omega^2 A\,\mathrm{e}^{\mathrm{i}\omega t} + \text{c.c.} - \varepsilon(i\omega A + \dot{A})\mathrm{e}^{\mathrm{i}\omega t} - \varepsilon(-\mathrm{i}\omega A^* + \dot{A}^*)\mathrm{e}^{-\mathrm{i}\omega t} = 0 \; .
\end{aligned} \tag{16.3}$$

Let us first apply the slowly varying amplitude approximation and consider to this end the first bracket which multiplies $\mathrm{e}^{\mathrm{i}\omega t}$ in (16.3). We first note that the term $-\omega^2 A$ and its complex conjugate cancel with the corresponding terms occurring in the last line of the equation. Because we have assumed that $A$ changes much more slowly than $\mathrm{e}^{\mathrm{i}\omega t}$, we may also assume that $\ddot{A}$ is much smaller that $2\mathrm{i}\omega\dot{A}$. Therefore we shall neglected $\ddot{A}$. A similar consideration holds when we compare $\dot{A}$ with $\mathrm{i}\omega A$ so that we shall neglect $\dot{A}$ compared to $\mathrm{i}\omega A$. This leads us to the equation

$$\begin{aligned}
&2\mathrm{i}\omega\dot{A}\,\mathrm{e}^{\mathrm{i}\omega t} - 2\mathrm{i}\omega\dot{A}^*\mathrm{e}^{-\mathrm{i}\omega t} \\
&\quad + 2AA^*\mathrm{i}\omega A\,\mathrm{e}^{\mathrm{i}\omega t} + \mathrm{i}\omega AA^{*2}\mathrm{e}^{-\mathrm{i}\omega t} + \mathrm{i}\omega A^3\mathrm{e}^{\mathrm{i}3\omega t} \\
&\quad + 2A^*A(-\mathrm{i}\omega A^*)\mathrm{e}^{-\mathrm{i}\omega t} - \mathrm{i}\omega A^*A^2\mathrm{e}^{\mathrm{i}\omega t} - \mathrm{i}\omega A^{*3}\mathrm{e}^{-\mathrm{i}3\omega t} \\
&\quad - \varepsilon\mathrm{i}\omega A\,\mathrm{e}^{\mathrm{i}\omega t} + \varepsilon\mathrm{i}\omega A^*\mathrm{e}^{-\mathrm{i}\omega t} = 0 \; .
\end{aligned} \tag{16.4}$$

We multiply this equation by $e^{-i\omega t}$ and collect terms which are independent of $e^{i\omega t}$ and those containing powers of $e^{i\omega t}$. When we integrate over one period and assume that $A$ changes much more slowly than $e^{i\omega t}$ or its powers, we readily convince ourselves that the only terms that survive in (16.4) are those that do not contain any factor $e^{i\omega t}$ or its negative powers. This is the so-called rotating wave approximation which has been well-tested in spin resonance theory, in laser physics, and in other fields. We are then left with the equation

$$e^{i\omega t}2i\omega(\dot{A}+\tfrac{1}{2}A|A|^2-\tfrac{1}{2}\varepsilon A)=0 \qquad (16.5)$$

which can be expressed in the form

$$\dot{A}=\tfrac{1}{2}(\varepsilon A-A|A|^2) \ . \qquad (16.6)$$

This is the van der Pol equation appropriate under the above mentioned approximations.

## 16.4. A Network of Oscillators for Associative Memory

We shall again denote the activity of a neurone by $z$ but because we have to distinguish between different neurones we label them by the index $j$. $j$ may stand for the position of the neurone or/and its specific frequency. Now each neurone receives signals from other neurones so that we write the starting equation in the form

$$\ddot{z}_j+(z_j^2-\varepsilon_j)\dot{z}_j+\omega_j^2 z_j=S_j \ . \qquad (16.7)$$

Having in mind that we wish to make contact with our previous model of an associative memory, we choose the source term $S_j$ in a particular manner. It should depend on the outputs of other neurones in a linear and in a cubic fashion. Later on, we shall also take into account some time delay. These considerations lead us to write $S_j$ in the form

$$S_j(t)=\int_{t_0}^{t}(\sum_{j'} K_{jj'}(t-t')z_{j'}(t')dt'$$
$$+\int_{t_0}^{t}\sum_{j'j''j'''} K_{jj'j''j'''}(t-t')(z_{j'}z_{j''}z_{j'''})_{t'}dt' \ . \qquad (16.8)$$

For sake of simplicity we choose the kernel $K$ in the form

$$K_{jj'}(t-t')=C_{jj'}e^{-\gamma(t-t')} \ , \qquad (16.9)$$

and

$$K_{jj'j''j'''}(t-t')=B_{jj'j''j'''}e^{-\gamma(t-t')} \ . \qquad (16.10)$$

Note that in a more general formulation we would allow the constant $\gamma$ to depend on the indices $jj'j''j'''$. The coefficients $C$ and $B$ are constants whose explicit form we shall specify later. In the first step of our analysis we shall introduce the rotating wave approximation and the slowly varying amplitude approximation into the network consisting of (16.7) and (16.8). The treatment of the linear term is straightforward so we shall consider only the term in (16.8) which contains a product of three $z$ values. We make the hypothesis

$$z_j(t) = A_j(t)e^{i\omega_j t} + A_j^*(t)e^{-i\omega_j t} \tag{16.11}$$

and consider the generic term

$$(A_{j'}e^{i\omega_{j'}t} + A_{j'}^*e^{-i\omega_{j'}t})(A_{j''}e^{i\omega_{j''}t} + A_{j''}^*e^{-i\omega_{j''}t}) \times (A_{j'''}e^{i\omega_{j'''}t} + A_{j'''}^*e^{-i\omega_{j'''}t}) \ . \tag{16.12}$$

Having multiplied out the brackets, the rotating wave approximation tells us that we need consider only those combinations of

$$\omega_{j'} - \omega_{j'} \qquad \omega_{j''} - \omega_{j''} \qquad \omega_{j'''} - \omega_{j'''} \tag{16.13}$$

which have three different indices $jj'j''j'''$ and whose sum comes close to the frequency $\omega_j$ which occurs on the left-hand side of (16.17). This leads us immediately to the following combinations of frequencies and their corresponding multiplying factors in (16.12)

$$\begin{array}{l|l} \omega_j \approx \omega_{j'} + \omega_{j''} - \omega_{j'''} & A_{j'}A_{j''}A_{j'''}^* \\ \omega_j \approx \omega_{j'} - \omega_{j''} + \omega_{j'''} & A_{j'}A_{j''}^*A_{j'''} \\ \omega_j \approx -\omega_{j'} + \omega_{j''} + \omega_{j'''} & A_{j'}^*A_{j''}A_{j'''} \end{array} \tag{16.14}$$

After inserting (16.14) in (16.8) we have to integrate over time. This integral can be written in the general form

$$\int_{t_0}^{t} e^{-\gamma(t-t')}f(t')e^{i\Omega t'}dt' = f(t)\frac{1}{i\Omega+\gamma}(e^{i\Omega t_0} - e^{i\Omega t_0}e^{-\gamma(t-t_0)}) \ . \tag{16.15}$$

In the following we shall consider the network for time differences $t-t_0$ for which

$$\gamma(t-t_0) \gg 1 \ . \tag{16.16}$$

This allows us to neglect the second term in the bracket in (16.15). Keeping only resonant terms as indicated in (16.14) and applying the slowly varying amplitude approximation in complete analogy to Sect. 16.3, we obtain our basic equations in the form

$$\dot{A}_j - \tfrac{1}{2}(\varepsilon_j A_j + A_j|A_j|^2) = \frac{1}{2i\omega_j}\left(\sum_{j'}\frac{1}{i\omega_{j'}+\gamma}C_{jj'}A_{j'}e^{i(\omega_{j'}-\omega_j)t}\right. + \sum_{j'j''j'''}B_{jj'j''j'''}[\ ]_{j'j''j'''} \tag{16.17}$$

where we have used the abbreviation

$$
\begin{aligned}
[\ ]_{j'j''j'''} = &\{\mathrm{i}(\omega_{j'}+\omega_{j''}-\omega_{j'''})+\gamma\}^{-1} A_{j'}A_{j''}A^*_{j'''}\mathrm{e}^{\mathrm{i}(\omega_{j'}+\omega_{j''}-\omega_{j'''}-\omega_j)t} \\
&+\{\mathrm{i}(\omega_{j'}-\omega_{j''}+\omega_{j'''})+\gamma\}^{-1} A_{j'}A^*_{j''}A_{j'''}\mathrm{e}^{\mathrm{i}(\omega_{j'}-\omega_{j''}+\omega_{j'''}-\omega_j)t} \\
&+\{\mathrm{i}(-\omega_{j'}+\omega_{j''}+\omega_{j'''})+\gamma\}^{-1} A^*_{j'}A_{j''}A_{j'''}\mathrm{e}^{\mathrm{i}(-\omega_{j'}+\omega_{j''}+\omega_{j'''}-\omega_j)t} \ .
\end{aligned}
\tag{16.18}
$$

Quite obviously the second term in (16.18) can be obtained from the first term by interchanging $j''$ and $j'''$, and the third term can be obtained by exchanging $j'$ with $j'''$. Thus we may make the replacement

$$
\sum_{j'j''j'''} \rightarrow \sum_{j'j''j''} \underbrace{(B_{jj'j''j'''}+B_{jj'j'''j''}+B_{jj'''j''j'})}_{B'_{jj'j''j'''}}
\tag{16.19}
$$

or, in final form,

$$
\begin{aligned}
[\ ]_{jj'j''j'''} = &\sum_{j'j''j'''} B'_{jj'j''j'''} \\
&\times\{\mathrm{i}(\omega_{j'}+\omega_{j''}-\omega_{j'''})+\gamma\}^{-1} A_{j'}A_{j''}A^*_{j'''} \ .
\end{aligned}
\tag{16.20}
$$

In order to make contact with our treatment of an associative memory in Chap. 5, we specialize the equations (16.17, 20). We identify the index $j$ with an index referring to localization and thus replace $j$ by $l$. We then write the activity of a neurone at site $l$ in the form

$$
z_l = A_l\mathrm{e}^{\mathrm{i}\omega_l t} + A^*_l\mathrm{e}^{-\mathrm{i}\omega_l t} \ .
\tag{16.21}
$$

Making use of the pattern vectors $v_{kl}$ and their adjoints $v^+_{lk}$ as introduced in Chap. 5, we write the coefficient $C_{ll'}$ in the form

$$
C_{ll'} = -\omega_l^2\left(2\sum_k \lambda v_{kl}v^+_{l'k} - \varepsilon_l\delta_{ll'}\right) \ .
\tag{16.22}
$$

The coefficients $B_{ll'l''l'''}$ read

$$
B_{ll'l''l'''} = \omega_l^2\left(2\sum_{kk'} B_{kk'}v^+_{l'k'}v^+_{l''k'}v^+_{l'''k}v_{kl} - \tfrac{1}{3}\delta_{ll'}\delta_{l'l''}\delta_{l''l'''}\right) \ .
\tag{16.23}
$$

We shall assume that $v$, $v^+$ are real so that $C$ and $B$ also real. This can be achieved by assuming $\gamma \ll \omega_j$. The rather lengthy equations can be considerably simplified when we now introduce *new amplitudes* $\xi$ which are defined by

$$
\xi^l_k = \sum_{l'} v^+_{kl'}A_{l'}\mathrm{e}^{\mathrm{i}(\omega_{l'}-\omega_l)t} \ .
\tag{16.24}
$$

Note that the upper index $l$ in $\xi$ does not indicate a power but serves as an additional label. By means of this abbreviation we may write the resulting equations in the form

$$
\dot{A}_l = \sum_k \lambda v_{kl}\xi^l_k - \sum_{kk'} B_{kk'}[2|\xi^l_{k'}|^2\xi^l_k + (\xi^l_{k'})^2\xi^{l*}_k]v_{kl} \ .
\tag{16.25}
$$

Our goal now is to study the properties of these equations. In a first step we make the hypothesis

$$A_l = \varrho_l e^{i\phi_l} \ , \tag{16.26}$$

which transforms (16.25) into

$$\begin{aligned} \dot{\varrho}_l + i\dot{\phi}_l \varrho_l = \sum_k \lambda v_{kl} \bar{\xi}_k^l - \sum_{kk'} B_{kk'} \\ \times [2|\bar{\xi}_{k'}^l|^2 \bar{\xi}_k^l + (\bar{\xi}_{k'}^l)^2 \bar{\xi}_k^{l*}] v_{kl} \equiv T_l \ , \end{aligned} \tag{16.27}$$

where we have used the abbreviation

$$\bar{\xi}_k^l = \sum_{l'} v_{lk'}^{+} \varrho_{l'} \underbrace{e^{i(\omega_{l'} - \omega_l)t + i\phi_{l'} - i\phi_l}}_{e^{i\bar{\phi}_{l'} - i\bar{\phi}_l}} \ . \tag{16.28}$$

Our aim is to derive closed equations for $\bar{\xi}_k^l$. To this end we make a hypothesis which is suggested by the experimental findings on neurones mentioned above. This hypothesis (16.29) can be substantiated by a detailed mathematical analysis which we shall present below. Here we assume that frequency locking between the different oscillators at locations $l'$ and $l$ occurs. This means that

$$\bar{\phi}_{l'} - \bar{\phi}_l = \text{const} \ , \tag{16.29}$$

i.e. that the relative phases are time independent. In the relation (16.28) we now choose a specific $l = l_0$ and take the time derivative. Because of (16.29) we then immediately obtain

$$\frac{d\bar{\xi}_{k_0}^{l_0}}{dt} = \sum_l v_{k_0 l}^{+} \dot{\varrho}_l e^{i\bar{\phi}_l - i\bar{\phi}_{l_0}} \ . \tag{16.30}$$

According to (16.27) the time derivative of $\varrho_l$ is determined by the real part of the right-hand side of ((16.27), i.e.

$$\dot{\varrho}_l = \mathrm{Re}\{T_l\} \ . \tag{16.31}$$

We now evaluate the right-hand side of (16.30) by means of (16.31) using the explicit form (16.27). Starting with the linear term in (16.27) and its complex conjugate, we obtain

$$X_1 = \tfrac{1}{2} \sum_l v_{k_0 l}^{+} e^{i\bar{\phi}_l - i\bar{\phi}_{l_0}} \sum_k \lambda v_{kl} \bar{\xi}_k^l \ , \tag{16.32}$$

which, using the definition of $\bar{\xi}_k^l$ [cf. (16.28)] can be cast into the form

$$X_1 = \tfrac{1}{2} \sum_l v_{k_0 l}^{+} \lambda \sum_k v_{kl} \bar{\xi}_k^{l_0} \ . \tag{16.33}$$

Because of the orthogonality relation (5.10) of Chap. 5, (16.33) can be transformed into

$$X_1 = \tfrac{1}{2}\lambda \tilde{\xi}^{l_0}_{k_0} \ . \tag{16.34}$$

When we use the complex conjugate linear part of (16.27) and insert it into (16.30), we obtain

$$X_2 = \tfrac{1}{2}\sum_l v^{+}_{k_0 l}\, \mathrm{e}^{\mathrm{i}\bar{\phi}_l - \mathrm{i}\bar{\phi}_{l_0}} \sum_k \lambda v_{kl} \tilde{\xi}^{l*}_k \ , \tag{16.35}$$

which, again using (16.30), can be expressed as

$$X_2 = \tfrac{1}{2}\sum_k \lambda \sum_l v^{+}_{k_0 l} v_{kl}\, \mathrm{e}^{2\mathrm{i}(\bar{\phi}_l - \bar{\phi}_{l_0})} \tilde{\xi}^{l_0^*}_k \ . \tag{16.36}$$

By means of the abbreviation

$$\sum_l v^{+}_{k_0 l} v_{kl}\, \mathrm{e}^{2\mathrm{i}(\bar{\phi}_l - \bar{\phi}_{l_0})} = M_{k_0 k} \tag{16.37}$$

the final result for $X_2$ (16.35) reads

$$X_2 = \tfrac{1}{2}\sum_k M_{k_0 k} \lambda \tilde{\xi}^{l_0^*}_k \ . \tag{16.38}$$

We now turn to a study of the nonlinear terms resulting from equation (16.30) with (16.31) and (16.27). We readily obtain

$$\begin{aligned} Y_1 &= -\tfrac{1}{2}\sum_l v^{+}_{k_0 l}\, \mathrm{e}^{\mathrm{i}\bar{\phi}_l - \mathrm{i}\bar{\phi}_{l_0}} \\ &\quad \times \sum_{kk'} B_{kk'} [2|\tilde{\xi}^l_{k'}|^2 \tilde{\xi}^l_k + (\tilde{\xi}^l_{k'})^2 \tilde{\xi}^{l*}_k] v_{kl} \\ &= -\tfrac{1}{2}\sum_{k'} B_{k_0 k'} [2|\tilde{\xi}^{l_0}_{k'}|^2 \tilde{\xi}^{l_0}_{k_0} + (\tilde{\xi}^{l_0}_{k'})^2 \tilde{\xi}^{l_0^*}_{k_0}] \end{aligned} \tag{16.39}$$

and

$$\begin{aligned} Y_2 &= \tfrac{1}{2}\sum_l v^{+}_{k_0 l}\, \mathrm{e}^{\mathrm{i}\bar{\phi}_l - \mathrm{i}\bar{\phi}_{l_0}} (-1) \\ &\quad \times \sum_{kk'} B_{kk'} [2|\tilde{\xi}^l_{k'}|^2 \tilde{\xi}^{l*}_k + (\tilde{\xi}^{l*}_{k'})^2 \xi^l_k] v_{kl} \ . \end{aligned} \tag{16.40}$$

By steps completely analogous to those used previously, we can express (16.40) as

$$Y_2 = \tfrac{1}{2}\sum_k M_{k_0 k} \sum_{k'} (-1) B_{kk'} [2|\xi^{l_0}_{k'}|^2 \tilde{\xi}^{l_0^*}_k + (\tilde{\xi}^{l_0^*}_{k'})^2 \xi^{l_0}_k] \ . \tag{16.41}$$

It is now time to simplify the notation. To this end we make the replacements

$$\tilde{\xi}_k^{l_0} = \xi_k \ , \quad k_0 \to k \ . \tag{16.42}$$

Using the results (16.34, 38, 39, 41), our basic equations read

$$\begin{aligned} \dot{\xi}_k = \tfrac{1}{2}(\lambda \xi_k - \sum_{k'} B_{kk'}[2|\xi_{k'}|^2 \xi_k + (\xi_{k'})^2 \xi_k^*] \\ + \sum_{k''} M_{kk''}\{\lambda \xi_{k''}^* - \sum_{k'} B_{k''k'}[2|\xi_{k'}|^2 \xi_{k''}^* + (\xi_{k'}^*)^2 \xi_{k''}]\}) \ . \end{aligned} \tag{16.43}$$

In analogy to Chap. 5 one may readily convince oneself that the right-hand side of equation (16.43) can be written as a derivative of a potential, or more precisely, in the form

$$\dot{\xi}_k = -\frac{1}{2}\left(\frac{\partial V}{\partial \xi_k^*} + \sum_{k''} M_{kk''} \frac{\partial V}{\partial \xi_{k''}}\right) \ . \tag{16.44}$$

Introducing the vector $\xi$ with components $\xi_k$, we may write (16.44) in the form

$$\dot{\xi} = -\frac{1}{2}(\nabla V + M(\nabla V)^*) \ , \quad (\nabla V)_k = \frac{\partial V}{\partial \xi_k^*} \ , \tag{16.45}$$

where the matrix $M$ has the elements $M_{kk'}$ defined by (16.37).

Let us consider a number of special cases. If the phase differences $\bar{\Phi}_l - \bar{\Phi}_{l_0}$ are randomly distributed, we may invoke the so-called random phase approximation, a well-known concept in solid state physics. In such a case we may assume that

$$M_{kk'} \simeq 0 \tag{16.46}$$

for all $k$ and $k'$.
The equations (16.43) then reduce to

$$\dot{\xi}_k = \tfrac{1}{2}\{\lambda \xi_k - \sum_{k'} B_{kk'}[2|\xi_{k'}|^2 \xi_k + (\xi_{k'})^2 \xi_k^*]\} \ . \tag{16.47}$$

Because $\xi_k$ may be complex, we make the hypothesis

$$\xi_k = r_k e^{i\chi_k} \ , \tag{16.48}$$

where $r_k$ and $\chi_k$ are real functions of time. In order to make contact with the results of Chap. 5, we shall allow $r_k$ to take either positive or negative values

$$r_k \gtrless 0 \ . \tag{16.49}$$

To this end we impose the condition

$$-\frac{\pi}{2} \le \chi_k \le \frac{\pi}{2} \ . \tag{16.50}$$

Inserting (16.48) into (16.47), multiplying both sides by $e^{-i\chi_k} r_k$ and taking the imaginary part of the resulting equation, we arrive at

$$r_k^2 \dot{\chi}_k = -\tfrac{1}{2} \sum_{k'} B_{kk'} r_k^2 r_{k'}^2 \sin[2(\chi_{k'} - \chi_k)] \ . \tag{16.51}$$

Note that $B_{kk'} = B_{k'k}$. Quite evidently the right-hand side can be written as the derivative of a potential function $W$ so that

$$r_k^2 \dot{\chi}_k = -\frac{\partial W}{\partial \chi_k} \ , \tag{16.52}$$

where $W$ is given by

$$W = \tfrac{1}{8} \sum_{kk'} B_{kk'} r_k^2 r_{k'}^2 \cos[2(\chi_{k'} - \chi_k)] \ . \tag{16.53}$$

In making each of the above steps we have assumed that

$$r_k \neq 0 \ . \tag{16.54}$$

We may now interpret (16.52) as the equation of motion of a set of particles with coordinates $\chi_k$ which move in an overdamped fashion in the potential $W$, where the damping constants are in general different, and are given by $r_k^2$. Provided

$$B_{kk'} > 0 \ , \tag{16.55}$$

and more specifically

$$B_{kk'} = B - C\delta_{kk'} \ , \tag{16.56}$$

and there are several $r_k$ of about equal size, one can easily show that, by a proper choice of

$$\chi_k = \chi_k^0 = \text{const} \ , \tag{16.57}$$

$W$ acquires an absolute minimum. Thus we arrive at the essential equations

$$\dot{r}_k = \tfrac{1}{2}(\lambda r_k - \sum_{k'} B_{k'k} r_{k'}^2 r_k (2 + \cos[2(\chi_{k'} - \chi_k)])) \ , \tag{16.58}$$

which have the same basic properties as (5.33). Thus we have shown that the network of oscillators may act as an associative memory.

Let us now turn to the case in which (16.46) is not fulfilled. In this case it is a harder task to treat the differential equations (16.45) but we may still study the fixed points, i.e. we consider

$$\nabla V + M(\nabla V)^* = 0 \ . \tag{16.59}$$

Equation (16.59) implies that the complex conjugate of the left-hand side of this equation also vanishes

$$(\nabla V)^* + M^* \nabla V = 0 \ . \tag{16.60}$$

From these two equations (16.59, 60) we can easily eliminate $\nabla V^*$ so that we find

$$(1 - MM^*)\nabla V = 0 \ . \tag{16.61}$$

Provided

$$(1 - MM^*) \neq 0 \ , \tag{16.62}$$

we find

$$\nabla V = 0 \tag{16.63}$$

and

$$(\nabla V)^* = 0 \ . \tag{16.64}$$

We decompose these vector equations into their components, multiply the equation

$$\frac{\partial V}{\partial \xi_k^*} = 0 \tag{16.65}$$

by $e^{-i\chi_k}$

$$e^{-i\chi_k} \frac{\partial V}{\partial \xi_k^*} \tag{16.66}$$

and take the imaginary part

$$\mathrm{Im}\left\{ e^{-i\chi_k} \frac{\partial V}{\partial \xi_k^*} \right\} = 0 \ , \tag{16.67}$$

In complete analogy to the treatment of (16.47), we find that the fixed points are situated at

$$\chi_k = \chi_k^0 = \text{const} \tag{16.68}$$

provided

$$r_k, r_{k'} \neq 0 \ . \tag{16.69}$$

When we now study the real part of (16.66) and use (16.67), we can readily convince ourselves that the same fixed points result as for the order parameter equations of Chap. 5. This means that the pattern recognition process takes place much in the same way as described in Chaps. 5 – 7.

We may summarize the results of this section as follows: Under the assumption that frequency locking occurs, the network of oscillators shows the same behavior is that of the static network described in Chap. 5.

To conclude this section let us briefly discuss the limiting case

$$M = 1 \ . \tag{16.70}$$

A look at (16.43) reveals that

$$\dot{\xi}_k = \text{real}. \tag{16.71}$$

Putting

$$\xi_k = u_k + \mathrm{i}\, v_k \tag{16.72}$$

we can thus immediately state that

$$\dot{v}_k = 0 \ , \tag{16.73}$$

i.e. the imaginary part does not change in time and the network may operate with real $\xi$'s.

## 16.5 Frequency Locking of Two Oscillators

In order to illustrate the essential aspects of frequency locking, we first treat a special case of (16.25). We consider only one spatial mode, i.e. $k = 1$, and two local oscillators, $l = 1$ and $l = 2$. To simplify the notation, we drop the index $k$ of $v_{kl}, v_{kl}^{+}$. Thus we have

$$\xi_1^1 = v_1^+ A_1 + v_2^+ A_2 \mathrm{e}^{\mathrm{i}(\omega_2 - \omega_1)t} \ , \tag{16.74}$$

$$\xi_1^2 = v_1^+ A_1 \mathrm{e}^{\mathrm{i}(\omega_1 - \omega_2)t} + v_2^+ A_2 \ . \tag{16.75}$$

Dropping the indices $k, k'$ of $B$ and putting $\Delta = \omega_2 - \omega_1$, we may write (16.25) in the form

$$\begin{aligned} \dot{A}_1 = {} & \lambda v_1 (v_1^+ A_1 + v_2^+ A_2 \mathrm{e}^{\mathrm{i}\Delta t}) \\ & - B v_1 [2 | v_1^+ A_1 + v_2^+ A_2 \mathrm{e}^{\mathrm{i}\Delta t} |^2 (v_1^+ A_1 + v_2^+ A_2 \mathrm{e}^{\mathrm{i}\Delta t}) \\ & + (v_1^+ A_1 + v_2^+ A_2 \mathrm{e}^{\mathrm{i}\Delta t})^2 \, (v_1^+ A_1^* + v_2^+ A_2^* \mathrm{e}^{-\mathrm{i}\Delta t})] \ . \end{aligned} \tag{16.76}$$

When we multiply out the products of the right-hand side of this equation, we obtain terms independent of $\mathrm{e}^{\mathrm{i}\Delta t}$, and terms proportional to

$$\mathrm{e}^{\mathrm{i}\Delta t} \ , \quad \mathrm{e}^{-\mathrm{i}\Delta t} \ , \quad \text{and} \quad \mathrm{e}^{2\mathrm{i}\Delta t} \ .$$

When, as in (16.26), we set

$$A_l = \varrho_l e^{i\phi_l} , \tag{16.77}$$

a little analysis reveals that the former terms

$$(e^{i\Delta t})^n , \quad n = 0, -1, +1, +2 \tag{16.78}$$

must be replaced by

$$(e^{i\tilde{\Delta}})^n , \tag{16.79}$$

where

$$\tilde{\Delta} = \Delta t + \phi_2 - \phi_1 . \tag{16.80}$$

Now, by using (16.77), we can express (16.76) in the form

$$\dot{\varrho}_1 + i\dot{\phi}_1 \varrho_1 = a_1 + b_1 e^{i\tilde{\Delta}} + c_1 e^{-i\tilde{\Delta}} + d_1 e^{2i\tilde{\Delta}} \tag{16.81}$$

where the coefficients $a_1, b_1, c_1, d_1$ are functions of $\varrho_1$ and $\varrho_2$.

Taking the imaginary part of (16.81) and dividing the resulting equation by $\varrho_1$, we arrive at an equation for $\dot{\phi}_1$ of the following form

$$\dot{\phi}_1 = \alpha_1 \sin \tilde{\Delta} + \beta_1 \sin (2\tilde{\Delta}) . \tag{16.82}$$

In complete analogy, we obtain $\dot{\phi}_2$ as

$$\dot{\phi}_2 = -\alpha_2 \sin \tilde{\Delta} - \beta_2 \sin (2\tilde{\Delta}) . \tag{16.83}$$

Because the $\phi$'s occur in the combination (16.80) in the sin functions, we subtract (16.82) from (16.83) and introduce $\tilde{\Delta}$ (16.80) as a new variable. This leads to

$$\frac{d\tilde{\Delta}}{dt} = \omega_2 - \omega_1 + \alpha \sin \tilde{\Delta} + \beta \sin (2\tilde{\Delta}) . \tag{16.84}$$

The coefficients $\alpha = \alpha_1 + \alpha_2$ and $\beta = \beta_1 + \beta_2$ are still functions of the real amplitudes $\varrho_1$ and $\varrho_2$. In the following we shall treat $\varrho_1$ and $\varrho_2$, and thus $\alpha$ and $\beta$, as fixed parameters.

We now wish to study the solutions of (16.84) and to look for the fixed points, for which

$$\frac{d\tilde{\Delta}}{dt} = 0 . \tag{16.85}$$

The resulting equations can be readily solved by a graphical plot. For small $|\omega_2 - \omega_1|$ there clearly exists a fixed-point solution in which $\tilde{\Delta}$ is time independent. In this case $\phi_1 + \omega_1 t$ and $\phi_2 + \omega_2 t$ differ by a time-independent factor, i.e. $A_1$ and $A_2$ are frequency locked – they oscillate at a common frequency. The

Fig. 16.1

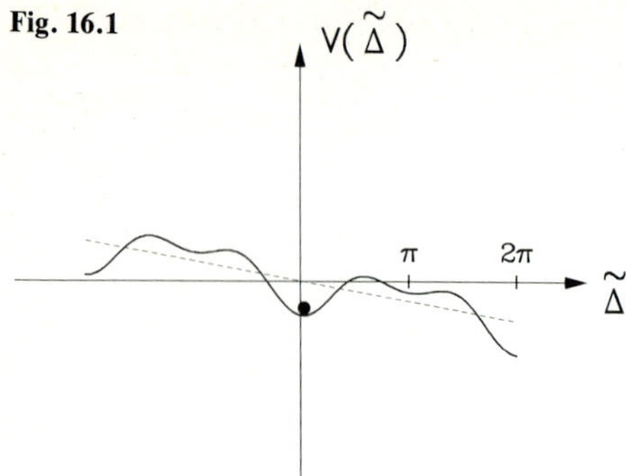


**Fig. 16.1.** The potential function $V(\tilde{\Delta}) = a\tilde{\Delta} - b\cos\tilde{\Delta} - c\cos(2\tilde{\Delta})$ for parameter values $a = -0.15$, $b = 0.5$, $c = 0.3$. Note that the minima are shifted but do not disappear when $a$ or $b$ or $c$ are transformed into their negative values provided $a$ is small enough

Fig. 16.2 Fig. 16.3

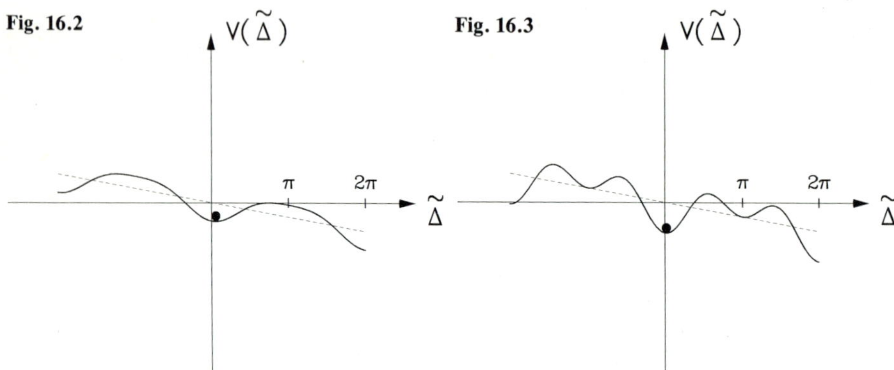


Fig. 16.4 Fig. 16.5

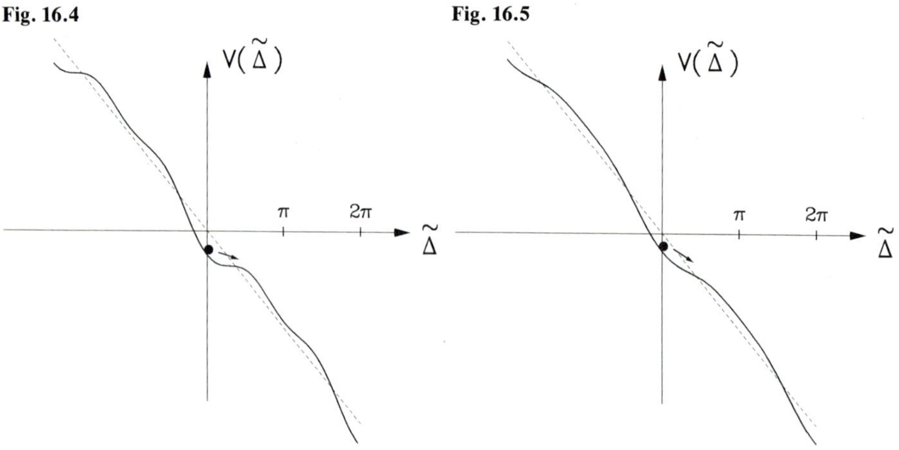


**Fig. 16.2.** As Fig. 16.1 but for parameter values $a = -0.15$, $b = 0.5$, $c = 0.1$

**Fig. 16.3.** As Fig. 16.1 but for parameter values $a = -0.15$, $b = 0.5$, $c = 0.5$

**Fig. 16.4.** As Fig. 16.1 but for parameter values $a = -1$, $b = 0.5$, $c = 0.3$. In this case, frequency locking is no longer possible, i.e. the phase $\tilde{\Delta}$ keeps growing

**Fig. 16.5.** As Fig. 16.1 but for parameter values $a = -1$, $b = 0.5$, $c = 0.1$. Here too frequency locking is no longer possible

stability of this fixed-point solution and even the global behavior can readily be found by exploiting our trick of using a potential $V$. We thus write

$$\frac{d\tilde{\Delta}}{dt} = -\frac{\partial V}{\partial \tilde{\Delta}} , \tag{16.86}$$

where

$$V = -(\omega_2 - \omega_1)\tilde{\Delta} + \alpha \cos \tilde{\Delta} + \frac{\beta}{2} \cos(2\tilde{\Delta}) . \tag{16.87}$$

This potential is plotted in Figs. 16.1 – 5. If $|\omega_2 - \omega_1|$ is small enough, the potential possesses local minima indicating that the fixed points are stable. On the other hand, when $|\omega_2 - \omega_1|$ exceeds a critical value, $\tilde{\Delta}$ simply becomes larger and larger, and no frequency locking is possible. We finally remind the reader that frequency locking is also called mode-locking.

## 16.6 Frequency Locking of Several Oscillators

Having prepared the ground in the previous section, we now discuss the general case. We first form (16.24) and insert it into the right-hand side of (16.25). Evaluating the products in (16.25), we obtain some terms that contain no complex factors, and others which involve

$$e^{i(\omega_{l'} - \omega_l)t} , \tag{16.88}$$

$$e^{i(\omega_{l'} - \omega_l)h} e^{-i(\omega_{l''}\omega_l)t} e^{i(\omega_{l'''} - \omega_l)t} \tag{16.89}$$

We then make the ansatz (16.26).

In extension of (16.78 – 80) we find, that $\Delta_{l'l} \equiv (\omega_{l'} - \omega_l)\, t$ in (16.88, 89) must be replaced by

$$\tilde{\Delta}_{l'l} = (\omega_{l'} - \omega_l)t + \phi_{l'} - \phi_l . \tag{16.90}$$

The generalization of (16.81) reads

$$\begin{aligned} \dot{\varrho}_l + i\dot{\phi}_l\varrho_l = a_l + \sum_{l'} b_{ll'} e^{i\tilde{\Delta}_{l'l}} \\ + \sum_{l'l''l'''} c_{ll'l''l'''} e^{i(\tilde{\Delta}_{l'l} - \tilde{\Delta}_{l''l} + \tilde{\Delta}_{l'''l})} . \end{aligned} \tag{16.91}$$

Taking the imaginary part of (16.91) and dividing the resulting equation by $\varrho_l$, we obtain an equation of the form

$$\dot{\phi}_l = \sum_{l'} \alpha_{ll'} \sin \tilde{\Delta}_{l'l} + \sum_{l'l''l'''} \beta_{ll'l''l'''} \sin(\tilde{\Delta}_{l'l} - \tilde{\Delta}_{l''l} + \tilde{\Delta}_{l'''l}) . \tag{16.92}$$

Subtracting equations (16.92) from one another for different $l$ values ($l_1$ and $l_2$), and introducing the new variables $\tilde{\Delta}_{l'l}$ according to (16.90), we obtain the appropriate extension of (16.84)

$$\begin{aligned}\frac{d\tilde{\Delta}_{l_1 l_2}}{dt} &= \omega_{l_1} - \omega_{l_2} \\ &+ \sum_{l'} (\alpha_{l_1 l'} \sin \tilde{\Delta}_{l' l_1} - \alpha_{l_2 l'} \sin \tilde{\Delta}_{l' l_2}) \\ &+ \sum_{l' l'' l'''} (\beta_{l_1 l' l'' l'''}) \sin (\tilde{\Delta}_{l' l_1} - \tilde{\Delta}_{l'' l_1} + \tilde{\Delta}_{l''' l_1}) \\ &- \beta_{l_2 l' l'' l'''} \sin (\tilde{\Delta}_{l' l_2} - \tilde{\Delta}_{l'' l_2} + \tilde{\Delta}_{l''' l_1}) \ . \end{aligned} \tag{16.93}$$

What then are the fixed points? If $\omega_{l_2} - \omega_{l_1} = 0$ for all $l_1, l_2$, an obvious fixed point is

$$\tilde{\Delta}_{l_1 l_2} = 0 \quad \text{for all } l_1, l_2.$$

When $|\omega_{l_2} - \omega_{l_1}| \neq 0$, but is still small, we may assume, at least in general, that $\tilde{\Delta}_{l_1 l_2}$ is small for all $l_1, l_2$. But in that case we may replace the sin functions by their arguments. In the case $d\tilde{\Delta}_{l_1 l_2}/dt = 0$, we are left with a set of linear, inhomogeneous equations for $\tilde{\Delta}_{l_1, l_2}$. A little analysis shows that we may choose exactly as many equations as there are independent variables. Since the coefficients $\alpha$, $\beta$ are generally unrelated, the corresponding determinant does not usually vanish. We thus find time-independent solutions for $\tilde{\Delta}_{l_1 l_2}$. But their time independence means frequency locking. When $|\omega_{l_1} - \omega_{l_2}|$ continues to increase, the equations (16.91) can eventually no longer be fulfilled because the sin functions remain bounded – i.e. the frequency locking is destroyed. A discussion of the stability of the frequency-locked state is beyond the scope of our present analysis.

# 17. Concluding Remarks and Outlook

## 17.1 Pattern Recognition Is Pattern Formation

Probably the most salient feature of this book is its exploitation of the profound analogy between pattern recognition and pattern formation. In this concluding chapter I wish to go one step further by claiming that pattern recognition *is* pattern formation. In making this statement I am referring mainly to pattern recognition by humans. To understand the implications, we must immediately address the question of what sort of patterns are being formed.

By means of the analogy with fluids we saw that a neural network can store internally a whole set of possible patterns which may be evoked ('remembered') because of some external cues. In this way the "outer world" may be reconstructed internally by supplying lacking material, or apparently lacking material. This is achieved by experience or expectations which are stored in one way or another within the network. This interpretation is not only supported by the mechanisms of the "neural" net described in here; it can also be substantiated by Kaniza figures (Kaniza 1990). According to Baumgartner (1987) there is even physiological evidence that neurones that are not directly excited from the outside may start to fire and thus serve to complete a firing pattern corresponding to a full line instead of line segments only. Our ideas lead to a new interpretation of the role of internal evocations of internal images, a strongly debated field in the cognitive sciences. In our interpretation the images evoked by thought processes may be more or less the same as those evoked by the outer world, but the cues are different. Clearly there are quantitative differences between externally and internally evoked images: for externally evoked images only much smaller portions must be supplemented, at least in general.

Our results shed new light on the concept of *gestalt*. Gestalt appears here as the ability of the brain to fill in lacking material irrespective of certain transformation properties. In other words, gestalt is a concept which relies heavily on invariance properties. It is beyond the scope of this concluding section to make further speculations, for instance, on the extent to which the cognitive abilities of the brain are due to genetic programming or, alternatively, to some kind of self-organization during its ontogenesis. We leave open the answer to this and also the following questions: Does the brain repeat, or mimic, or reflect the unfolding of structures of the outer world in its activity patterns or in its morphogenesis? Such questions can only be anwered by close cooperation between theory, neurophysiology, and psychology, and we believe that synergetics and its concepts of pattern recognition may play an increasingly influential role in this interplay between the disciplines.

## 17.2 Attractor States and Beyond

In this book we have seen that there are several possible realizations of the general concept by which pattern recognition is treated as pattern formation. We remind the reader of the algorithm of Chap. 5 which was implemented on a serial computer. It was possible to encompass learning in this algorithm in the sense that it included appropriate adaptation of specific coefficients (parameters) which were themselves used in the algorithm or program. On the other hand, we saw that this algorithm also lends itself to a simple realization on a fully parallel network. The latter may consist of one layer of specific neurones or of two layers (with a third layer serving as an output layer). In the two-layer model, the second layer was composed of a kind of generalized grandmother cells, which in the terms of synergetics represent the individual order parameters. Learning can be achieved in the one-layer network by the well-known Hebbian mechanism, but in the two-layer network a new type of learning may also appear, namely, the formation of new grandmother cells. This type of learning might by called non-Hebbian learning.

The fact that the algorithm can be realized by means of a sequential computer as well as by parallel nets shows that there is in princple no difference between these realizations except for speed, with the parallel realization being much faster. But what appears to be important in the context of the cognitive sciences is the fact that the whole approach does not imply any symbolic manipulations. (Note that, in the context of the synergetic computer, numbers represent quantities and not symbols.) Even logic, for instance the XOR operation, can be represented as a process in a dynamical system.

All the realizations we have discussed so far are based on the abstract idea that the state of the system may approach one of several attractor states. If such a state is reached, the system's task is accomplished, e.g. the pattern has been recognized. This is also the basic principle used in parallel distributed processes, but in general these involve so-called spurious states, which are totally avoided by our approach here. Furthermore, in this book, we have gone beyond the recognition of simple objects, such as faces; we have shown how our computer can recognize scenes and how it can deal with ambiguous patterns. Here it turned out that the *dynamics of the attention parameters* is relevant. In the case of scene selective attention and also in the oscillating perception of ambiguous patterns, we found that certain attention parameters saturated. In this way attention could be focussed on different objects. But at this stage the original concept of attractors had been abandoned. The parallel processes take place continuously and do not approach a final state. These findings are a strong indication that in the brain an enormous subconscious reprocessing, filtering, decomposition, and composition of percepts goes on. This is also supported by the experimental findings of saccadic eye-movements.

One may further speculate that there is a continuous shuffling and reshuffling of information into or from the short term memory and into and from the long term memory whereby this shuffling or reshuffling is at least partly governed by attention. There is clearly an enormous amount of work still to be done to incorporate such features into the computer models developed in this book.

## 17.3 Some Problems Left for the Future

Even is we focus our attention on vision only, a number of important points were not touched upon in this book. An important issue is that of stereopsis. Any theory dealing with this subject has to take into account the fundamental and beautiful experimental findings of Julesz (1971) on random dot stereograms. It may well be that Julesz's model involving coupled magnets can give an important lead in the construction of a theoretical approach to the understanding of pattern recognition as pattern formation. Another important aspect is that of color vision where we refer the reader to the early ideas of Land (1959) and recent work of Rubner and Schulten (1990). It does not appear to be difficult to translate their approaches into the approach used in this book, but we leave open the question of whether other fundamentally different approaches to color vision exist.

Since the question of internal representation was alluded to in Sect. 17.1, a few words are in order with respect to future research on this subject. We refer here to the beautiful experiments of Shepard and Metzler (1971) on internal rotation. In these experiments test persons were shown certain images which were rotated with respect to their normal orientation. It turned out that the time needed by the test persons to mentally adjust the images into some kind of normal position depends on the angle of the rotation. It appears that such findings can be modelled within our framework although work on this is still in progress. Another example to which our approach may be applied is that of mental maps as studied by Kosslyn (1983).

Finally we mention an important area of future research which may well benefit from the ideas outlined in this book, namely the field of perception-motor action. As we have seen here, a network is capable of supplementing incomplete data once a number of initially given cues are presented. While these cues may be given by sensory inputs, the missing data may refer to the performance of specific actions, such as locomotion or speech. Thus certain initially given cues may supplement the whole perception-motor pattern. It is worth pointing out that such motor patterns are governed by just a few order parameters as was shown elsewhere by Haken et al. (1985). Note that the formation of perception-motor patterns may circumvent pattern recognition, for instance, motor action can take place without or with delayed recognition.

As these few comments serve to show, application of the concepts of synergetics to cognition is in full swing and we are clearly just at the beginning of an exciting phase of development. The competition between the bottom-up approaches offered by neural computers and the top-down approach offered by synergetics will certainly lead to far-reaching new insights into cognition.

# Bibliography and Comments

There exists a vast literature on the subjects of neurocomputers, pattern recognition, and cognition. The references alone would fill more than a volume. In the following, I have thus included only those references that were used in the preparation of this book, and those which offer an introduction to alternative approaches.

## 1. Goal

The following selection of books may serve to elucidate the general background.

H. Gardner: *The Mind's New Science. A History of the Cognitive Revolution* (Basic Books, New York 1985)
S. Grossberg: *Studies of Mind and Brain* (Reidel, Boston 1982)
H. Haken, M. Stadler (eds.): *Synergetics of Cognition*, Springer Ser. Syn. (Springer, Berlin, Heidelberg 1990)
D.O. Hebb: *The Organization of Behavior. A Neurophysiological Theory* (Wiley, New York 1948)
A. Newell, H.A. Simon: *Human Problem Solving* (Prentice-Hall, Englewood Cliffs, NJ 1972)
R. Pfeifer, Z. Schreter, F. Fogelman-Soulie (eds): Connectionism in Perspective (North-Holland, Amsterdam 1989)
R. Rosenblatt: *Principles of Neurodynamics* (Spartan Books, New York 1962)
D.E. Rumelhart, J.L. McClelland, and the P.D.P. Research Group: *Parallel Distributed Processing: Explorations in the Microstructure of Cognition*, Vols. 1 and 2 (Cambridge University Press, Cambridge 1986)
T.J. Sejnowski, C.R. Rosenberg: Complex systems **3**, 145 (1987)
P.D. Wasserman: *Neural Computing, Theory and Practice* (Van Nostrand Reinhold, New York 1989)

### 1.1 Why a New Computer Concept?

The synergetic computer described in this book represents an alternative to some other concepts, notably that of neurocomputers (or connection machines). Here are some important references on neurocomputers (and related concepts):

L.B. Almeida: *Neural Computers.* Proceedings of the NATO ARW on Neural Computers, Düsseldorf (Springer, Berlin, Heidelberg 1987)
S. Amari: IEEE Trans. **C-21**, 1197 – 1206 (1972)
D.J. Amit, H. Gutfreund, H. Sompolinsky: Phys. Rev. A **32**, 1007 – 1018 (1985a)
D.J. Amit, H. Gutfreund, H. Sompolinsky: Phys. Rev. Lett. **55**, 1530 – 1533 (1985b)
E.R. Caianiello (ed.): *Parallel Architectures and Neural Networks* (World Scientific, Singapore 1988)
E.R. Caianiello: J. Theor. Biol. **1**, 209 (1961)
K. Fukushima: A neural network for visual pattern recognition. Computer, March 1980, pp. 65 – 75
K. Fukushima: Cognitron: A self-organizing multilayered neural network, Biol. Cybern. **20**, 121 – 136 (1975)
K. Fukushima: Neural networks **I**, 119 – 130 (1988)
J.J. Hopfield: Proc. Natl. Acad. Sci. **79**, 2554 – 2558 (1982)
W.S. McCulloch, W.H. Pitts: Bull. Math. Biophys. **5**, 115 – 133 (1943)

M. Minsky, S. Papert: *Perceptrons: A Introduction to Computational Geometry* (MIT Press, Cambridge, MA 1969)
R. Rosenblatt: *Principles of Neurodynamics* (Spartan Books, New York 1962)
F. Rosenblatt: Psychological Review **65**(6), 386 – 408 (1958)

For still other concepts see:
W.D. Hillis: *The Connection Machine* (MIT Press, Cambridge, MA 1985)
G. Carpenter, S. Grossberg: The art of adaptive pattern recognition by a self-organizing neural network, Computer, March 1980, pp. 77 – 87

For the concept of the Turing machine see:
A.M. Turing: Proc. London Math. Soc. Series 2, **42**, 230 (1936)

**1.2 What is Synergetics about? Pattern Recognition as Pattern Formation**

H. Haken: *Advanced Synergetics. Instability Hierarchies of Self-Organizing Systems and Devices.* Springer Ser. Syn. Vol. 20. 2nd printing (Springer, Berlin, Heidelberg, 1987)
H. Haken: *Synergetics. An Introduction.* 3rd ed. Springer Ser. Syn. Vol. 1 (Springer, Berlin, Heidelberg 1987)
H. Haken: *Information and Self-Organization.* Springer Ser. Syn. Vol. 40 (Springer, Berlin, Heidelberg 1988)
H. Haken: In *Computational Systems, Natural and Artificial.* Ed. by H. Haken. Springer Ser. Syn. Vol. 38 (Springer, Berlin, Heidelberg 1987)
E.L. Koschmieder: Adv. Chem. Phys. **26**, 177 (1977)
A.T. Winfree: Private communication

**1.3 Cognitive Processes and Synergetic Computers**

See references to Sect. 1.2 and
M.L. Minsky: *The Society of Mind* (Simon and Schuster, New York 1986)
A. Newell, H.A. Simon: *Human Problem Solving* (Prentice-Hall, Engelwood Cliffs, NJ 1972)
P. Smolensky: Behavioral and brain sciences **11**, 1 – 23 (1988)

# Part I Synergetic Computers

## 2. What are Patterns?

A. Babloyantz: In *Complex Systems – Operational Approaches*, ed. by H. Haken, Springer Ser. Syn. Vol. 31 (Springer, Berlin, Heidelberg 1985)
C.N. Banwell: *Fundamentals of Molecular Spectroscopy* (McGraw-Hill, London 1983)
F. Close, M. Marten, Ch. Sutton: *Spurensuche im Teilchenzoo* (Spektrum der Wissenschaft, Verlagsgesellschaft, Heidelberg 1989)
M.C. Escher: *Graphik und Zeichnungen* (Heinz Moos, München 1975)
A. Fuchs, H. Haken: In *Dynamic Patterns in Complex Systems*, ed. by J.A.S. Kelso, A.J. Mandell, M.F. Shlesinger (World Scientific, Singapore 1988)
H. Grohe: *Otto- und Dieselmotoren*, 9th ed. (Vogel, Würzburg 1981)
W. Landscheidt, A. Schlüter: *Bauzeichnungen*, 9th ed. (Bauverlag, Wiesbaden, 1977)
D. Lehmann: Private communication
J. Lissner: *Radiologie* I, 3rd. ed. (Ferdinand Enke, Stuttgart 1986)
G.K. Scheibelreiter: Naturwissenschaftliche Rundschau **10** (1979)
P. Thurn, E. Bücheler: *Einführung in die Röntgendiagnostik*, 7th ed. (Thieme, Stuttgart 1982)

## 3. Associative Memory

A now classic book is
T. Kohonen: *Associative Memory and Self-Organization*, 2nd ed. (Springer, Berlin, Heidelberg 1987), where many further references may also be found

## 4. Synergetics – An Outline

H. Haken: *Synergetics. An Introduction*, 3rd ed. Springer Ser. Syn. Vol. 1 (Springer, Berlin, Heidelberg 1983)
H. Haken: *Advanced Synergetics. Instability Hierarchies of Self-organizing Systems and Devices.* 2nd printing. Springer Ser. Syn. Vol. 20 (Springer, Berlin, Heidelberg 1987)

### 4.1 Some Typical Examples

M. Bestehorn, H. Haken: unpublished
H. Haken, J.A.S. Kelso, H. Bunz: Biol. Cybern. **51**, 347–356 (1985)

## 5. The Standard Model of Synergetics for Patterns Recognition

H. Haken: In *Pattern Formation by Dynamical Systems and Pattern Recognition*, ed. by H. Haken, Springer Ser. Syn. Vol. 5 (Springer, Berlin, Heidelberg 1979)
H. Haken: In *Computational Systems, Natural and Artificial*, ed. by H. Haken, Springer Ser. Syn. Vol. 38 (Springer, Berlin, Heidelberg 1987)
H. Haken: In *Neural and Synergetic Computers*, Proceedings of the International Symposium, Schloss Elmau, ed. by H. Haken, Springer Ser. Syn. Vol. 42 (Springer, Berlin, Heidelberg 1988)
H. Haken: *Synergetics. An Introduction*, 3rd. ed Springer Ser. Syn. Vol. 1 (Springer, Berlin, Heidelberg 1983)

## 6. Examples: Recognition of Faces and of City Maps

A. Fuchs, H. Haken: Biol. Cybern. **60**, 17–22 (1988a); 107–109 (1988b)
A. Fuchs, H. Haken: In *Dynamic Patterns in Complex Systems*, ed. by J.A.S. Kelso, A.J. Mandell, M.F. Shlesinger (World Scientific, Singapore 1988a)

## 7. Possible Realizations by Networks

See references to Chap. 5 and
H. Haken: In *Computational Systems, Natural and Artificial*, ed. by H. Haken, Springer Ser. Syn. Vol. 38 (Springer, Berlin, Heidelberg 1987)

## 8. Simultaneous Invariance with Respect to Translation, Rotation and Scaling

A. Fuchs, H. Haken: Biol. Cybern. **60**, 17–22, (1988a); 107–109 (1988b)
A. Fuchs, H. Haken: In *Dynamic Patterns in Complex Systems*, ed. by J.A.S. Kelso, A.J. Mandell, M.F. Shlesinger (World Scientific, Singapore 1988a)

### 8.1 An Approach Based on Fourier Transforms and Logarithmic Maps

A. Fuchs, H. Haken: Biol. Cybern. **60**, 17–22 (1988a)

For related work see also
R.A. Altes: J. Acoust. Soc. Am. **63**, 174–183 (1978)
J. Altmann, H.J.P. Reitböck: IEEE Transactions on Pattern Analysis and Machine Intelligence, Vol. Pami-**6**, no. 1 (1984)
B. Fischer: Vision Res. **13**, 2113–2120 (1973)
H.J. Reitböck, J. Altmann: Biol. Cybern. **51**, 113–121 (1984)
H.J. Reitböck, T.P. Brody: Information and Control **15**, 130–154 (1969)
E.L. Schwarz: Biol. Cybern. **25**, 181–194 (1977)
G. West, H.J. Reitböck: Elektronische Informationsverarbeitung und Kybernetik **15**, 10, 507–512 (1979)

### 8.2 Numerical Calculations

A. Fuchs, H. Haken: Biol. Cybern. **60**, 107–109 (1988b)

### 8.3 A Second Approach to the Invariance Problem

A. Fuchs, H. Haken: Pattern formation and pattern recognition as dual processes, in *Dynamic Pattern in Complex Systems*, ed. by. J.A.S. Kelso, A.J. Mandell, M.F. Shlesinger (World Scientific, Singapore 1988a)
A. Fuchs, H. Haken: Biol. Cybern. **60**, 17–22 (1988a)
R. Hönlinger: Diplom Thesis, Stuttgart (1989)

## 9. Recognition of Complex Scenes. Scene Selective Attention

See references to Sects. 8.1, 2

## 10. Learning Algorithms

### 10.2 Learning of the Synaptic Strengths

H. Haken: Lectures given at the University of Stuttgart (1988)

### 10.3 Information and Information Gain

H. Haken: *Information and Self-organization*, Springer Ser. Syn. Vol. 40 (Springer, Berlin, Heidelberg 1988)

### 10.4 The Basic Construction Principle of a Synergetic Computer Revisited

See references to Sect. 10.3

### 10.5 Learning by Means of the Information Gain

In this section I essentially follow Sect. 12.4 of
H. Haken: *Information and Self-organization*, cited above

For the special case of spin-glasses see:
D.H. Ackley, G.E. Hinton, T.J. Sejnowski: A learning algorithm for Boltzmann machines: Cognitive Science **9**, 147–169 (1985)
The numerical results and figures are due to R. Haas, Diplom Thesis, Stuttgart (1989)

### 10.6 A Learning Algorithm Based on a Gradient Dynamics

H. Haken, R. Haas, W. Banzhaf: Biol. Cybern. **62**, 107–111 (1989)

## 11. Learning of Processes and Associative Action

In this chapter I essentially follow Sect. 12.5 of
H. Haken: *Information and Self-organization*, cited above

# Part II Cognition and Synergetic Computers

## 12. Comparisons between Human Perception and Machine "Perception"

### 12.1 Introductory Remarks

H. Haken, J.A.S. Kelso, H. Bunz: Biol. Cybern. **51**, 347–356 (1985)
W.J. Levelt: *Speaking. From Intention to Articulation* (MIT Press, Cambridge, MA 1989)
G. Schöner, H. Haken, J.A.S. Kelso: Biol. Cybern. **53**, 247 (1986)

#### *12.2.1 Rotation Invariance*

A. Fuchs, H. Haken: Biol. Cybern. **60**, 17–22, 107–109 (1989)

#### *12.2.3 Decomposition of Scenes*

S. Del-Prete: *Illusorismen, Illusorismes, Illusorisms*, 3rd ed. (Beuteli, Bern 1984)

### 12.3 Recognition of Low- and High-Pass Filtered Faces

This section is based largely on

R. Hönlinger: Diplom Thesis, Stuttgart (1989) and
R. Hönlinger, A. Fuchs, H. Haken: To be published

For experimental studies see

A. Fiorentini, I. Maffei, G. Sandini: Perception **12**, 195–201 (1983)
A. J. O'Toole, R. B. Millward, J. A. Anderson: Neural Networks, Vol. I, No. 3 (1988), who also propose an alternative theoretical interpretation

## 13. Oscillations in the Perception of Ambiguous Patterns

In this chapter I essentially present the theory developed in

T. Ditzinger, H. Haken: Biol. Cybern. **61**, 279–287 (1989); **63**, 453–456 (1990)

Further references include:

J.A. Anderson, J.W. Silverstein, S.A. Ritz, R.S. Jones: Psychol. Rev. **84**, 413–451 (1977)
F. Attneave, Sci. Am. **225**, 62–71 (1971)
A. Borsellino, A. DeMarco, A. Allazetta, S. Rinesi, B. Bartolini: Kybernetik **10**, 3, 139–144 (1972)
J. Botwinick: Am. J. Psychol. **74**, 312–313 (1961)
B.R. Bugelski, D.A. Alampay: Can. J. Psychol. **15**, 205–211 (1961)
W. Eichler: Z. Sinnesphysiol. **61**, 154–193 (1930)
G.H. Fisher: Am. J. Psychol. **80**, 541–547 (1967)
E.H. Gombrich: Illusion in Nature and Art. In: *Illusion in Nature and Art*, ed. by R.L. Gregory, E.H. Gombrich (Duckworth, London 1973)
H. Gräser: *Spontane Reversionsprozesse in der Figuralwahrnehmung*. Dissertation, Trier (1977)
H. Haken: In *Computational Systems, Natural and Artificial*, ed. by H. Haken, Springer Ser. Syn. Vol. 38 (Springer, Berlin, Heidelberg 1987)
W.E. Hill: *My Wife and my Mother-in-Law*. Puck (1915)
J. Jastrow: *Fact and Fable in Psychology* (Houghton Mifflin, New York 1900)
A.H. Kawamoto, J.A. Anderson: Acta. Psychol. **59**, 35–65 (1985)
W. Köhler: *Dynamics in Psychology* (Liveright, New York 1940)
P. Kruse: Delfin **11**, 35–58 (1988)
R.W. Leeper: J. Genet. Psychol. **46**, 41–75 (1935)
T. Lorscheid, K. Hofmeister: Perception **9**, 113–114 (1980)
K. Marbe: Phil. Stud. **8**, 615–637 (1893)
L.A. Necker: London, Edinburgh, Philos. Mag. J. Sci. **3**, 329–337 (1832)
J. Orbach, D. Ehrlich, H.A. Heath: Percept. Mot. Skills **17**, 439–458 (1963)
E. Pöppel: *Lust und Schmerz. Neuronale Grundlagen menschlichen Verhaltens* (Severin Siedler, Berlin 1982)
W. Porterfield: *A Treatise on the Eye. The Manner and Phenonema of Vision* (Hamilton and Balfour, Edinburgh 1759)
E. Rubin: *Visuell wahrgenommene Figuren* (Gyldendalske, Copenhagen 1921)
H. Schröder: Poggendorffs Annalen der Physik und Chemie 181 (1858)
M. Stadler, H. Erke: Vision Res. **8**, 1081–1092 (1968)
H. Wallach, P. Austin: Am. J. Psychol. **67**, 338–340 (1968)

### 13.2 Properties of Ambivalent Patterns

Most of these properties were listed in

J.A. Anderson et al. *op. cit.*
C.H. Fisher: Measuring ambiguity, Am. J. Psychol. **80** (1967)

*13.7.1 Introduction*

A. Borsellino et al.: Perception **11**, 263 – 273 (1982)
J. Price: Psychonomical Science **9** (12), 623 – 624 (1967)

*13.7.3 Results*

R. Duda, P. Hart: *Pattern Classification and Scene Analysis* (Wiley, New York 1973)

## 14. Dynamic Pattern Recognition of Coordinated Biological Motion

The theoretical results of this chapter are based on the papers

H. Haken, J.A.S. Kelso, A. Fuchs, A.S. Pandya: Neural Networks **3**, 395 (1990) and R. Haas, A. Fuchs, H. Haken, E. Horvath, A.S. Pandya, J.A.S. Kelso: Recognition of Dynamic Patterns by a Synergetic Computer, to be published

Further references are

G. Bingham: J. Exp. Psychol.: Human Perception and Performance **13**, 153 – 177 (1987)
J.E. Cutting, D.R. Proffitt: In *Intersensory Perception and Sensory Integration*, ed. by R.D. Walk, H.L. Pick (Plenum, New York 1981)
T. Ditzinger, H. Haken: Biol. Cybern. **61**, 279 – 287 (1989)
A. Fuchs, H. Haken: In *Dynamic Patterns in Complex Systems*, ed. by J.A.S. Kelso, A.J. Mandell, M.F. Shlesinger (World Scientific, Singapore 1988a)
A. Fuchs, H. Haken: Biol. Cybern. **60**, 17 – 22, 107 – 109, 476 (1988b)
S. Grossberg: Psychological Review **87**, 1 – 51 (1980)
H. Haken: *Synergetics. An Introduction*, 3rd. ed. Springer Ser. Syn. Vol. 1 (Springer, Berlin, Heidelberg 1983)
H. Haken: In *Pattern Formation by Dynamical Systems and Pattern Recognition*, ed. by H. Haken, Springer Ser. Syn. Vol. 5 (Springer, Berlin, Heidelberg 1979)
H. Haken: In *Computational Systems – Natural and Artificial*, ed. by H. Haken, Springer Ser. Syn. Vol. 38 (Springer, Berlin, Heidelberg 1987)
H. Haken, J.A.S. Kelso, H. Bunz: Biol. Cybern. **51**, 347 – 356 (1985)
H. Haken, M. Stadler (eds.): *Synergetics of Cognition*. Springer Ser. Syn. Vol. 45 (Springer, Berlin, Heidelberg 1990)
H. Haken, W. Lorenz: To be published
E. Hoenkamp: J. Human Movement Studies **4**, 59 – 69 (1978)
D.D. Hoffman, B.E. Flinchbaugh: Biol. Cybern. **42**, 195 – 204 (1982)
J.J. Hopfield: Proc. Natl. Acad. Sci. **79**, 2554 – 2558 (1982)
G. Johansson: Perception and Psychophysics **14**, 201 – 211 (1973)
J.A.S. Kelso: Bull. Psychon. Soc. **18**, 63 (1981)
J.A.S. Kelso: Am. J. of Physiol. **246**, R1000 – R1004 (1984)
J.A.S. Kelso, J.P. Scholz: In *Complex Systems – Operational Approaches*, ed. by H. Haken, Springer Ser. Syn. Vol. 31 (Springer, Berlin, Heidelberg 1985)
J.A.S. Kelso, G.S. Schöner: Springer Proc. Phys. **19**, 224 – 237 (1987)
J.A.S. Kelso, G. Schöner, J.P. Scholz, H. Haken: Physica Scripta **35**, 79 – 87 (1987)
J.A.S. Kelso, S. Wallace, J. Buchanan: *Phase Transitions in Single Multijoint Limb Patterns* (Society of Neuroscience, 1989)
J.A.S. Kelso: Phase transitions: Foundations of behavior, in *Synergetics of Cognition*, ed. by H. Haken, M. Stadler (Springer, Berlin, Heidelberg 1989)
J.A.S. Kelso, A.S. Pandya: In *Mechanics, Control and Animation of Articulated Figures*, ed. by D. Zeltzer, N. Badler, B. Barsky (Morgan Kaufmann, 1989)
T. Kohonen: *Self-Organization and Associative Memory*, 2nd ed. (Springer, Berlin, Heidelberg 1987)
S. Runeson, G. Frykholm: J. Exp. Psychol.: Human Perception and Performance **7**, 733 – 740 (1981)
S. Runeson, G. Frykholm: J. Exp. Psychol.: General **9** (4), 580 – 610 (1983)
G. Schöner, J.A.S. Kelso: Science **239**, 1513 – 1520 (1988)
G. Schöner, W. Jiang, J.A.S. Kelso: J. Theor. Biol. in press
J.T. Todd: J. Exp. Psychol.: Human Perception and Performance **9** (1), 31 – 42 (1983)

# Part III Logical Operations and Outlook

## 15. Realization of the Logical Function XOR by a Synergetic Computer

This chapter is based on

H. Haken: Progr. Theor. Physics Supplement, Complex Dynamics in Nonlinear Systems, **29**, 399 (1989), eds. K. Kawasaki, Y. Kuramoto, H. Okamoto

The impossibility of using the perceptron to perform the XOR operation was demonstrated by M. Minsky, S. Papert: *Perceptrons* (MIT Press, Cambridge, MA 1968)

## 16. Towards the Neural Level

### 16.1 Neurones Fire and May Mode-Lock

R. Eckhorn, H.J. Reitböck: In *Synergetics of Cognition*, ed. by H. Haken, M. Stadler, Springer Ser. Syn. Vol. 45 (Springer, Berlin, Heidelberg 1990)
W.J. Freeman: *ibid*
C.M. Gray, P. König, A.K. Engel, W. Singer: *ibid*
H.J. Reitböck, R. Eckhorn, M. Arndt, P. Dicke: *ibid*
Further references may be found in the above contributions

### Sects. 16.2 – 5

The main results of these sections are based on unpublished work by the author.

## 17. Concluding Remarks and Outlook

G. Baumgartner, E. Peterhaus, R. von der Heydt: In *Computational Systems – Natural and Artificial*, ed. by H. Haken, Springer Ser. Syn. Vol. 38 (Springer, Berlin, Heidelberg 1987)
H. Haken, J.A.S. Kelso, H. Bunz: Biol. Cybern. **51**, 347 – 356 (1985)
D.O. Hebb: *The Organization of Behavior. A Neuropsychological Theory* (Wiley, New York 1948)
B. Julesz: *Foundations of Cyclopean Perception* (University of Chicago Press, Chicago, 1971)
S.M. Kosslyn: In *Cognition and Categorization*, ed. by E. Rosch, B.B. Lloyd (Hillsdale, NJ 1978)
S.M. Kosslyn: *Image and Mind* (MIT Press, Cambridge, MA 1980)
S.M. Kosslyn: Psychological Review **88**, 46 – 66 (1981)
S.M. Kosslyn: *Ghosts in the Mind's Machine: Creating and Using Images in the Brain* (Norton, New York, 1983)
S.M. Kosslyn, T.M. Ball, B.J. Reiser: J. Exp. Psychol.: Human Perception and Performance **4**, 47 – 60 (1978)
H. Land: Experiments in color vision, Sci. Am. **200** (1959)
J. Rubner, K. Schulten: Biol. Cybern. **62**, 193 – 199 (1990)
R.N. Shepard, T. Metzler: Science **171**, 701 – 703 (1971)

# Subject Index